Lessons
Out of School

Books by John E. Upledger, D.O., O.M.M.

A Brain Is Born:
Exploring the Birth and Development
of the Central Nervous System

Cell Talk:
Talking to Your Cell(f)

CranioSacral Therapy

CranioSacral Therapy II:
Beyond the Dura

CranioSacral Therapy:
Touchstone for Natural Healing

SomatoEmotional Release:
Deciphering the Language of Life

SomatoEmotional Release and Beyond

Your Inner Physician and You:
CranioSacral Therapy and SomatoEmotional Release

Lessons Out of School

*From Detroit Gangs to New
Healing Paradigms—Life Stories of*
Dr. John E. Upledger

As told to
Barry S. Kaplan, M.D., & Charles Stein

North Atlantic Books
Berkeley, California

Published by

North Atlantic Books	UI Enterprises
P.O. Box 12327	11211 Prosperity Farms Road, Ste D-325
Berkeley, California 94712	Palm Beach Gardens, Florida 33410

Cover photograph by CJ Walker
Cover and book design by Paula Morrison
Printed in the United States of America

Lessons Out of School: From Detroit Gangs to New Healing Paradigms—Life Stories of Dr. John E. Upledger is sponsored by the Society for the Study of Native Arts and Sciences, a nonprofit educational corporation whose goals are to develop an educational and crosscultural perspective linking various scientific, social, and artistic fields; to nurture a holistic view of arts, sciences, humanities, and healing; and to publish and distribute literature on the relationship of mind, body, and nature.

Library of Congress Cataloging-in-Publication Data

Upledger, John E., 1932–
    Lessons out of school : from Detroit gangs to new healing paradigms : life stories of Dr. John E. Upledger / by John E. Upledger, with Charles Stein.
        p. cm.
        ISBN-10: 1-55643-615-7 (pbk.)
        ISBN-13: 978-1-55643-615-4 (pbk.)
    1. Upledger, John E., 1932– 2. Osteopathic physicians—Biography.
    3. Osteopathic medicine. I. Stein, Charles, 1944– II. Title.
        RZ332.U64A3 2006
        615.5'33'092—dc22

                        2004000253

1 2 3 4 5 6 7 8 9 UNITED 12 11 10 09 08 07 06

To all my Teacher-Patients, all of those who have tolerated me and those who have supported me I offer love and thanks. Mine has been and continues to be a wonderful life. Thank you all from my rather healthy heart. And to my wife Lisa who supports me in most of what I am doing (sometimes she disagrees with me in a very humanitarian way).

Acknowledgments

I want to thank Barry Kaplan for asking the first questions and starting the ball rolling; his interviews of me were the genesis of this book. I want to thank Charles Stein for asking good questions and listening to my answers carefully enough to ask even better questions. Thank you to Cathy Cash Spellman, Laura Leslie, and Jed Bickman for help with interviewing and transcribing. And finally, I want to thank Richard Grossinger for shepherding this project through stormy weather, for fixing the music and smoothing out the chops.

Contents

Family, Early Childhood, and School

I was born at home in Detroit, Michigan, at 12:05 p.m. on February 10, 1932. "Home" was a big two-story house owned by my mother's father. It wasn't a very fancy house. To give you an idea of its quality: my grandfather sold it in 1949 for $3,800. My mother and father and I lived there during the years of my early childhood, as did my maternal grandmother, my maternal grandfather, and Phyllis, one of my two half sisters.

I didn't know very much about my father's history until after he died. Dad didn't talk much about his past. For instance, he never told me how old he was. Whenever I asked him, he just said he was thirty-nine—Jack Benny-style! He died in March of 1946, a few weeks after I turned fourteen.

Soon thereafter, I started taking odd jobs around Detroit, and I ran into a couple of his old friends. I was surprised to find out how much I didn't know. It turned out that ours was his *third* family. I don't know a thing about the first one. However, I do know about the second because, at the time that he married my mother, he already had two daughters by that wife: Phyllis, who lived with us for a few years; and Eleanor, who was a bit older and went on her own soon after my father married my mother.

Apparently Dad had done very well for a while. He had been part-owner of a bank in Detroit, part-owner of the Whittier Hotel there, and part-owner of a car dealership. His prosperity was not long-lived, however. In 1928, his second wife died of colon cancer at the age of twenty-eight. At about the same time, the Great Depression hit and he lost everything. He really was up against it and had to start his life all over again.

I don't know anything about how he got involved with Eleanor Bernice, my mother. They were married, I believe, in 1930, but I'm not even sure of that. It's just something my mother let drop occasionally. I do know my dad was totally broke at the time and thus, when he and my mother got married, they moved into her parents' house. I was born there, as I mentioned, in '32.

My early life was kind of strange. There were many undercurrents. I can guess the origin of some of these as an adult, but to a child they were totally mystifying. Even now, I cannot make up a good story to explain the circumstances that led to my father's and mother's meeting and courtship. They seemed so mismatched. By the time I came on the scene my mother was already very, very dominant and also very, very angry. My father was always having to play the peacemaker, placating her. He had to be especially careful about his behavior because he was living on foreign territory.

My mother was unhappy to *be* a mother. She wanted to be a musician. It wasn't easy for a woman to make it in the professional world in those days, and she apparently hadn't planned on getting married. Having a husband and a child got in the way bigtime. Back in the late '20s and early '30s, she led a little band called *Bernice and the Syncopators,* probably playing flapper music. Then she was Mrs. Edwin C. Upledger. How it happened I have no idea.

My maternal grandfather, John Peter Cave, was a very practical, outspoken guy. I have inherited some of his genetic material,

I suspect. It isn't clear exactly where he hailed from. He told me he came from Montreal. At one time he had been a bartender there. When he started courting my grandmother, he was working for Detroit Edison. He strung electrical wire and used to say, "I've climbed every electric pole between Detroit and Port Huron." That's about sixty miles. Well, he was that kind of a storyteller, but I'm sure he climbed quite a few. He also worked for a while in the "brass works" in Detroit. Now, exactly what *that* was, I don't know, but the job involved a lot of filing and sanding of brass and eventually he contracted lung disease, no doubt from inhaling the filings. They told him that it was tuberculosis and he was going to have to go to a sanitarium. He told them to go to hell, "All I need is a little fresh air, and I know how I'm going to get it!" He did. He slept all that winter on the front porch in a sleeping bag. When spring came around he was healed. My mother, my grandmother, and some of the people in the neighborhood all confirmed his story.

After that he never worked for a company again. He did freelance stuff as an electrician, a carpenter, and a plumber. He put in the wiring for a couple of excursion boats that still travel the Detroit River between Detroit, Belle Isle, and Cleveland.

He also conducted small manufacturing ventures. For instance, he brewed beer and prepared wine in the basement of our house, and he taught me how to help him. At age three, I was an assistant brewmaster and vintner! Then he got a contract somewhere—I'm not sure how this happened—to produce a nasty little concoction he called "Blue Death." Blue Death was an insecticide sold in little cans. I was mixing chemicals before I was even in kindergarten. I learned how, if you mix stuff up with other stuff in just the right way, it changes color and becomes imbued with interesting properties! As we just poured one thing into another, they mixed and mingled and turned blue. We'd make a washtubful of it and put it in the cans. Apparently there was a thriving local market for the product.

It's possible that this manufacturing enterprise actually killed him. He died of liver toxicity some years later. In the research I've done, I've discovered that, if you absorb harmful chemicals through your skin, it can be as much as twenty years before you get sick. Of course, I don't know whether there was a connection here or not, but I do know that there were some serious organic solvents in that Blue Death concoction.

Besides embroiling me in his business enterprises, Grandpa used to take me with him on all sorts of adventures and excursions, and he wasn't particular as to whether my parents approved. One set of escapades involved a dairy farm outside of Detroit—I don't know exactly how far, but it was a nice drive in Grandpa's old, Model T Ford. We used to go out there to get me fresh milk. I just loved that farm buttermilk!

I remember hearing my dad and grandfather getting into a serious row about these unauthorized trips. This was about the time when pasteurization was first being introduced to prevent disease, and they must have been arguing about that. Dad didn't want Grandpa to take me out there anymore ("You gonna get the kid sick drinking that raw stuff!"), but as soon as Dad would go to work some days, Grandpa Cave would pile me into the Ford and off we'd go. As we'll see, this was pretty much par for the course. Meanwhile my mother wasn't paying much attention.

Grandpa was also compelling, as I look back, for a number of his inventive eccentricities, many of them stomodeal. He used to suck all of the marrow out of cooked bones that were in the stew pot. He would also put two pin holes in raw egg shells and suction the stuff out of them.

He owned a full set of upper and lower false teeth that he had purchased through the Sears & Roebuck catalogue. Sears & Roebuck offered teeth in "small, medium, and large," so they weren't exactly built to fit an individual's mouth. Grandpa ordered medium. Of course they were terribly uncomfortable, so he carried them in his pocket and inserted them only when he needed them to eat.

Grandpa also rolled his own cigarettes. After his teeth were pulled, he had a hard time holding a cigarette in his mouth, so he provided himself with a device made out of an old-fashioned clothespin. He cut off the part of the wooden pin that would normally clip onto the clothes line. Only the body of it was left. He drove a large hole for the cigarette in one end and connected it through to a small hole in the head of the pin. He could grip the clothes-pin head with his gums and suck in the smoke through the bore.

Grandpa was a rumrunner. He had a sailboat and he used to cross the Detroit River right to Windsor, Canada, and you could buy all the booze you wanted there. He had a pretty good sized sailboat, twenty feet or something, and he used to put what he called 'pig iron,' big pieces of raw iron, in the bilge to act as a weight and then, when he got to Canada, he'd take it out and sell it for a little bit and put the liquor down there which gave him the weight to come back. He had that little thing running back and forth. Finally, something happened and his boat sank. I think it sank, but I'm not sure. That was after the police got onto him and they were following him. Maybe he sank it himself just to get out of it!

Grandpa also had strong opinions. I remember sitting on his lap while he listened to news broadcasters—you know, the Walter Winchell-type guys that yak, yak, yak, yak, yak. And Grandpa would just be cussin' up a storm and telling me just how bad these politicians were and how Roosevelt was nuts because he threw milk in the Detroit River while everybody was starving. I inherited a very rebellious and skeptical attitude.

I have some new insights into why my mother was as dominating and difficult as she was, and it also has something to do with why my grandpa was such a great companion for me. Grandpa had wanted a son, not a daughter; yet Mom turned out to be his only child. As my sister Phyllis imparts it to me (she and I have remained very close), my mother tried to be a son to him by denying that she was female. She didn't want to be a woman—that's all there was to it. Even in our household when I was, perhaps, ten or eleven—anyway, old enough to notice it—she used to do the carpentry work while my dad did all the paperwork. But she did give birth to me. Grandpa got a grandson and my mother had to accept the idea that she was female. That made her angry at *me* from the very beginning. When I was a tiny infant, she abused me almost without mercy. My sister says the hard treatment began when I was only a few days old.

Well, I was tough enough—I guess because of my grandfather—not to become too dysfunctional, even though this abuse went on for two or three years. She would spank my behind mercilessly if I messed my pants and cried or if I created a disturbance for any reason. I learned two things very fast: not to feel her abuse, emotionally or physically; and to be very, very, very quiet. I found out that no matter how uncomfortable I was or how much I wanted to do something, if I made noise, my mother might come in and whack the hell out of me. So I learned how to be quiet and remain unnoticed as far as possible. Even if she really hurt me, I wouldn't cry. I can still hear her words echoing in my head. "If you cry, I'll give you something to cry for." *I'll give you something to cry for.* I remember that so clearly.

One of the things that made me so mad at my mom was our

dog had pups in the basement. There were four puppies. They were mutts, but the mother was a Toy Collie. My mom was so powerful—she made my dad drown them in the sump pump in the wintertime. They were just born, one day old, and she made him drown them all. In the old days they had these pumps in the basement; she made him drown them in that. I wasn't old enough to do any objecting or anything. I was standing there listening, crying a little bit. I knew the puppies are going to be killed.

Anyway, a lot of stuff like that went on. I don't know whether or not my father knew about it. I think he probably *could* have known, but he chose not to. I don't think that he ignored it; I think that he *chose* nonconsciously to deny it.

I didn't dwell on any of this abuse as I was growing up or during my young adulthood, but eventually memories started coming back to me. When they did, at first I thought I was a little bit nuts—what I was remembering was so bizarre—but Phyllis has confirmed a good bit of it.

The memories started to come sometime in the 1980s when I was about fifty years old. They surfaced during my work in Somato-Emotional Release. I started remembering things like getting stuck with a long pin—I could see it very clearly. My mother used to stick me with a big sail needle. When I asked my sister Phyllis about it, she said, "Yeah, she used to do things like that. There'd be some blood in your diapers, so whatever you're remembering is probably right." Phyllis and I shared a bedroom while I was little, so she was in a pretty good position to be aware of what went on.

Phyllis was always very good to me. My dad would intentionally let money fall out of his pocket into the couch and my sister would retrieve it and then take me for a walk to get ice cream cones. But if Mom found out about it, she would intervene. Too

7

much fun, I guess! When I was about three years old, she chased Phyllis out of the house and in effect evicted her. She was eleven when I was born, and now she was about fourteen. One day she was swinging me around in the air, the way people do with little kids, and I guess her hand slipped. I fell and dislocated my shoulder. My mother used that as an excuse to get rid of her. She was gone within two or three days. My mother had already banished my older half-sister, Eleanor. Phyllis went to live with her and stayed there until she got married about five years later.

Mom's meanness actually wasn't focused exclusively on me. At times it even had a weird, creative dimension to it. For instance, she used to like to bake meringue pies. Sometimes, when I was very little, I would find one in the kitchen. I'd figure out a way to climb up on the kitchen table and help myself to, well, a fistful! One day I found a beautiful fresh pie, this time not high up on the kitchen table, but on the floor of the back porch, where it was inexplicably easy to get to. I was about to dig in when Mom came running and screaming like crazy. Though the pie was decked out beautifully—handsomely embellished like some party desert—it seems she had seasoned the dish with a generous modicum of rat poison. Rats and other pests were running rampant in the vacant lots near the house and sometimes braved it onto the porch, and she would have none of that! Another few seconds and I'd have been a goner. But think about it: what kind of a person would bake a beautiful meringue pie that no one would ever so much as lay their eyes on—just to fill it with rat poison—as if the rats gave a hoot about her powers as a designer of pies!

When I talk about my mother, people say, "Oh God! How could she have done such cruel things to you?" But I think, in retrospect, that she taught me a lot, whether you like her methods or not (and I obviously didn't like them at the time). I used to think maybe it could have been different, better somehow, but I've come to believe that in some sense it happened the way it had to; she was training me in the only way she knew how. She set me up to be tough! She set me up to get along with adversity: to be quiet when it pays to be quiet and to raise hell when it pays to raise hell!

You can see that there were various people who influenced me in my childhood: my mother, who used to abuse me, but trained me like an old war chief; my father, whom I loved dearly, who always had a way of making things okay, and who taught me how to be a soft, compassionate person; and my sister Phyllis, who was a playmate and confidante until she got thrown out. (When I was no more than a month or two old, my mother moved me into Phyllis's bedroom. She was then about eleven or twelve.) And, of course, there was my grandfather, who was both rebellious and handy— and practical as all get out. He taught me how to get along in the world. And finally there was my grandmother, that is, my mother's mother. She was just pure, unadulterated love. She didn't have another thing going for her but, oh God, she was love all the time. And I can particularly remember when she'd make soup. If I didn't have a second bowl, she'd say "Awwwww, you don't like my soup? Awwww...," and she'd cry a little bit.

On the other side of one of the walls in the bedroom I shared with Phyllis, there was a nice old upright piano, and every night just after I'd gone to bed, Grandma would sit down and play on it— always the same song. I think it was the only thing that she could play. Eventually I found out its name: it was called "Still Alarm," a pretty strange title, it seems to me now; but I've never been able to trace where it came from or learn what it was about or anything else concerning it. I've never come across the song since that time, but I probably heard it every single night for the first three years of my existence. And I loved it. Still do. It made me very happy going to sleep; the piano was just on the other side of the wall from my bed and, when I heard it, I knew it was time to go to sleep.

I don't know what my grandfather's heritage was. The only thing he ever told me was that he was from Montreal, as I mentioned before. I used to think the name "Cave" was English, but I recently learned that it's French.

Grandmother Ella was a first-generation immigrant from Germany. She was a member of a large family. I had many uncles and aunts on her side, but we never saw much of them because my grandmother and my mother were both rather prudish—they didn't believe in partying and things like that, and most of the uncles I knew were big-time, beer-drinking, German party guys. My Uncle Fred (of whom my mother and grandmother particularly disapproved) once remarked, "It's too bad the family never gets together unless there's a funeral."

As far back as I can remember, I was into music, and Fred did have something incidental to do with my development as a musician. I played in a band even in elementary school; I started my own dance band in high school. We played for dances, wedding receptions, and parties. Uncle Fred had nine children. As they grew up and got married, he hired me to bring my little band in and play for the wedding parties, one after the other.

My father, Edwin, was the son of a colonel in the Prussian army named Julius Up*legger*. I only know this because it says so on my father's birth certificate. He never talked about it. My father put the "d" in the name. I'll tell you why in a minute. His father was dead long before I was born. My father's mother was named Mary Wall and she came from Vienna, so my heritage is Prussian, Austrian,

German, and French, or whatever my mother's father was.

All I know about Mary Wall was that she and my grandfather came to the United States and started a farm seventy to a hundred miles north of Detroit. I think my dad had six or seven brothers and sisters, but he was the only one in the family who graduated from high school.

My dad didn't like being part of that family. He didn't like being the son of a Prussian colonel, so as soon as he could, he cleared out and moved to Mount Clemens, just outside of Detroit, where he became a bank teller. And that's how he came to change the spelling of his name to Up*ledger* instead of Up*legger:* now he was a banker rather than a soldier! That's really all I knew about my father's background until after he died. The main reason for this lack of information was that my mother didn't want me to know anything about his previous life. It was as if he *had* no life previous to being with her.

When I was little, my dad used to tell me that I should be an attorney because I was always so contrary. I seem to have been born with an ability to argue, so he thought I'd be a natural in court. It was probably said of lots of kids then, as lawyering was coming into vogue, but for years I assumed I *would* be an attorney, just because he used to tease me that way.

———

Kindergarten

My schooling was a little out of whack age-wise right from the beginning. I was always in classes with kids older and bigger than I was. I attended the Marxhausen School from kindergarten through 6th grade. It was on Cadillac Avenue where we lived, about three blocks down the road. The problem was, I was born in February of 1932, and they wouldn't accept me into kindergarten in the fall 1936 because I wasn't five yet. They *did* let me start in January of the next year when I had just about "come of age"! The school was big enough that they could have a class that started like that in the middle of the year. So I entered kindergarten in January and had to do the second half of it in the fall of the following school year.

Turning five was really important for me and not only because I started school. I finally got to take accordion lessons. I'd been longing to play since before I was three years old. Here's how it happened.

We had a party at our house on New Year's Eve, 1934–35, and one of the guests brought his accordion over. It was fascinating. I called it a "stomach squeezer." I wanted one. My dad took that very seriously and tried to get me a teacher so he'd feel it wasn't a waste to buy one, but he couldn't find anybody willing to take on a three-year-old. However, Wurlitzer's, the music store in downtown Detroit, would start a child on their fifth birthday. So for my birthday, I got an accordion and my first lesson.

In spite of my initial enthusiasm and a true desire to play the instrument, I soon grew unhappy with my teacher. She was making me play everything just the way *she* thought it should be. I already had my own ideas about how I wanted the music to come out, but she would slap my hand with a ruler when I didn't play a piece her way.

Now, Wurlitzer's carried popular sheet music that was always displayed prominently on a nice rack, and my Dad was aware that I eyed it because I talked about it when I came home. He bargained with me, "Every time you get a star on your lesson, I'll buy you one dollar's worth of sheet music." You could get three song sheets for a dollar so, while I was learning to play the way that the lady with the "handslapper" was teaching me, I was also getting popular songs. Here's a list of some of the songs I remember learning from sheet music then: "Mexicali Rose," "I Got Rhythm," "South of the Border," "Melancholy Baby," "Yes, We Have No Bananas," "Strike Up the Band," "Blueberry Hill," "Come Back to Sorrento." A bit later, after World War II broke out, I remember getting numbers like: "Stage Door Canteen," "Coming in on a Wing and a Prayer," "Johnnie Got a Zero," "You're a Sap, Mr. Jap," "Johnnie Doughboy Found a Rose in Ireland," "The White Cliffs of Dover."

Every day, after I finished practicing my lesson, I could spend as much time as I wanted playing away and singing to myself. Strangely, even though mother was a musician, she never took an active role in my music. Well, that's not exactly true. She tried to make me play the violin when I was very little and, boy, does that hurt your fingers. I've hated the violin ever since. I still don't even like to *hear* a violin. She also played the piano, and my father used to sing once in a while. In fact, he was the end man in a minstrel show every year.

Though my dad was the one who really initiated and supported my musical education, it was my mom who had to drive me to Wurlitzer's. She didn't like having to do it and was usually in an irritable mood during the outing. She kind of had the "soccer mom" syndrome years before it was recognized as an entity. Part of her irritation was finding a parking space. One day, right next door to Wurlitzer's on Broadway Avenue, she noticed a perfect spot. The only trouble was that a car was double-parked in front of it in a way that made it impossible to get our car in properly. Apparently, the guy who owned the double-parked car had run into the jewelry store next to Wurlitzer's—"just for a minute." But we weren't going to wait for that minute! Mom decided to push his car out of the way with her own. The driver must have left the ignition on and the car in gear—old-fashioned cars with manual shifts could be parked that way. When Mom gave the car a nudge, it started up even though there was no driver in it and slowly made a ninety-degree turn. It crossed Broadway and drove itself into a large parking lot across the street, bumping into and bouncing off of three or four cars in the process. By now a whole gang of fellows were running out of the parking lot, and a few of the people in the bumped cars jumped out too, and they were all screaming their heads off at this car that had no driver in it!

My mom did get a ticket for doing that. The guy who ran out of the jewelry store got a ticket as well.

During my first year in kindergarten, the whole class was brought to see *The Wizard of Oz,* my first movie. I was only five, but I swear to God I fell deeply in love with Judy Garland singing "Over the Rainbow." I was swooning. "Over the Rainbow" is still one of my favorite songs.

Once my erotic life was initiated by Judy Garland, it wasn't satisfied with young ladies in the pictures. Very soon I developed a crush on a little girl in our kindergarten class named Barbara. Barbara lived about two blocks past my house, and I used to walk her home in what, I must say, was a very courtly fashion. One day we were holding hands en route, and a whole bunch of kids sort of gathered around us and, when they saw Barbara and me holding hands, they started taunting: "Kiss her! Kiss her! Kiss her!" We stopped at the corner near her house, and I did just that; I had the first kiss of my life with a girl. The guys were bouncing around, taunting us, and going berserk at the exhibition. For days after that, I got a whole lot of razzing, but so what! It was really fine, that kiss.

There's one very sad story etched in my memory from what I think must have been the summer after I started kindergarten. It was my first experience of the death of a human being. It also came with my first experience of the way adults try to cover over the fact of death in a way that just makes it more terrible and puzzling.

Cadillac Avenue was a four-lane thoroughfare and, of course, I had strict orders not to cross the street. There was nice little girl who lived across the road from us and, even though she was probably a couple of years older than I was, she wasn't supposed to cross the street either, so we just used to wave and holler at each other, and we became friends even at that distance. One day we decided that one of us would risk the traffic (and our parents' anger if we got caught) so we could play together. Since she was older than I was, she decided that she would cross the street and come to my side. She watched the traffic carefully and mindfully ran across at just the right moment. We got to play with each other and everything was fine. After a while, however, she suddenly realized her mother was overdue to come outside. How she sensed this I don't know, but she was gripped by a sudden panic, dropped what we were playing with—I don't remember what it was—and ran out into the street, this time without any of the care and mindfulness she showed on first coming over. No doubt all of her concern was on getting home before her mother found her missing, rather than on the traffic. Off she ran. I watched in a kind of paralyzed horror, as if the world had slid into a dream. A car was coming. She got to the far side of the street before it hit her and threw her up in the air. She came down and landed on its front.

Of course there was a big ruckus. Her mom came running out

and some man picked her off of the hood and took her into another car that, I presume, carried her off to the hospital. When the police arrived, they asked me how fast the car that hit her was going. That's all they wanted to know. As if at age five I could judge such a thing. I'm going back there now, and I'm feeling a little guilt in my heart because I think I should have gone over to see her. But I remembered my dad was always saying that you drive thirty miles per hour on Cadillac Avenue, so that's what I told them—I said with great authority the car was going thirty miles an hour. And they took that down like good cops. I never saw her again and I could only assume she got killed. Because of me. She was running home to make like she wasn't disobeying her mom. Nobody ever told me anything about what happened to her. And I didn't ask.

First Grade

I finished kindergarten at Christmastime, 1937 and then, in January 1938, I was put into first grade. This staggering of the grades, so I would always begin a new one in the middle of the winter, continued as long as we lived on Cadillac Avenue.

I'll never forget my first-grade teacher, Mrs. Hart. She was very kind and affectionate to me. One morning I must have looked really down. Probably my Mom had whacked me one up-side the head or been mean to me in some other way. Mrs. Hart noticed it and, in front of the whole class, lifted me into her lap and started reading the story we were into as if she were reading it just to me. Her kind attention was a perfect antidote to my mother.

During the second semester of first grade, I had my first experience of the violence of "street life." In fact, there seemed to have been some sort of "organized crime" among the ten-year-olds. We lived in an Italian neighborhood, and I was to learn later that there was definitely a mafia presence in our part of Detroit. One day as I was walking to school, a couple of the guys in the fourth or fifth grade slowly came up on both sides of me and started walking next to me very menacingly at exactly my pace. They must have had fathers that were in the mob or something because they worked me over like they definitely knew what they were doing although, as it turned out, they didn't score with me. As they walked up on either side of me, they each said, "Okay, kid, we want your lunch money." I was carrying, maybe twenty-five cents or something like that. I told them emphatically, "You can't have my lunch money." They insisted and tried to take it by force, but I wouldn't give it up, and we started to struggle. Before we came to serious blows, some other kids came along, and my two assailants got distracted by them and seemed to lose interest. This wasn't the end of it, however: later that afternoon, when I was coming home from school, they joined me again. They had gotten greedier, "We want your money, and we're gonna take your lunch money every day, so you better have some."

I resisted, but this time they mastered me. A bigger group joined them, and they wedged me in the backyard of one of their houses, stood me up on one side of the yard against a tree, and produced a rifle. I remember a commotion, nervous laughter, and then, when the rifle appeared, silence. The atmosphere of an execution settled on the scene. The kid who seemed to be the leader of the group said, "I'm gonna count to ten, and you can either run or we'll shoot you. I . . . 2 . . . 3 . . ."

It's a little unclear in my mind why things were developing the way they were. In retrospect, it seems they became more interested in humiliating and terrifying me than in taking my money. "4 . . . 5 . . . 6 . . . 7 . . ." I was literally paralyzed with fear. I couldn't run. I've never forgotten the lesson of that. In such a situation you've just got to do something to prevent paralysis from setting in or you're sunk. 8 ... 9 .... 10!

The gun never fired.

They were probably as terrified as I was.

A couple of guys came over and started laughing. Someone said, "Aw—it's just a bee-bee gun." It was a bee-bee air rifle, but I hadn't known that until that moment. Then they walked me out of the yard at gun point and just said, "Get out of here." They never bothered me again. I don't quite know why. While scared to death, maybe I inadvertently proved my courage, my non-conscious willingness to die, so I was a dangerous, unpredictable hombre. But it was my *first* experience as the subject of an execution! (There was to be another many years later, as you'll hear.)

At about the same time that I was learning about the dangers of life on the street, I was working at my accordion and doing pretty well with it. My mother decided to take me downtown to the Broadway Capitol Theater one Sunday morning to compete to get into an "amateur contest." I was working on "March of the Wooden Soldiers," and I thought I could impress the lady by playing the thing just as fast as I could to show her how much facility I had. I must have raced the *music* right out of the piece because the woman had the good aesthetic sense to disqualify me. I was playing *too* fast. There's a difference between music and machismo—even in the first grade!

Second through Sixth Grade

I started the second grade in January 1939. Its second semester started in September but, in December, we moved to St. Clair Shores outside of Detroit. Even though we had very little money, my dad and grandfather had managed to buy three empty lots of land there, and Grandpa had built a house on one of them for us to live in.

Once we'd moved to St. Clair Shores, the not-so-great consequences of being out of sync with my age group began to set in. The school at St. Clair Shores didn't let you enter a new grade mid-year, so I either had to go back and take the second part of the second grade over again, or skip the first semester of grade three and go right into the second semester. They decided that I should skip. This was no problem academically, but now I was the youngest and smallest kid in the class and, of course, that meant I got picked on and bullied a lot. I needed friends in the neighborhood apart from school.

The day after we moved into the new house I noticed a big pile of dirt out in the back yard covered with new-fallen snow. It looked as big as a mountain, though it probably wasn't more than eight feet high. I rolled a bunch of snowballs up the mound so they got bigger and bigger, and gathered them into a structure that I called my "fort." I worked on it for hours—as long as I could—until it got too dark. I went to sleep thinking about nothing but getting up in the morning and going out to work on it some more. I thought this would win me the admiration of the kids around the block and we'd become great friends.

First thing the next morning, I looked out the window, and there indeed were about eight or nine neighborhood kids out there, all sliding down the mound on sleds. They were paying no attention at all to my beautiful fort, admiringly or otherwise. They in fact had pretty much obliterated it. I was furious and was about to go out and make one-man war on these intruders, but Mom intervened, "Just remember, John, you're going to be playing with these kids as long as we are living here, so maybe you should go out and make friends with them anyway, even if they didn't notice your fort."

I must say that this was one time that my Mom actually helped me out with some decent advice. I did what she suggested. I started having fun. We had sled races down the hill and I got to be buddies with everybody.

As I came to know all the kids in the neighborhood, I began to be aware that one thing we all had in common was a fascination with firearms. My dad was very opposed to having guns and other weapons in the house. He never lectured me or tried to interfere with anything I found interesting, but he did find a very sensitive and effective way to teach me about what it means to kill.

I was eight years old. It was the spring of the first year after we moved out to St. Clair Shores. There were empty lots all over the neighborhood where we used to hang around and play—the two lots on our property as well as other ones. One day I bought a bee-bee gun from one of the kids. I think I paid a quarter for it. It was a single-shot Daisy air rifle. I knew my father didn't like guns, and I thought he wouldn't approve of my purchase, so I hid it in the field next to our house.

It wasn't too long, however, before my father saw me with it. He said, "Okay, you've got a gun. Bring it into the house. Don't be deceptive. Don't lie about it." So I brought the bee-bee gun into the house. I would take it out occasionally and practice hitting various objects—spots on a tree trunk, old cans—that kind of thing.

One Sunday morning, I got up early and looked out the kitchen window. I saw a bird flying about in the backyard. I ran and got my gun and shot at the bird. To my astonishment it fell to the ground. My father was standing right behind me. When he spoke, there was no anger in his voice. He said, "John, that was a really good shot. Now let's go see what you killed." He took me outside and had me pick up this little bird. And I . . . God, I felt so bad . . . I've never shot another thing in my life. And I never will. I don't even feel comfortable fishing.

My Dad really made an impact on me with the way he did that. He made me understand what *compassion* really is. Well, he didn't *make* me understand it, but he offered me the chance to discover it. He showed me the natural outcome of my behavior rather than punishing me. In fact, he seldom punished me. He always preferred to teach me in ways like that.

Another way that I learned kindness from my Dad was through his refusal to participate in the prejudice and race-hatred that was so common in the world when I grew up. In St. Clair Shores, there was an old nightclub called "Blossom Heath" that the Detroit Tigers used to frequent. Around the time we moved there, it was being sold to a group of black people. Before too long the good white folks of St. Clair Shores had set a bomb to it. That was my first lesson in racial "integration." I was eight years old. I kept asking my father why the white people did that and he, as distressed and incredulous as I, repeated, "I don't know. I don't understand why people do these things. They are very bad things to do."

Another thing that happened when I was about eight years old, was that my father got involved in the political life of Roseville, Michigan, a northern suburb of Detroit not far from St. Clair

Shores. Roseville had a marching band, and by now I was a pretty competent little accordion player. I had graduated from the child's accordion and was playing a full-sized instrument. So my dad got me into the band. There I was, weighted down under a huge accordion, marching and playing Sousa. Initially, I tried strapping the thing on a bigger kid in front of me so I could just follow along, but that didn't work, so I had to learn how to carry it myself.

Next, Dad got me into playing with high-school kids in a dance band. I was this little tyke in the fourth grade playing with high-school kids! It was kind of strange, but I loved it. One Sunday afternoon, we were practicing at some kid's house and I overheard one of the guys saying, "We're going to have to replace Johnny in the band—we need a piano player."

I said, "Hey! I play the piano."

We did have a piano at our house—the one my grandmother used play "Still Alarm" on night after night when I was little and which we took with us when we moved from Cadillac Avenue. The truth is, I'd actually never touched it, but I did *that* day! First time! I knew how to play the right hand from the accordion. I could replicate most any melody you wanted because my dad had bought me all that sheet music. And the left hand—I thought, "Well, I'll just wing it! Pum, pum, pum, pum! Like that." The only way I could improvise that left hand was from the accordion, where I had learned to push the buttons on the left side for rhythm. It supports what I'm playing on the right side. I thought, 'I'll do the same thing on the piano.' I didn't hit all good notes but I didn't hit all bad notes, and I hit them so that the drummer would know the rhythm. And they said, "Oh well, okay, we can try." So I went home and I practiced like heck with my left hand.

The next week I was a little better at it, and pretty soon I'd learned how to play a boogie-woogie bass, and that made me some sort of sensation—this little kid playing boogie-woogie. That was big stuff back in those days. On the piano, you use your left hand to create a kind of secondary bass line that gives rhythm to what you're doing with your right. So I taught myself the boogie bass line, and I could play it while playing anything else. The chord progression is usually in C—it's C, F, G. You hit eighth notes— a C with your fifth finger and then an octave above with your thumb. Then you go into F, with those two fingers and the thumb going on eighth notes. The thumb always follows the fifth finger. And if you can do that while standing on your head, then you can start playing Boogie. Boogie was hot, and I became somewhat of a showpiece for the older guys. Soon they were actually getting jobs because I was playing the piano for them. It was the beginning of a career!

I think the first time I ever got paid to play was when my dad took me to a Christmas party at Warner Aircraft where he was working. I played my accordion, and he passed the hat for me. I made eight dollars and change. WOW! It was really something. However, by the time I was twelve, I was making pretty good money playing both the piano and the accordion. In fact, I didn't give up accordion until about twenty-five years ago. And it wasn't that I gave it up it, really. It was just that the bellows on the old thing were all taped up and it finally just gave out! By then I was done with it musically. I like piano a lot better anyway. But in my day I made a lot of money playing accordion—especially around Detroit, with all the Polish people there. I'd play polka weddings and get a pretty penny.*

---

*Actually, I just got a new accordion a couple of years ago. I play it a little now!

One last story before we move on to junior high.

Doesn't every boy, at some point in his young life, yearn almost desperately to fly? One dreams of being Peter Pan, Superman, or at least Batman. Well, I was no exception. One day in, it must have been the sixth grade, I decided to do something about this longing to take to the air. Now there are various ways that you could go about becoming airborne: you could invent an anti-gravity device; you could construct an airplane; but the most obvious and practical way, it seemed to me, was to imitate birds. All you needed was a pair of wings.

Unhampered by any knowledge of aerodynamics, I got hold of some wood and set to work. I built a frame that was pretty much modeled after the wings on the Batman emblem. I procured some sort of cloth material and nailed it onto the frame and, as soon as no one was home to stop me, I set out to put myself in flight.

There was a maple in the backyard with a tree house in it and steps going up to it. I took the wings up there, and feeling like something between a fledgling blue jay and Batman himself, leapt out of the tree house, flapping my wings like mad. FLAP RATTLE SHRIEK!*&^%^%$#@—THUNK. It must have been a fifteen- or twenty-foot fall. Well, my wings were irreparably disabled, but I myself just landed on my bottom, no worse for the experiment. I never tried flight again.

Junior High School

Another major scientific, or rather "technological," exploit of mine took place a year or so later during my first year in Junior High School. I don't know where I got the idea that I needed to manufacture gun powder, but it came from somewhere. I wasn't interested in packing it into bullet shells; I just wanted to see if it would explode. My science for this work was a bit more precise than for the flying caper. I had come upon the chemical formula and basic instructions for preparing the compound, probably in a chemistry laboratory handbook of some kind, and I concocted up a Campbell's soup can full of a mixture of sulfur, potassium nitrate, and charcoal. I had gone to the local drugstore and bought the ingredients, which they quite conveniently sold over the counter. My laboratory was our garage. Once the car was gone and Mom and Dad were nowhere to be seen (Grandpa wasn't a party to this escapade, so he must have been off somewhere, too), I set up a proper experiment. I mixed up the ingredients in the correct proportions and put a match to the whole batch at once. It flared upwards. It practically ripped the roof off the garage. Once again, I escaped any damage to my person, but I sure caught heck when my folks got home.

Life in Junior High was pretty good for me. I did fine academically, and socially I was well-accepted. My music business was booming. By now I had my own little dance band, and we used to play for school dances—both junior high and high school. Actually, we played for about half of them. The music director of the high school band had his own group that worked the rest of them, and he wasn't particularly fond of me because I was taking gigs away from him.

My band was called "Six Jacks and A Queen"—six male musicians and a girl singer. ("Queen" obviously didn't mean what it does today.) The "Six Jacks" consisted of one trumpet and three saxophones, drums, and me on the piano. We played, for the most part, arrangements of dance tunes that I got at Wurlitzer's. There were dances on Wednesday afternoons in the gym, but our band didn't play at those, so I got to dance a bit and learn how to get along with the girls.

On the day that I graduated from junior high, I had a little adventure with fishing—I actually caught a fish! It was not an exhilarating experience.

My friends and I kept a little rowboat on an inlet at Lake St. Clair about a mile's walk from school. In this cove we also kept what you call a "catfish line." You pound two stakes into the bottom of the lake in the shallows a bit offshore. You run a line between the stakes, and you hang bait on hooks in the water from the line every two feet or so and just leave it there overnight, or for however long you want to.

Well, after the graduation ceremony, even though we were in our little suits, I said to my buddies, "Come on—let's go and check out the line." We didn't really expect anything—there had never been a fish on one of the hooks before—but it was always fun just going to look. We got to the inlet, took off our suit jackets, rolled up our pant legs, and got into the rowboat. There, on one of the hooks, was an enormous catfish, still alive and thrashing about, wild and desperate. Later when we measured it, it was twenty-eight inches long. But now we were terrified! There we were, four of us crowded in the back end of the boat, with the catfish in the bow. It looked so ferocious we were sure it was going to attack and bite us. Eventually one of the guys got the courage to take the hook out of its mouth and whack it on the head with an oar. That slowed it down, and it died quietly enough on the floor of the boat.

We rehooked the fish and attached it on a line to an oar and walked with it all the way back to a dairy bar we knew that was a few blocks from the lake. It had those two u-shaped counters that dairy bars have—I'm not sure what they're for—but the proprietor let us put the oar across them with the fish dangling there behind the counter and everyone staring at it admiringly. We nonchalantly downed our malted milks, and off we went to my house and to my dad to find out what the devil we were supposed to do now! Dad showed us how to clean it. He spiked it up to a tree and then slit its gut and took all its innards out and stripped its skin off too.

Now here's the point of this story. Ever since my Dad gave me the gentle lesson about death when I shot the little bird from the kitchen window, I'd felt very unhappy about killing anything. I hadn't made up my mind about fishing, but then I'd never caught a fish before; and now that I'd done it, I didn't like it. It gave me a twang. Later in life I took my own kids fishing a few times, but I really didn't like that either, and eventually I absolutely quit.

It used to be said that fish don't really feel pain but, when you see one squirming and thrashing like a soul in torment, you just can't believe it. And as a matter of fact, I recently read an article in the scientific journal *Nature,* saying that they've finally discovered that fish *do* feel pain. Indeed. Humans are always trying to kid themselves, when they are inflicting suffering, that somehow it isn't really happening. When I was a medical intern, we had to perform circumcision on infants and they'd squirm like hell, but the doctors insisted that they were too young to feel pain. Give me a break. Pain is pain, and we all know exactly what it looks like.

High School

High school at first was a really difficult time for me. Being "skipped" way back in grade school continued to have annoying consequences. I was only thirteen when I became a freshman and I was too young to play football even on the junior varsity team. I went to sign up, and at first it looked like I was going to make the team. The coach even went as far as issuing me a uniform. Then he looked at my papers and saw that I wasn't old enough. My buddies were all on the team—all the guys I'd been playing sandlot games with for years—and I had to sit on the sidelines and watch. It drives me wild to think of it even now. I turned fourteen in the middle of winter, but of course football season was over and I had to wait for the following year.

I did make JV basketball though. I was actually a pretty good shooter. One special night that winter, my Dad was in the stands. Usually, during warm-ups everybody got to take a couple of shots, but for some reason that night the coach let us keep shooting until we missed. I sunk eighteen in a row! Finally, the coach came up and spun me around, and of course after that I missed. My Dad was up there standing in the bleachers cheering away. I was so proud. This was the last time he ever saw me play. A month later he was dead.

It happened late one Friday night in March just after I'd turned fourteen. Unexpectedly. I had played catch with him that afternoon when he came home from work. I had permission to go with some other guys to a movie that evening. I came home at about ten o'clock and everything was all right. I went to sleep. But in the middle of the night, suddenly my mother was yelling, "Wake up! Wake up! Wake up!"

I ran into the living room. Dad was lying on the couch, and my mother was sitting over him rubbing his chest frantically. "Call Dr. Markum," she commanded.

I grabbed the phone book and fumbled to find his number, but I was just so scared I couldn't read the damn thing—I could hardly make out the letters. "Ma," I cried, "I can't find the number!" So she left my Dad and grabbed the phone and called the doctor herself. The doctor said to call the fire department or the police or some-body—which doesn't quite make any sense unless she knew that he was dead already and had told the doctor so. I didn't really understand what was going on, but then she put the phone down and went back into the living room and started screaming at me and calling me vicious names and saying it was all my fault, that I had killed my father because I couldn't find the number. Eventually, the police or the firemen came—anyway, guys in uniform—and pronounced him dead and took him away. And she kept on rais-ing hell with me, swearing that my father had died because I couldn't read. God, it was awful. I carried that around with me for quite some time.

My father had his funeral, and some of his buddies asked me to be a pallbearer. That was a real hit for me; here I am carrying my father's casket. I don't know what happened during the funeral, but after the funeral I was crying uncontrollably, so my two half sisters took me to a pool hall and had me shoot pool to try to keep me from crying. It worked. I thought in retrospect that maybe that was-n't a good thing to do because I should have just cried it out, whereas they thought the best thing they could do was stop me from cry-ing. I cried my bloody butt off and then they got me in there, played the jukebox, shot some pool. At age fourteen, I didn't get in a pool hall much.

After my father's death, I became really angry and depressed, and I guess not only because I lost a great Dad, and not only because my mother continued to blame for his death. Fourteen is a rotten age to have your father die. No doubt I was primed to be down on the world in general, and this was the clincher. After he died, my mother took a job working for West Wright Realty. She got a reasonable salary. But she really just spent all her time locked in the front room reading novels. I had less and less to do with my mother. I was playing the piano and also cutting grass and shoveling snow, so I was self-sufficient and my mother was self sufficient, except that I lived in her house and didn't make any rent payments or anything. Whatever I needed, I got my own money for. I don't think I ever asked her for money.

After a week or two of my darkening the atmosphere with my depression, my mother got anxious about my newly acquired surly attitude and decided I needed "counseling," so she sent me to the minister, a Reverend McConnel. This did not do the trick. Church in general has never meant anything to me. I used to play the piano for the church's youth group on Sunday mornings, mainly so I wouldn't have to attend McConnel's tedious services. I told the good Reverend how mad I was at God for taking my dad away. He did not find this an appropriate attitude. He didn't even reprimand me or try to turn me around with some sage religious bromides. He just said that until I changed my mind, I needn't bother coming back. So much for the wise counsels of the Church. I never went back—not until I had my own kids, and then we went to the Unitarian Church where you can basically believe whatever you want.

My anger did not pass away quickly, but it did get channeled into a variety of activities: sports, music, hanging out with street gangs, generally misbehaving and—maintaining my own motor car. I'll get to the car later.

In my sophomore year in high school, I finally got to play on the junior-varsity football team and did very well as a linebacker. I was strong and quick and didn't mind contact. In my junior year, on the main team, I was a starting linebacker and found myself in the middle of the very first defensive play of the opening game. We were playing in Utica, Michigan, which is a farming community, and their team was populated by strapping country boys, a bit out-sizing us suburban cityslickers. Their fullback was a big, big guy. I was tough, but I weighed, oh, about 160 pounds, and I was resolved to get this guy. Right after the snap of the first play of the game, there he was, coming through a hole in our line, so I gave him everything I had—helmet smash against thigh pad. When I woke up, it was the fourth quarter! After that the coach was very careful about whom he let me line up against. He probably thought I'd kamikaze myself to death.

The following year—my senior year—very early, before the season even started, we were playing a practice game against ourselves, and a guy came through the line and broke my right femur. Looking at it in retrospect, I'd say that at this point I had enough intelligence and sense of myself to decide that this was enough football for me. Still, I was used to being in good physical condition and didn't want to stop training, so after my leg came out of the cast, I asked my doctor what I should do to get back in shape. I'd been inactive for about six weeks, though fortunately my femur had fractured just above the knee and my knee joint had stayed intact. Doc said, "Roller skates!"

Now I think he was actually kidding, but I took him seriously. I went to Eastward Park Roller Rink and I started skating. Pretty soon some of the girls there got me taking dance lessons, and I won a bronze medal in roller-skate dancing. Actually, that was kind of boring because there wasn't much you could do, dance-wise. But I did get good enough on skates to join a roller-hockey team.

I really loved playing roller hockey. This wasn't a high-powered, intra-mural, macho sport like football where you half-expect to decimate your body for the team. It was often a largely improvised kind of thing. The biggest kick we used to get was on Friday night when our team would take on all comers, and we would play with a football for a puck and brooms for hockey sticks.

Roller hockey, incidentally, was also a really great way to meet girls. There were always nice-lookin' females in short skirts skating around the roller rink. I had my first really serious dates from being on the roller-hockey team. The girls didn't play—they'd just hang around and watch. Most of them were roller skaters, but they didn't play roller hockey.

During the first part of high school, I was maybe fourteen or fifteen; I started playing a lot of accordion at Polish weddings in my area. On Friday nights they'd have the big party before. We'd play for about four hours. They always rented a giant hall, at least when we played, and we'd have a band of maybe five of us. They would have this huge, long buffet table with Polish sausage and everything that you could think of that was ethnic. We could drink beer if we wanted to. There were always a lot of good-looking girls there, so I was flirting a ton with them.

Usually these weddings would have well over a hundred people. Major partying went on. We'd play from maybe four in the afternoon until midnight. A long stay. On Sunday morning, to make up for hangovers from the whole big wild party, we'd probably show up around one or two in the afternoon and play till five. You'd bust your ass, I'll tell you. The only thing I can remember is by late Saturday night or Sunday, I could catch a nap while playing my accordion. I'd get a tap on the shoulder, saying, 'Wake up—we're getting out of this now.' I didn't even know I was sleeping, but I guess I was playing the damned thing subconsciously or something.

Meanwhile, my career as a jazz musician was taking a rather serious turn. By the time I was halfway through high school I was playing fairly regularly with jazz groups in downtown Detroit. We had some really good stuff going down there jazz-wise. As soon as I was about fifteen or sixteen, I started regularly playing with black musicians. I had fake I.D. papers that said I was twenty-one, so playing in clubs was no problem.

My mother had no idea what I was up to, but it was never even an issue. My dad was dead, so it was just her. After he died, she kind of went into her front bedroom and didn't come out very much. She didn't try to get me to do anything. She felt totally incompetent as a parent, I think. My grandfather couldn't have cared less about the false papers. If he had known, he would have encouraged me. But I didn't tell anybody what I was doing.

St. Clair Shores was just on the edge of Detroit, and there was a twenty-five-cent bus to get there. On Sunday afternoons, I'd go downtown and play music in a place called "Paradise Valley," which was "black and tan," that is, black and white mixed. It was Detroit's version of Harlem. I'd get on the bus about noon, play in jam sessions with the black groups, and come home around six. What I learned was that the Blacks expressed their feelings in their music. I learned to put my emotions into my piano playing. This was a kind of lesson that I later applied to my hands-on work. I started the Sunday sessions before my father died.

The black musicians let me sit in pretty much as a curiosity at first—this young white boy who can play boogie-woogie on the piano—but pretty soon I could hold my own musically. I found that I got along with black people in general very well, and I was just accepted as a musician.

By the way, there was quite a bit of marijuana-smoking among the musicians, but, for some reason, I refused point blank to indulge. The 1940s equivalent of "just say no," however, didn't prevent me from skipping school whenever I felt like it! I started playing hooky in about the 10th or 11th grade, once or twice a week. I'd take a bus downtown and go to one of those theaters where they alternate a movie with live music. You could go in at noon and come out at midnight for a buck and a quarter. Some really great music happened there—Frank Sinatra, Jazz at the Philharmonic, Errol Garner, Illinois Jacquette, Sammy Davis Jr., George Shearing. I figured it was a pretty serious part of my musical education, but the truth is, I wasn't planning very much for my future. Apart from playing music, which in any case was always happening in the present, I didn't think a lot about what I wanted to do with my life. It had pretty well been decided by my dad that I was going to be a lawyer because of how contrary I was and how well I could argue.

After my dad died and I got really, really angry and skipped class an awful lot (though I still managed to do well grade-wise), I went on the streets and hung out with gangs and did the stuff you weren't supposed to do.

Today gangs murder each other. In those days gang members did not carry guns. In fact, if a guy was caught with a gun, it was taken away by the other gang members and thrown in the river. A few guys carried knives, the switchblade kind that you can flip open. As a matter of fact I was one of those. The knives were used mainly to bully, to bluff your way through something. The weapon that was used the most was a pair of socks—one inside the other because that was stronger—filled with pebbles, and you hit people with it, mostly the body, not the head. We didn't do robberies or murders. We did a lot of drinking under age. We didn't so much rumble as bluff. Two gangs would arrange a meeting at the corner of say, Field and Jeff, and we'd yell at each other, threaten each other, and once in a while someone would get punched. It was like a turf war; we'd stand nose to nose and decide who was going to have that turf. Basically gangs were groups of guys who got together and had parties. What was illegal was the underage drinking and assemblage in spots we weren't supposed to be. I guess we were showing off to the girls that we were tough.

I ended up in my own gang, just a bunch of guys hanging out, really. I got to know this kid Walter real well. He heard me on piano. I'm playing jazz clubs and parties then and he thought that I'd get along with his best buddy Rudy. Rudy was one of these hardass mothers. He was living in the East Side of Detroit. His old man was from Germany, a tough sucker too. He came over in the beginning of second World War (1941 or '42) and by the time 1946 or '47 rolled along, he had a couple of tool-and-die shops. They were manufacturing parts for automobiles and tanks. He used to beat the living shit out of Rudy. German fathers do that. He used to smack him with a poker. Rudy was a weight lifter by this time, rugged as nails. Anyway we got to be pretty good buddies. He introduced me to bodybuilding and that kind of stuff.

So there were these two guys and myself, and we almost put this gang together from the three of us. Another member was Duke. His old man was a drunk and he used to beat him too. Then there was Hank. Hank's father was a door-to-door milkman. We used to drive his truck once in a while. A gal named Jean used to be kind of thick with us, and her dad had a little "nightclub" on the beach and we could commandeer it periodically, have our parties there. When my mother wasn't home, we'd have a bash at my house. So we called ourselves a gang, the Slim Bo Rockets; home bases was 9 Mile and Mack. We didn't fight much, but enough to be recognized by the other gangs; they respected our territory.

Once we had an arranged meeting with the Mack and St. Jean Gang (the gangs were named after their streets). At this particular rumble I was working with the Cass Avenue Gang. One guy's father had an egg route. He had a delivery truck. We also had a guy, Crazy Louie. He was huge by our standards in those days, over six feet, very muscular, and he was a little, shall we say, retarded. Unbeknownst to the guy's father, we took the panel egg truck, and we put Crazy Louie in the back. We put chains on each ankle and each wrist. Crazy Louie would do almost anything for a Baby Ruth candy bar. That's what we paid him to allow us to chain him up. We came to the site of the rumble and we were totally outnumbered. We had about ten or twelve, and they had at least thirty. Mack and St. Jean was their turf, and we wanted to let them know we were not afraid of them. We got out of the truck and our cars, and we started yelling at these guys. When things were getting really heated up, we opened the door to the panel truck, and Louie came bounding out with his chains on, and behind him came guys holding the chains, one for each wrist and ankle. He jumped out, waving his chains around, making noises like a gorilla. The guys were behind him, holding the chains, pulling on them so that he can't get away. The Mack and St. Jean guys just took off running. We stood on their corner for a little while, laughing and calling them cowards and chickens. Then we got in our cars and panel truck and took off, and that was the end of the war between Mack and St. Jean and Cass, at least for that night.

I went as a guest at this one party with my buddy Rudy. There must have been twenty or thirty guys there. Frankie Suma had just gotten out of juvenile home; he showed up with a gun. He got a little drunk and was waving his twenty-two-caliber pistol around. Rudy goes up to him and says, "Give me the gun, Frankie."

Frankie says, "No."

Rudy rips his shirt open and says, "If you're going to shoot me, make sure I'm dead, because I'm going to kill you." Frankie put the pistol down. I've never forgotten that.

Let me tell you, I'm pretty sure I survived that period of my life because of the ability I developed escaping my mother: *becoming very quiet.*

To survive on the streets of Detroit, you had to be good. You had to be able to be a shadow. You had to be able to not stick out. I think the first time I was attacked on a street in Detroit, I was about ten. It wasn't a very serious attack. A drunk came out of an alleyway and tried to get me, and I took off running. He chased me but couldn't catch me. Around then I realized that if I wasn't obvious, I wouldn't be attacked. When I was with the gangs, I always managed to fade into the woodwork when it was appropriate.

Not that I wasn't bold enough. In fact, I always insisted on having things my own way. It's just that I would look for rather subtle ways to get them! For instance, I actually was a member of three street gangs in Detroit at the same time in three different parts of town! Well, you weren't supposed to go into a given territory if you weren't a member of the right gang, but this kind of limitation wasn't for me, so I figured, "Okay, I'm gonna be in three gangs because I wanna go here, here, and here!" And I managed to do that, and they never found out, just because I was very good at not appearing at the wrong place at the wrong time.

Here's another illustration of the same point. After high school, I went away to Alma College for a year, but then I came back to Detroit to Wayne University and was living at home temporarily. Some guys from one of the gangs came to my house and said, "John, we really need you. We got a big rumble coming up with this West Side gang and we need all the guys we can get."

"Naw, I don't do that anymore."

"Oh c'mon, man."

Well, there were three of them out there, so I went. They said, "You've been gone for a year. We want you to go find out who's who—they won't know you."

There were about five carloads of us, and we went over to this other territory where there was a bunch of guys over on the corner. One of our guys said to me, "Find out if those are the guys that are the problem for us. They don't know you, so you and Polski go on and walk over there and find out who they are."

Okay. We walk over there, and Polski asks if they know Petrak. Petrak was a bigshot in our gang.

"You guys are from Petrak?" they replied.

"No, no, no." But they weren't having my denial.

At this point it looked like it was going to start getting rough. There were about ten to twelve of the West Side gang and they began grabbing us by the fronts of our shirts and passing us around and giving us little, nasty slaps. We were about to get our asses kicked royally when suddenly the police showed up and started shooting at the sky. That got everybody's attention. I really didn't want to be involved with the cops. I looked down the street and I saw a bus coming. It was about thirty yards to the bus stop from where I was—there in the middle of the scrape—so I walked very quietly backwards over to the bus stop so they didn't know I was leaving. I got on the bus and went to the back and looked out the window and saw the cops arresting everybody. And I just kind of waved. That could be the end of a Western. It was beautiful.

After that, I never got into another gang thing!

I never actually got into *serious* trouble from hanging out with gangs. It was hard to get in real trouble in those days. I did spend my share of nights in jail, but it never went on the record. They just locked you up to "teach you a lesson." What exactly that lesson was, I never quite found out!

I was actually much younger the first time I got thrown in jail. It was during World War II. A house in my neighborhood had a light that kind of blinked on and off in the upstairs window. About half-a-dozen of us got together and decided that the guy who lived there must be a German spy, so on Halloween we peppered his house with tomatoes and raised a general commotion. He must have called the police because they came and got us. It was strange that we were arrested, we thought, because, according to us, we were being good, patriotic citizens, exposing a German spy. The police didn't see it that way though, when I explained it to my dad, he got the idea, so I didn't get punished at home for that. As it turned out, I don't think he was a German spy. I think we were wrong. But hey—during wartime, you can't take any chances!

During my rebellious teenage days, I got thrown in jail quite a bit for fighting, but just for overnight, or maybe for four or five hours—that kind of thing. The police weren't like they are now. It wasn't anything serious. I've never stopped to count it, but I was incarcerated for a few hours maybe twenty times during those years. Something like that. But never since the cops have gotten tough.

Another aspect of being a teenager was the inevitable involvement with motor vehicles. This was Detroit after all. About two months after my father died, I convinced my mom to let me buy a car. In Michigan at that time, you could get a learner's permit at age thirteen and a regular license at fourteen years of age. I got my license and bought a '35 Ford for $375 of my own money from the guy next door. It turned out to be a real dog, but I learned a lot from trying to keep it on the road. First of all, the headlights weren't working very well, so I sent away to Sears & Roebuck and got a new wiring loom and spent about two days trying to figure out where all these wires were supposed to go. The lights were wired to a gadget that rotated around the post of the steering wheel and controlled the bright lights, dim lights, horn, and so on. The loom was the wiring piece that you hooked onto the bottom of the steering column. It was almost impossible because the wires already installed in the Ford were all black, but the new ones were color-coded and it wasn't possible to follow the codes. I'd push the light switch and the horn would start blowing, I'd push the horn and the lights would flash. The only way to get it right was by going through all the combinations trial-and-error style. It was a major headache. Once I had my car in the lot with the engine running, and the salesman said, "Who are your fenders waving at?" My front fenders were so loose they were flopping up and down as the motor ran. I learned a lot—if nothing else, not to assume that you will be able hook up something that you buy from a catalogue by just following directions!

Besides the lights not working, the engine was no great shakes. Eventually, it got so bad that I couldn't drive up the slight incline that went into our garage. I think what really happened was that the spark plugs had gotten so beaten up that they just couldn't fire very well, but I assumed that something was wrong with the valves. At that point I decided to give up on the thing and sold it to a junkyard for $56. The guy next door wanted to know what happened to it and, when I told him, he said, "Gee, too bad you didn't bring it over. I would have fixed it." I don't know about that. I'd had that old Ford on the road for about a year, so I figured I'd gotten my money's worth, and now I wanted a new toy.

For $125 I bought a '32 Ford from a parts dealer. By now I thought I was an experienced automotive engineer, see, so I could risk putting a buggy together practically from scratch. It turned out to be a real fun car. It didn't have a motor when I got it, so I sent to Sears & Roebuck for a rebuilt four-cylinder, and my buddy Rudy and I put it together.

I used it for all kinds of things, including making a little extra money. In St. Clair Shores, we had bad rains every spring, and the main intersection would flood, and you'd always see a lot of cars stalled there until the water subsided. I attached a 2 x 12 plank on the front of my car as a bumper, and I put the battery on the front seat where it wouldn't get wet and hung out with my vehicle at the intersection waiting for cars to stall. I could go through about two feet of water so I'd push these guys out and charge them a dollar. I'm not so proud of this, but when I used go out with a couple of guys at night, like after a Sunday music gig, we'd take my car over to the city parking lot, where they park their trucks and stuff, and we'd siphon gas out of the big Caterpillars and trucks and fill up my tank. We'd wait until ten at night and then go out with our gas can and siphoning tube. Once we had fuel, we could go out cruising all over the place. I grew up pretty fast.

One Sunday morning I woke up to find that my '32 Ford was gone. I called the police to report a car stolen. They came over to question and possibly arrest me! The Ford had been used to rob a liquor store and then abandoned. The police thought I might be the perpetrator. It turned out to be a couple of guys I knew and who knew my car.

Eventually I abused that car so badly that its engine broke down entirely. I put another engine in it and kept it going for a while. In time, I had enough to buy a '41 Mercury. I was a sort of teenage hustler. The money mostly came from musical gigs and odd jobs like towing stalled vehicles.

During that high-school period, we had a dance to play for on most Friday or Saturday nights. The alto sax man in the group was, I think, about twenty, and I was about sixteen or seventeen, and we were all eager to experience a bit more of "the world." We found out that we could get a box at the burlesque show in Detroit after we finished our job. It was about a twenty-minute drive downtown. They had three burlesque houses there. Of course I was under age, so the sax man would buy the tickets for all of us. We had a lot of fun at the shows. Once I fell in love with a beautiful stripper. I even went so far as to get some flowers and wait at the exit from the theater for her, but she wouldn't give me a tumble.

I was also playing for a lot of dances—every Wednesday night at the Civic Center. I really fell in love with this girl—she was gorgeous and was sort of digging on me. Then we found out we were cousins! My Uncle Fred was her father. That I didn't know initially and then she told me and all of a sudden—phew! My uncle had a talk with me; he said it's illegal for you to marry your cousin in Michigan. So we continued being friends.

Uncle Fred had nine kids and he only got nine by going to bed a lot. He probably thought, same blood, I was going to be pretty sexually active too. I was, what, sixteen, I guess. That was Doris and, damn, she was beautiful. I danced with her a little bit and then all of a sudden, I asked, "What's your last name?"

She said, "Tappert."

I said, "Oh my God, who's your father?"

She said, "Fred."

"Damn, that's my uncle." It was my mother's maiden name.

After that I did get in a fling with this girl named Cookie. This was my last year in high school. I'd go over to her two-story house and hit the horn and she'd come running out and we'd go to the movies, usually the drive-ins. But once in a while I went in her house to get her, and her mama let me know I wasn't wanted. One time mama started dusting me out of the house with a broom; she wasn't trying to hit me, just shoo me out of the place. Her father was telling me that if he ever caught me messing around with his daughter, it would be too bad for me. But we did break the rules a good bit. I had my 1932 Ford then, my second car, and I had fixed it up so it had two seats up front that could go down. We rigged that so we could make out in the car. We went out on Belle Isle—that's an island on Detroit River, a lover's lane sort of place. We were having a good time and I think she was on top of me when, all of a sudden, a flashlight comes in the window. It's the cops. I have to hand it to her: she was under age, and it would've been statutory rape, but she got me out of trouble. When they found out she was fifteen, and threatened to take me to jail, she started acting so tough, putting on her garter belt and all that stuff. I told the cops I was going to go to college and, when I graduated, we'd all get married. The cops saw how she was acting and one of them said, "I'd advise you to get rid of this babe," then walked away.

We broke up before graduation. I had given her my ring, but my mother asked me to get it back from her so I could wear it for graduation. For some reason this was a really big deal to her, and we busted up over that. I think after we broke up, she put on about twenty pounds. She wasn't nearly as attractive then.

As a high-school senior, I wrote a regular column on music for the school paper—mostly on jazz concerts—and I also wrote articles opposing racial segregation. The jazz column was my idea, and it was a great success. That's when I started seeing a lot of jazz shows, so I enjoyed it, and it became a regular feature of the high-school paper. For all my extra-curricular cutting up and my being generally disrespectful of school, I still appeared to be a rather respectable high-school citizen by the time I left in 1949. I got great grades, graduated salutatorian, and got honor certificates in geometry, sociology, international relations, and journalism. When I went to the honors assembly, I had no idea that I was going to get any awards. I was wearing some beat-up peg pants with about a thirteen-inch cuff at the bottom and a t-shirt with a pack of Lucky-Strikes rolled into the sleeve, looking like the classic teenage rebel. Had I known I was going to be honored, I would have dressed the same way. I walked up on stage about five times, delivering a visual message that you don't have to be conformist in order to do well.

During senior year, everybody was deciding to go to college, but it never occurred to me to think about it until it was almost too late to apply. I finally remembered that my dad always assumed I would go to college, so I went to the library and picked up the college directory. Alma College started with "A." It was the first one I saw. I applied to it and was accepted. It was in Alma, Michigan. My mother thought it was wonderful because it was a Presbyterian college.

The summer before I went away, I worked for my grandfather, building a house for him and Grandma on one of the two vacant lots next to our house. Grandpa hired me for seventy-five cents an hour to carry the cement blocks and do all the heavy work, while he built his new home. He let me put the chimney up by myself, but somehow I got it spiraled. It looked strange, but it functioned all right. Grandpa said, "That's good. That'll be your trademark."

Grandpa did have a temper. When I was putting the roof on (Grandpa was about seventy and didn't want to go up on the roof), I was trimming corners off of the joist with a little hatchet. He told me to use his big hatchet. It would be quicker. I refused, and he threw it at me! Fortunately, I saw it coming and ducked.

In spite of my grandmother's and my mother's prudish views about drinking, Grandpa was something of a drinking man, though he had to do his drinking on the sly! He used to love beer, though truly, I don't remember him ever getting really drunk. He did have his special brand—Seebowaing it was called—made from spring water in northern Michigan. That and peppermint schnapps were his favorites.

The house we built had a utility room three steps down from the kitchen. My grandmother had fallen down and broken her hip and was on a walker, so she couldn't go down steps anymore. I asked Grandpa, "Why the steps? Grandma can't get down there."

He said, "You'll see."

Then he put a potty down in there—a little toilet—and he built a partition around it with doors like you'd see in a public restroom. After that summer I went away to school and, when I came back to visit, Grandma and Grandpa had moved in. As soon as he and I were alone, Grandpa winked and took me to see the utility room.

Do you remember a beautiful, popular painting called "September Morn?" It's a picture of a nude, blonde, nymph-like girl in water about up to her knees or lower. He had this poster hanging on the inside of the toilet door, and he'd put a bottle of schnapps in the toilet tank! So he had his little private sanctuary!

College

After the summer, it was off to Alma, and almost immediately Alma was a crisis for me.

Alma, Michigan, was a little farm town, and I'm really a city kind of guy. One problem was financial. I was used to playing for my supper, so to speak, and I couldn't even make a buck playing the accordion in this place. I had maybe three gigs during the whole first semester. The only other income I had was a check once a month from my father's Social Security for $13.25. And I was supposed to live on that! My mother received $35 per month. By Christmas time I'd had enough of Alma, and I negotiated a transfer to Wayne University in Detroit because I wanted to be back in the city. I had to stick out the year in Alma, but by the summer before my second year, I was back home.

I remember at Alma, how sophomores have to do something to the freshmen. I knew that was happening. We were supposed to climb the flagpoles and get the flags down; otherwise the sophomores would punish us in some way. I'm from Detroit and they're talking about this big campus war they're going to have between the sophomores and freshmen, so I went back home and returned in a car with about five guys, gang members. We knocked the shit out of those sophomores. Everyone on campus saw these strange guys from Detroit pulling the sophomores down and sitting on them. The Dean found out about it and pulled me into his office. I said that I thought this was a battle to win. I didn't know it was just a fun little thing.

I departed from Alma with almost a "straight A" average, and I don't know how the hell I did it because I probably didn't attend class more than fifty percent of the time. Though I couldn't get much paying work in Alma, I did play music. I was seventeen when I entered college, but there was a bunch of older guys at Alma who were back from the service—World War II veterans in school on the GI Bill. This was 1949. And it was the same old thing. I could play jazz piano, so these guys would take me around to bars and clubs. We'd go to Saginaw and I'd play the piano. They were my "buddies" so they'd get to pick up women, pretty much on my charisma! And I must say, I had a pretty good deal going, because these guys, who were in their mid-twenties, were taking me with them the whole time. I'd get back to Alma usually about Tuesday and leave again on Thursday. I had weekends that went Friday through Monday.

The summer before I started at Wayne, an old friend of my Dad who worked at Chrysler's marine engine plant in Detroit got me a job there. His name was Sam Penny. Working at Chrysler taught me a lot about relations between workers and management, and between black and white workers on the assembly line. My job was putting screws in the top of oil pumps. I'd do a whole bunch of them and then go and read a book for a while until the production line caught up with me. Pretty soon the union representative came up to me and said, "Kid, if you want to keep your job all summer, you're going to have to slow down. It took us a long time to get Chrysler to agree to a slower rate of production, and you're makin' it look like it's going *too* slow."

Well, I didn't do too well at slowing down, so what happened was, Mr. Penny came to my rescue and they transferred me and turned me into an "inspector." Now I was turning the wheels on the oil pumps to make sure they were functioning properly. That was okay, but very soon they closed the oil-pump line down and moved me over to an altogether different production line.

Speed was an issue at this new task too, but in a different way. There were seven of us on this new line, three black guys on one side where the line started, three white guys on the other at the end of the line, and me in the middle. The three white guys had automated machinery, so their rate of production was fixed. But the three black guys and I worked on hand machines, so we could control our own pace. Production was paid on a piece-work basis, so if the white guys on the end of the line had to work overtime to get their work done, they didn't get paid overtime for it.

The three white guys were real "rednecks" and not at all friends with the blacks, and I could see at once that it was going to be possible for me to ally myself with one or the other of the two groups but not both. The truth was, it was really very natural for me to make friends with the blacks. They were much more fun to be with. The choice was obvious.

We became buddies pretty quickly, and that meant that there really was no way I could relate socially to the white group, as I mentioned. But the problem wasn't just social. The black group and I, if we wanted to, could do our tasks on the production line faster than the automated white guys, but we could also, if we chose, work more slowly. My three black buddies had the idea that we should all work nice and slow so the white group would have to work overtime. No big deal, just a little payback.

My friendship with my black co-workers went beyond the line. They started taking me out to bars—the "Black and Tans" that I mentioned before. The "leader of the pack," so to speak, was a fellow I would guess to be in his late thirties or early forties. His name was Ray Secrest. It was Ray who invited me to go "nightclubbing" with these guys. Well, though I was only eighteen and the drinking age was twenty-one, I could usually get away with it because I still had the fake identification documents that I had acquired to play in music bars. It was good enough to get into the places, but it was risky if there were cops around, especially for a white kid in a black hangout.

Well, one Friday night Ray said, "Come on out with me and my buddies." So I went and met them all in an alley. One guy came up and gave me a big hug, actually weeping. I said, "What's going on?"

He said, "Well, man, it's just that I never get to be friends with a white guy. You seem like a nice fellow and I'm just moved."

We went to a place called "The Gay Black and Tan." (That was, of course, before "gay" meant homosexual. It just meant a good time.) A small combo was playing there, and people were dancing, but you had to go through the narrow barroom to get to the dance floor. The bar itself was long and narrow, and there was one row of booths behind the bar stools where people were sitting and drinking. We all went directly to the back to listen to the music. After we were there for a while, I got up and sat in with the band—a black group of course—and I had a great time playing with those guys.

Not for long though. After a while, there seemed to be some kind of a fracas going on in the long skinny part of the place. We could see the bartender leaning over his bar and beating some guy on the head with something like a billy club and screaming at him to get out of the place.

The dude left, but ten minutes later he was back, brandishing a long knife and threatening the bartender. Everybody at the bar and the booths was scurrying to get to the dance floor and out of the way. Up at the front of the place, there was the guy with his knife and the bartender facing off across the bar. Suddenly the bartender reached down under the bar and pulled out a gun and shot the guy!

Now remember, I'm the only white in the place, and I'm thinking, "Oh boy, the cops are gonna be in here in a minute and I'm gonna be in deep trouble. I'm a minor and they'll spot me because I'm white, and I don't know whether they'll accept my fake I.D. or not."

Meanwhile, I notice that my buddy Ray is up at the narrow end of the place cruising the deserted booths, nonchalantly scooping the loose coins off the tables! He's not worried about any of this—he's just taking advantage of the fracas to rake in a little extra change. When he finished his rounds, he remembered me.

There was a very attractive waitress in this joint that I thought was rather neat. Ray grabbed me and called her over and said to her, "You take care of my friend here and make sure the police don't find him." She said "sure" and took me into the lady's room and had me put my feet up on top of the toilet and sort of squat there until the whole thing blew over.

Well, it was really wild. The black women kept coming in and laughing and saying, "You know that little white boy? He's in HEE-ah!"

After I don't know how long—it seemed like maybe an hour—the cops had come and gone. The guy was wounded but not dead, and they had hauled him out of the place. The waitress came and got me out of the lady's room and we all just went right on with our good time.

Later that evening we went to a kind of old garage, and lo and behold, the great blues singer Muddy Waters, was sitting in the center of the place singing and playing his guitar.

When the summer was over I started at Wayne University. That place was right up my alley. At that time it wasn't "Wayne State" yet. It was just "Wayne University," which was a city school. The State took it over a bit later while I was in the Coast Guard. When I came back in '57, it was "Wayne State."

During my first year at Wayne, I had a buddy from Alma who transferred on purpose with me. He was a big black guy, a football player, named Freddy Hayes, and no doubt he was at Alma because white, middle-America Alma needed to have a token black on their roster (it was before the days when colleges filled their football teams with black athletes, but recent enough so that the "appearance" of integration was a good idea). But he and I became good friends, and we wanted to stay together when I was going to Detroit, so he transferred too. He was a year or so older than I was and was already thinking about what he wanted to do after graduation, which was law school—and Wayne University was a likely place.

Pretty soon after school began, I joined a fraternity. I was still under the drinking age, of course, but you could always get a beer in the frat house, so one day I took Freddy into the basement and we hung out for a while and had a beer or two. Nobody said that there was a problem with any of this while we were there, but the next day my dear brothers made it clear that the "brotherhood" of the "fraternity" did not extend to black people, and therefore it was inappropriate for me to have one as a guest in the house. I was flabbergasted. I didn't quit the fraternity, but my enthusiasm for frat life definitely cooled and, whenever I saw the opportunity, I made my brothers uncomfortable on the race issue. For instance, when they had their summer prom dance toward the end of the school year, I took a black girl for my date. And that made me very popular, as you can imagine.

You know, when you're up for joining a fraternity, there are a lot of pranks played on you and idiotic tasks that you have to per-form, all under the general rubric of "hazing." Well, during, I think, my second year at Wayne, a good buddy of mine named Moe was in the process of being hazed. Moe was a student in automotive engineering and a generally clever and capable guy. He got tired of the stupidity of the hazing process, so, on the night of his ini-tiation, he turned the tables on the "pledge-master"—the obnox-ious character who had been in charge of hazing him. This pledge-master owned a Volkswagen that he was very proud of because, since it was so small, it could get in and out of places more imposing vehicles were incapable of negotiating. Well, Moe decided to show this character just how maneuverable that little bug could be. He got three or four guys to help him completely disassemble it and carry it up stairs to the third floor of the frat house and then put it back together again. The pledge-master and the rest of the fraternity brothers spent hours trying to figure out how the VW got up there, and more hours trying to get it out again.

Some time later, my friend Freddy, who was now a law student, was working as the hotel manager of a black hotel six or eight blocks off the Wayne campus. At that time I was playing the piano in Paradise Valley, which was located pretty close to the hotel, and I was accustomed to stopping by and seeing Freddy at the hotel after a gig when he was on the night shift. I might just walk in at about 2:30 in the morning and hang out for a while.

At this time, I owned a black 1949 Ford that I drove to school and to work. Unfortunately for me, the Ford looked pretty much like a police car. One night while I was visiting Freddy, in walks a guy with a rather imposing get-up and a very sexy entourage. He was sporting an oversize cashmere overcoat, and at least three females hung on his arms. Two wary-looking body guards straddled this already menacing tableau. Freddy had told me about this guy, who was simply known as "The King." This "King" was a king*pin* of the neighborhood drug business, and he was renting the whole top floor of the hotel.

"Good morning," says Freddy.

The King doesn't mince words. He ignores Freddy and drags his whole company right up to *me*.

"You're a narc and we're gonna take *care* of you."

I said, "I'm not a narc, I'm not even twenty-one yet."

Why I thought my under-age status would reassure him that I wasn't a narcotics agent I have no idea. Presence of mind in a tough situation, my hallmark, no doubt.

"You're a narc. You look like a narc and you got a cop car out there, so we gonna *do* you."

For the second time in my short life, I thought for sure I was witnessing the scene of my own execution. Lunch money all over again. The King certainly would have "done me" if Freddy hadn't leapt over the desk with a baseball bat that he stashed there for just such circumstances. He so startled the King and his girls and his men that for two seconds they actually listened to him. He talked real fast and convinced them that I was his old friend and not a narcotics agent and that, if they wanted to "do me," they'd have to bloody up the hotel lobby with his blood as well as mine. This was not, I think, what they had in mind, and so I escaped underworld retribution again.

Rudy and I had this house; we paid a little bit of rent, not very much, and I was playing the piano at the beachcomber nightclub. Two waitresses were hanging around, and they asked me if they could come over and see my house. One was in her thirties and the other was a little Greek girl. Rudy comes home and sees them sitting in the living room. It was hot and so they were stripped down to their underwear and I was serving beers. Rudy says, "I like that little Greek girl. Come on, babe, let's go on to the bedroom."

She says, "Ten dollars." And he paid her.

I dropped them back when I needed to leave. I thought Rudy was an idiot for paying her but, when I came back, I gave him two bucks so I could say, "Here, Rudy; here's my twenty percent."

We had a good time living in that house.

Rudy also played the accordion, but he never did any professional playing. Sometimes we'd parade down the street with our accordions after we'd got a couple beers in us. We'd do it right at sunrise, and the neighbors would complain about these two drunks running early in the morning with accordions.

When I wasn't playing music, keeping Rudy out of trouble, or dodging the underworld, I was working pretty hard on my studies. I majored in psychology—not for any particular reason except that, when I enrolled in my junior year, I had to pick a major. I figured that if I was going to be a lawyer, probably psychology would help me in the courtroom.

It took me four years, including the one at Alma, to earn my B.A. Wayne had twenty-five thousand students at the time that I was going there, and I think somewhere on the order of eight thousand were part-time. They were working their way through school. It was an ideal environment for me, since I had to work too, even though I was full-time in school. It was easy for me because I'd been working since I was just a kid. I could get plenty of gigs playing the piano in the clubs downtown.

Around this period I was starting to play with some really great musicians. If you're a jazz player and a guy really blows his bloody ass off and makes you go wow, you feel it inside of you. Kenny Burrell, he was one of those. We'd be laying down a tune, maybe a Fats Domino thing—"Blueberry Hill"; we'd knock out a couple of choruses of it and then all of a sudden it's his turn. I'd do mine; he'd do his, all over the place. Like that. That's the way it worked. It was such a privilege to be playing with him. Kenny was flat-out inspirational.

I met Kenny in a music-theory class at Wayne. One of the things we did was transcribe music from ear. I watched Kenny do this and was amazed. They'd put on a record like Chopin and we were supposed to write what we heard on blank music paper.

Burrell just sat there and copied it down perfectly. Theoretically, he was a music genius. He also looked great on stage. He talked like a black man but resembled a Spanish hipster; he had kinky hair—tall, thin, and bashful.

I started playing jam sessions every Wednesday afternoon at the student center at Wayne. Tommy Flannigan was also attending those sessions. As I recall, he became Ella Fitzgerald's piano man.

Kenny and I started working together; we got gigs at both white clubs and black clubs. It was interesting because Kenny himself was part white and part black, so he wasn't totally accepted by either community. He lived in a kind of no-man's land. But he was fun to be with and a great musician. He eventually became quite famous, and has been mentioned recently in *Downbeat* and *Playboy*. The cat is still performing.

Later on, I got to play piano on Monday nights at the Bowl-A-Drome. It was a bowling alley to which they had added a lounge. The music was in the lounge. They had a little stage about three feet high with a piano and enough room for four or five guys to jam—space for a drum set, etc. The bar was about forty feet long. These "jazz night" jam sessions were such that someone could just show up and say, "Hey man, can I come in?" A guy name of Frank Russelino arrived and tried out with us on trombone, in fact several Mondays in a row. I was at Wayne then, probably a third- or fourth-year student at that time, and I was playing piano every Monday night at the Bowl-A-Drome. Then this guy appears with his trombone and sits in, so I say, "Well, what do you want to do, man?"

He says, "Let's play 'Take Me Out to the Ball Game.'"

I say, "What!" But the son of a bitch was all over that trombone. Maybe two months later he announces, "Okay, I got my try-out with Stan Kenton." Kenton came to town and he was at the Masonic Temple, so we all went, the Monday-night guys, about five of us. Frank was having his audition. It was really neat because Art Pepper, alto sax man with Kenton, and Maynard Ferguson, were both just getting started too. Right before my eyes Maynard Ferguson blew his natural ass off. Maynard is fantastic.

When Pepper came up, they brought him to the microphone to play and he was so stoned they had to guide him there, but boy did he blow nice.

So Frankie got the gig. We were all "Yeah for Frank!"

I got to know Ferguson and still know him. I see him at concerts around here. He's very sick and I offer my services. He always says, "Well next time I get to town." His ankles are getting to be like soccer balls and his belly's sticking out—he's going to die. Art Pepper already died in Holland. He fell out the window in Amsterdam—he was stoned, landed in the street.

I knew some great musicians; we'd get together and blow. I was in that crew and we didn't have racial minds at all. It was good times.

Musical work of this kind actually didn't get in the way of my school work at all. I found that I was able to read my textbooks while playing the piano. The only requirement was that the drummer had to tap me on the shoulder with his drumstick when the end of the song was coming—otherwise I'd keep on playing my solo straight into the next chorus. Everybody thought it was pretty weird when they saw me studying while I was playing. I guess I learned to split my brain that way.

Besides playing gigs, I taught accordion at a certain music studio that shall remain nameless because it was a scam operation and it's out of business now. The studio sent door-to-door representatives into factory-worker neighborhoods. They gave hearing tests to children and announced to their proud parents that their child was a "musical genius." The parents were sold a series of ten lessons for their little prodigy on a beginner's accordion that they lent to the child for the purpose. My job was to get the student to be able to play "Jingle Bells" by the end of the fourth lesson. The studio door was kept ajar. The manager heard the "Jingle Bells" and entered the room "astonished" that a fourth-lesson student could play the song. I was to suggest that the beginner's accordion was holding back progress. Most of the time this produced a sale of a larger accordion at a great profit. I quit the studio after about six weeks, and I took eight students with me. I got wholesale accordions for them and went to their homes to give lessons. This worked out fine and my conscience was clear.

My mother had remarried during my senior year at Wayne University, about seven or eight years after my father's death. Nick was a Hungarian watchmaker, so I made some money selling watches and diamonds through his jewelry store. I also got two instant stepbrothers. Life was very cool.

Anyway, I began at Wayne in September of 1950 and graduated in June, 1953, but before I graduated—this was during the winter semester break at the end of '52 and the beginning of '53— a racially mixed group of four of us got a gig to go down and play in Sarasota, Florida. The guy that organized the group was named Gilbert Holliday (no relation to Billy). We drove in two cars because we had drums and other equipment. We arrived about two hours before we had to start to play, and we went into the bar to set up our stuff. At one point we took a break and went to sit down at a table and have a beer, but they wouldn't serve us. I asked, "What do we do?"

The bartender said, "You can stay here, but your friends will have to go out in the alley to drink theirs."

I said, "Okay, I'll go out in the alley with them." But that wouldn't do either. The point was, blacks weren't allowed to drink with whites. Period.

The next morning word had swept around town like a hurricane that I was a "nigger lover," and I couldn't get served anywhere. I went into a Walgreens and the waitress just ignored me. We stuck it out for two nights and decided we'd had enough. We jumped in the cars and drove back to Detroit without getting paid.

At the end of the spring semester of 1953, I graduated from Wayne. In October, I joined the Coast Guard.

Military, Medical School, and Early Practice

Coast Guard

Things were precarious for me after graduation because I had used up my educational deferment from military service. The Korean War was still going on, and I was expecting to be drafted any day. The jazz group I was playing with—and I was playing with a *good* jazz group—was looking for a new piano player because they didn't expect me to be around much longer. So I went to the draft board and said, "Take me, man. I'm just wasting my time here."

They said, "Well, we got to draw your name out of the hat. We can't just take you."

So I got a job with an outfit called the "Michigan Brake Exchange." I had to drive around in a pick-up and, if a big truck had trouble with its brakes on the road, I would go out and pull the wheel off.

I would bring the wheel or wheels into the shop, get them fixed, carry them back to the big truck, and put them back on. This was hard on my delicate, piano-playing fingers, so I didn't particularly want to spend too much time doing that. One day in October, I went down to the federal building in Detroit to enlist; this time I resolved not to take no for an answer. For some reason, I was in a real hurry to get going. I didn't want to wait even a short period of time. I tried the recruitment offices of all the different military services, asking, "Can you take me tomorrow morning?"

The Air Force said, "Well, it's going to take about four or five days."

I wouldn't even think about the Marines. I was mad at the Army because they wouldn't draft me. The Navy said, "Ehhh—about a week." But the Coast Guard said, "Be here tomorrow morning at eight o'clock. We'll give you your physical. If you pass, you'll be on a train going to Cape May, New Jersey, by ten o'clock."

I didn't tell my mother what was happening, but I did tell my sister Phyllis. She and her husband, Cliff, decided they wanted to give me a farewell dinner. It turned out to involve a risky caper that could very well have ended my military career before it started, and a lot else besides.

I spent most of the day packing what little gear I intended to bring with me and, early in the evening, went over to Phyllis and Cliff's. They suggested we go to a nice steak house they knew about crosstown. I said, "Great." We had a few glasses of champagne, got a little high, and took off.

Cliff was kind of a wild and impulsive guy—almost as wild as I was, even though he was about fifteen years older; he had somewhat settled down since he married my sister. They had just bought a new house in St. Clair Shores and were in the process of landscaping their front yard.

To get from St. Clair Shores to the steak house, we had to pass through Grosse Point, the hoity-toity part of town where the automotive company executives had their swanky estates. As we drove through, ogling the beautiful lawns and gardens, Cliff kept talking about how it was high time he to got his own landscaping done.

Suddenly Cliff spied the Grosse Point Police Station coming up on the right. It was all dark outside, but in front of the building there was a line of nice shrubs you could see in a distant street light. We were only about two miles from his house so, after about two seconds deliberation, he ordered my sister, who was driving, to turn us around and take us back to the house, where we could pick up some shovels and buckets and trowels. Off we went, got the equipment, and then zoomed back to the front of the police station where, like lightning, we liberated, oh, five or six shrubs. Hey, what could they do? I was about to go into the Coast Guard—so the hell with it. We stuck 'em in the back of the car, flew back to the house one more time, dug holes and planted the shrubs with a great flourish, and then went and ate our steak dinners. Never got caught. Stealing landscaping from out in front of a police station. It was about 8:30 at night. You'd think the cops would have been looking out there once in a while. The sidewalk was right out the front door and the shrubs were up to the sidewalk. I guess no one was paying attention.

The next morning I was at the Coast Guard recruiting office right on schedule. Though I hadn't told my mother I was leaving (I wasn't getting along real well with my mother and stepfather then), Phyllis must have done so, because my mother and stepfather, Nick, showed up at the railroad station after I had boarded the train, and there I was, waving out the window.

When I got to Cape May, they found out I was a musician, so they had me start a dance band for the officers' club. I was led to believe that I could just stay there for the whole four years of my enlistment but, after I finished boot training, it turned out that that wasn't how things were. I was assigned to regular Coast Guard duty, and there was no telling where I'd be headed. An ensign or somebody, I don't remember who, asked me if I wanted to take the test for Officer Candidate School. I said, "Naw, I don't want to be an officer."

"Well," he said, "you might get stationed somewhere you don't want to be. If the orders come and you don't like your duty station, you can go to Officer Candidate School. You can always resign later and tell them where you want to go, and they'll probably let you do it." Okay, good!

I took the test to become an officer and, as luck would have it, I scored high, so Officer Candidate School it was! It was a matter of months before orders came through to start Officer Candidate School, during which time I was moved from one place to another. First, it was to Ellis Island in New York.

Being in New York was great, mainly because I could hang out in Manhattan when not on duty. I quickly realized that it would be useful to have a car so, as soon as I had a couple of days off, I hopped a flight to Detroit to fetch my old '49 Ford, which was still more or less operational. I drove it to New York and parked it at the south end of Manhattan Island. Now I was a guy with a car—a rare thing for a young man around Manhattan. Of course, the car had no reverse gear, so theoretically you couldn't park the thing, but somehow I always managed to find spots where I could pull away without having to back up. I never did get it fixed.

I started playing piano off-duty at bars and began to get to know a lot of people. At one point, a French movie director approached me and actually asked me to desert the military and come to France and be an actor for him! Nicolas Spaniat. I thought about that for a while, but I realized I'd be a fugitive from then on and it probably wouldn't be worth it.

With a car you can pick up girls pretty easily, and I was getting, well, *familiar* with a whole lot of different women, mainly through my piano playing. One particular Puerto Rican named Alyce worked at a place called "Neary's Show Bar," and this Alyce had decided somehow that I was her private property, though this wasn't my view of our relationship at all. She couldn't speak English, and I couldn't speak Spanish, but we communicated in other ways, so to speak, but not too well on this point of personal proprietorship! Well, one night I happened to walk past Neary's Show Bar with two other girls on my arm—I had convinced them that I could give them a tour of the Manhattan jazz scene. Alyce was working within eye-shot of the front window and caught a glimpse of us. Out she came like a shot, right at me. She scratched the hell out of my cheeks and whacked me with her fists—just because I was walking down the street with these other girls.

I remained stationed on Ellis Island for about a month. Then I got sent to Jones Beach, the famous bathing resort on Long Island, New York. Unfortunately, it was the middle of January.

Once we arrived—four of us were being shuffled around together—it turned out they needed one guy at a lifeboat station on Fire Island, another island off Long Island. We drew straws and I lost. Now it was Fire Island in February. I don't know if you know how cold *that* is, but it's very cold. We had a nutty skipper on the island and he had us out rowing at four o'clock in the morning in Long Island Sound. He'd get drunk—maybe it would be four in the morning—and say, "Okay guys, drill time." We'd get in a boat and have to row. It would be about eight guys, four oars on each side. He'd call out, "Okay, let's move your asses." He'd be in the boat with us, yelling, "Heave, heave." The water was icy cold, somewhat rough. I don't remember us getting into high wind, just high water. Massive waves. The first time we went out there,

I didn't know we were going to be rowing. I didn't even think about having gloves. My hands were all chafed and freezing.

Also, every day you had to do four hours up in the lighthouse. If you saw something that didn't belong, you'd report it to the main desk where the skipper might be. I can remember one time, I was on duty from 4:00 a.m. till 8:00 a.m. in the tower and I saw this big silver thing coming. It was a few miles away from us. Shiny and round, it looked to me as if it could have been one of those UFOs. I called down and said, "I don't know what this is, but I think it's a UFO." It was going around, the sun was coming up and shining off of it, particularly on one side. I later found out that it was supposed to be a weather balloon that had broken loose from the Navy. I was the only guy there with a college degree, which, under the circumstances, was by no means an advantage. I stayed for a month and endured the continuous jibes of the skipper: "Okay, college boy! Get over here, etc., etc., etc.!"

Finally my orders came through for Officer Candidate School. I was to go to New London, Connecticut. When I got my papers, I said to the skipper, "Next time I see you, you might be taking orders from *me*." That was a lovely moment!

Mother's new husband was a man who had only finished the fourth grade, and his attitudes about education weren't much better than the skipper's. He would say to me stuff like, "What are you going to do with your degree? How much money are you gonna make?" AW, SHUT UP! JESUS! His name was Nicholas Petrocy and, while I was at Officer Candidate School, he was sent to prison.

Petrocy was a watchmaker by training, as I said, and he made his living from a jewelry store that he owned, but he also worked as a professional clown. One Saturday he and a buddy named Vic were clowning, and the following is what *I think* occurred. Vic had been driving drunk. Actually, I think they both were drunk. They were on Belle Isle, which is an island park in the Detroit River. Somehow the car must have gone out of control and they ran over and killed a little boy lying under a tree. Now this Vic had a bad heart, so my stepfather claims he took the rap for him and told the police that he was the one who was driving. The upshot was that he had to do two years for involuntary manslaughter at the Detroit House of Corrections. That was inadvertently lucky for me; I'll tell you why.

When word came that he was about to go to prison, they gave me a weekend pass to go home and say goodbye to him. I came back to the base that Sunday night. A certain Lieutenant Flanagan was the Officer of the Day. He was sitting behind the desk when I came in. I was pretty "up" from having had four days at home and seeing all the guys. I was feeling a little jaunty. But as soon as I saw Flannigan, I knew he was all pissed off about something. I said, "Gee Lieutenant, you look kind of upset. What's bothering you?"

He snarled, "Aw, this goddamn Coast Guard."

I said, "Well, what's the matter?"

"This is the third time they called me back."

"The third time they called you back?"

"Yeah." he said. "I'm a football coach and every time they need a new coach at the academy, they call me back. I was out there— I had a good job at a college over in Cincinnati!"

"Well, how'd they call you back?"

"Oh," he said, "when you take this commission, they've got you until you're sixty-five. They can call you back any time they want."

"Really?"

"Yeah, once you sign your name on that thing and accept a

commission they can call you back when you're sixty-four years old if they want you."

Monday morning I went in to see the captain. I said, "I'm sorry sir, I'm going to have to resign."

He said, "Well, why is that?"

I said, "Well, I don't think I have the ability to be an officer. I just don't have the self-confidence."

"Dammit, your grades are okay. Why don't you want to be an officer?"

"I don't think I could run a ship."

He said, "You must be queer."

"No, I don't think I'm queer."

"If you don't want to be an officer, then you must be one of them queers."

Then he said, "You go to the barracks and come back tomorrow. You let me know. Maybe you'll change your mind." Apparently, he was under some pressure to commission more ensigns.

I returned the next day and said, "No, I still want to resign."

He said, "Get out my office, you queer son-of-a-bitch."

I hightailed out of there and the yeoman (kind of like a male secretary) sitting in the outer office said, "Boy! You really got him, didn't ya!"

"Yeah!"

He said, "Where do you want to go?"

"Well, I'd like to go to Detroit and get on one of those navigational aid boats that goes up and down the river."

"You're *from* Detroit. I can't send you there."

"Okay."

Now, here was my second choice: after I told my brother-in-law Cliff that I was going into the Coast Guard, he volunteered that there were Coast Guard guys in Miami riding horses up and down the beach looking for submarines. During World War II, Cliff had been at Normandy with Patton, so he should know, right?

I said, "I want to go to Miami and join the Beach Patrol."

The guy said, "What the hell are you talking about? There ain't no goddamn Beach Patrol!"

So in the midst of this display of a bit of goofy defiance and a bit of macho insubordination, just when I wasn't paying attention, at the precise moment that spirit guides tend to slip one by you, I made a fateful choice. I remembered when I was in boot training that when I went into the sick bay for vaccinations and stuff, corpsmen were sitting around playing cards, smoking cigarettes, and putting a little hospital alcohol in their Coca-Cola. I said, "I think I want to become a hospital corpsman."

He said, "That I can do for you."

I packed up all my stuff—which was one big sea bag—threw it in the back of a truck, and they took me across the river to Groton, Connecticut. I had to work in hospital clean-up detail for about three weeks until class started. The class I took after those three weeks is quite simply how I came to be a doctor. I really loved it! I still consider it the most demanding and yet inspirational educational experience I've ever gone through. It was sixteen weeks—sixteen weeks to learn how to be a Coast Guard medic from ground zero. I studied anatomy, physiology, first aid, emergency, and pharmacy. We were in class from 8:00 a.m. until 5:00 p.m. and, after that, we had to make sure that the hospital was clean and perform other menial tasks until maybe 9:00 or 9:30 in the evening.

I finished at the top of the class. When it was over, I had qualified to serve on a boat by myself: "Independent duty"—no doctors.

Actually, I did so well that they were going to keep me on as a teacher, but I got in trouble with the law. Here's what happened: A guy named "Ski" and I were at a USO party and one of the girls there gave us her address and said, "Come on over." Well, we got about half drunk—maybe a little more than half drunk—and we decided at about two in the morning to pay her a visit. We drove to the address she gave us. The lights were all dark so we tried the front door and it was open. We didn't do anything *bad*. We were both hungry, so we found our way to the kitchen, sat down, and made sandwiches from stuff in the refrigerator. The kitchen was on the second floor. At about that time, her father, who was on the third floor, heard the noise and came running. We made a mad dash down the stairs. I tripped and fell, rolled down the stairs, stumbled out of the house, crossed the street, and jumped into my car. Of course, it wouldn't start!

Ski just ran and kept on running. I found a field, and even though it was wintertime, I lay down and went to sleep. The cops were out scanning the place with their flashlights, but they didn't spot me. I woke up in the morning and went to my car to see if I'd have any better luck getting it started, but as soon as I put my hand on the door handle, they nabbed me!

I spent a few hours in jail in New London, but the girl and her father didn't press charges, so I was released. It was all in fun, so to speak, but word did get back to the Coast Guard, so it was decided at the school that I probably shouldn't remain there on the faculty. The Coast Guard instead sent me to New Orleans.

After training was over, they gave me twenty days leave before I had to go to New Orleans. I stopped in Detroit where my mom was living in this house, remarried to that jeweler, Nick. I saw my Grandma, and every time she looked at me, she was crying. I said, "What's the matter, Grandma?"

"Oh, you gotta go, you gotta go." It was during the Korean War and I assumed she thought I was going to be in battle.

I said, "That's not where I'm going; I'm going to New Orleans."

She said, "That's not it, that's not it."

I said, "What is it, Grandma?"

She said, "Everybody thinks the world is round, but I know it's flat and you're going on a boat in the Gulf of Mexico, so you'll sail off the end."

I thought, 'Oh my God!' I said "Grandma, I'll tell you what; every night I'll go up to the top deck of the boat and I'll look for the edge. If the sun is over the edge, I'll see it illuminating. If I get a glimpse of that edge and we're heading toward it, I'll get in one of the rowboats and I'll row like the dickens the other way."

At New Orleans, I was stationed on Lake Ponchartrain for about two months. They put me to work in the sick bay and doing physicals on guys that wanted to enlist. Hey! I liked that: X-Rays and other technical stuff—a lot of fun. During those two months, I got to play piano at the Brass Rail for tips and free drinks. The Brass Rail was on Canal Street near Bourbon Street where all the strip shows are, and I got to know a lot of strippers. I finally received my orders to go to Panama City, Florida. I was to leave on the bus at nine o'clock the next morning, so that night I thought I'd go out and say goodbye to one of my favorite strippers. She worked to four o'clock in the morning at one of the clubs on Bourbon Street. That would leave me five hours before I had to catch the bus, during which time I thought we could have some fun.

I went to her club at about 2:00 a.m. and ordered a six-ounce beer. Even in those days they were charging $2 for a beer in a place like that. I was making a hefty $87.50 a month from the Coast Guard, plus whatever I could pick up playing the piano here and there, but I thought I'd nurse that one beer for a couple of hours until she got off work. Well, I don't know how much time went by, maybe a half an hour, when the bartender said, "You ready for a refill?"

I smiled. "No, I'm just working on this one."

He didn't return the smile. "You can't just sit here. You're going to have to order another beer because you're watching the show."

I said, "I don't think there's any law that says how fast I got to drink."

He argued a bit and then went off, I thought to attend another customer; but ten or fifteen minutes later, a couple of shore patrolmen walked in. They informed me that I'd have to order another beer or leave.

I said, "You know, I paid for beer and I'm not through with it, and I aim to sit here until I finish it. And you can't tell me how fast to drink it."

One of them says, "We'll be back in five minutes and you better be gone."

That's going to make me stay put for sure. In five minutes, they were back. One of them put his hand on my left shoulder and I just swung around and punched him in the face. I think I broke his nose. I wound up in the Coast Guard brig until they stuck me on the bus at 9 o'clock in the morning. That went on my service record and, when I got to Panama City, they penalized me by taking away a month's pay. All because I wanted to nurse a beer and see my stripper. And I didn't even get to say goodbye.

In Panama City, Florida, I was stationed on a 125-foot search-and-rescue vessel called the *Coast Guard Cutter Cartigan*. I was the only medic. They hadn't even *had* a medic in three or four months.

Though the *Cartigan* was stationed out of Panama City, we

used to go to New Orleans for dry dock. We did that maybe twice a year for a week at a time. Otherwise, the cutter would be at sea for ten days out of every thirty. Then we would come back in and be on two-hour standby. This meant that if there was an emergency on the water, we would be underway within two hours, so everybody in the crew had to be within two-hours calling distance to get back to the ship in time. We would do that for ten days. For the rest of the month, we did what we called thirty-minute "baker" standby. If you heard the ship's whistle blow, you had to be back and ready to sail right away, because the boat would be pulling out from the dock in thirty minutes and, if you missed it, you were AWOL.

That was our routine. When we were out on the water, most of the time we were boarding shrimp boats and other craft making sure that they weren't smuggling anything. But occasionally there were emergencies: storms and distressed vessels; and under those circumstances, I was the "doc."

My very first cruise was just such an emergency. There was a hurricane. The storm had snapped the towlines of a tugboat that was pulling a barge across the Gulf. It was 100 or 150 miles out. The tug went back to try to retrieve the barge, but the barge knocked a hole in its hull. The tugboat sank and eleven guys were in the water. It was an S.O.S., so we went out to the scene while the hurricane was still blasting. We were tossing like crazy on the waves, looking for men who had been in the water all night. I had no experience with anything like that whatsoever.

While the boat was rolling on the swell trying to find the men, I was on the bridge reading my corpsmen's manual! The executive officer said, "Whatcha reading, Doc?"

I said, "Right now I'm reading on frostbite. These guys have been out in the water all night."

He said, in a slow, deep, and sarcastic voice, "The water is seventy-eight degrees."

I blushed but kept my cool and said, "I'm from Detroit and the water's cold up there."

I'll always remember that day. It was a turning point in my life. We finally found the men. It was very dramatic. The sun had risen. It was probably around 7:00 a.m., and they had been watching our searchlights. There were eight of them clustered on a raft and three others in the water in life jackets that were tied to the raft. All of a sudden it really hit me that I was responsible for making sure that these guys were okay. It scared the living daylights out of me, so I took a walk around the deckhouse and came back. I wasn't scared anymore. It was just a question of "sit down, shut up, and tend to business." Eight of them turned out to be fine, two of them were clearly dead, and the other one—I just wasn't sure—so we did that old-fashioned artificial respiration where you lay 'em on their belly and you pump their ribs. We did that for a while until I decided he was dead, and we stopped; but then I saw he had a cut on the top of his head that started to bleed. Hell, he's still alive! So we started again. And we started and stopped like that for about an hour. I'm sure he actually was dead for longer than an hour before I could find it in my conscience to say, "Okay, let's give up, he's dead." I got a letter of commendation for that—for doing a good job with those guys.

On my very next cruise, a guy got a really bad bellyache. We couldn't get to shore because, again, we were out in the middle of a storm. I was thinking, "I'm not sure, but I think he's got appendicitis." So we called the Public Health—that was my consultation resource—the Public Health outfit in New Orleans. Technically, I wasn't serving under the captain of the ship; I was working for Public Health. But when I was out on the water, the captain was the boss—obviously. Well, the doctor back in New Orleans got on the horn, and he's talking to the radioman at his end who connects with the radioman on the ship, and they're sending Morse code back and forth. The doctor has me push at *McBurney's Point* (on the right side, halfway between the point of your pelvic bone and your belly button). With an appendicitis that point is always very tender. You push on it and the guy'll scream. So I push on that point and yep! The guy from the Public Health says, "Well, you're going to have to open him up." JESUS!!!

I laid this guy on the mess deck—the table we ate off of—that was the only place I could lay him down and have access to his body because on bunks there was all this stuff in the way plus a wall. This way I could get to him on both sides. I had no idea what I was going to be doing. I had Pappy, our radio man, move the receptor down with him so I could get instructions from the main office.

I got the executive officer, Mr. Pledger, to pour ether for me, and I got the cook, Jack Black Finch, to hand me the knives (because I figured he's a *cook*, so he ought to know about *knives*), and I actually took something out of this guy's belly. I *think* it was his appendix. As I understand it, he got ashore, healed up, and was okay. But I have no idea whether I took out his appendix or God knows what. I must say, though, that doing this was not only terrifying—it was a real thrill!

Soon after that, there was another surgical emergency. This one was with a buddy of mine. He smashed his thumb in the hatchway as it was closing while the ship rolled, and I had to amputate. The bones were all fragmented, and the tissue was mashed. I bandaged it first, and I put some tape around it, up higher by the palm of his hand. Then I put cellophane over it so I could watch it. We were out there for about two days; it turned black, and I decided I'd better take it off or he's going to have gangrene and that will do him in. That one I didn't even bother to radio in. I just eyeballed it. Then I took it off. There was blood all over the place. By that time, I was beginning to think that I wanted to be a doctor.

Here's one more experience that I had when I first got on the Coast Guard boat that was an important part of my path to the medical profession, harbinger of things to come. We were still in dock, probably during the first week that I was aboard. It was certainly before the tugboat-in-the-hurricane incident. I was called down below deck to see the steward. I was brand-new on the boat. You have to imagine a hospital corpsman coming onto a Coast Guard boat that hasn't had a medic for quite a while. Everybody was looking at me with *very* skeptical eyes, and believe me, I could feel it. The steward was lying on the deck down in the crew's quarters, and his leg was in tremendous pain. In corpsman's school, I'd been trained to take care of life-and-death situations, first aid, and all of that kind of stuff, but I didn't know anything about something like this. I had about fourteen or fifteen guys standing around just waiting for me to screw up, so I just put my hands on his leg and prayed within myself, "Please, let this turn out okay." And I could feel a lot of internal "energetic" activity going on in the steward's leg—energy running through it—and then suddenly his leg was okay, and he got up and walked away. After that, everybody trusted me! This is not something you forget. It's not something your cells forget.

Besides my initiation into medical practice aboard ship, any number of amusing things happened. When I first came on board, the skipper was a lieutenant named Alsup. The *Cartigan* wasn't a big boat at all—about 125 feet long, as I noted, and about 50 feet across the beam. There were forty-nine crewmen on board. One evening, we were out on one of our "soft" patrols, cruising off the coast of

Mexico to make sure that nothing was going wrong. Actually we were looking for prostitutes. Drug smuggling wasn't so big in those days, but there was plenty of prostitution on "the high seas." It was sort of natural because there were a lot of fishermen off the coast of Mexico who'd go out for a month at a time. The Mexicans would bring prostitutes out to the shrimp boats, and technically that was illegal.

Well, Lieutenant Alsup was a real, dyed-in-the-wool Baptist, so he relished this morality mission of ours. We all had out our binoculars. We were cruising about three miles out at sea, when along comes a vessel from the Mexican shore. This boat approached the shrimp boat and, sure enough, we could see two girls pass from one craft to the other. Alsup called out with great ceremony, "Prostitution on the High Seas," and off we went to intercept and board the shrimp boat. There indeed were the two women we had spied in our binoculars. It turned out, however, that they were married to two of the crewmen on the boat, so there was no crime!

It was under Lieutenant Alsup's command that the *USCG Cartigan* was once fired upon by a Mexican destroyer escort that, ironically, was a gift from the USA to Mexico after World War II. A U.S. shrimp boat was being boarded by Mexican military personnel. The Mexicans had been charging a large fee for permission to fish waters anywhere within nine miles of their coastline. International maritime law only honored a three-mile limit. Lieutenant Alsup spotted the boarding with his binoculars, and he radioed the Mexican boat to cease and desist. In response, the Mexican destroyer escort fired a large cannon across our bow. Lieutenant Alsup responded by inviting the Mexican ship's captain over for dinner. He notified U.S. authorities in Washington D.C., who must have communicated with the Mexicans at once because the dispute ended immediately.

Alsup was reforming everybody on the ocean morally, in particular *me*. He knew that I had walloped a shore patrolman, and his idea was that I needed to become a Baptist, so he worked at trying to convert me with relentless zeal. I'm not sure if he would have succeeded even if he had remained the skipper for my full two years, but I was spared finding that out because he retired a few months after I came on board. The new guy was a Lieutenant McElroy. On the day of the change of command, Alsup wanted to have everybody in formal regalia with uniforms "just so" when McElroy came to take command; but McElroy showed up in a civilian jacket and a beat-up pair of khakis and said, "Gentleman, you can forget all formalities. Lt. Alsup, you are relieved of command." Alsup left, swallowing his annoyance. McElroy was now in charge.

Alsup may have been very particular about spiritual matters, but he hadn't been big on keeping the ship in tip-top shape physically. Not long after McElroy took command, he summoned us all together and said, "This boat looks like a rust-bucket. We're going to take her out into the middle of the bay, drop anchor, and nobody goes ashore until she looks perfect. I live in town, so I'm taking the motor launch back to shore." He skippered us out into the harbor, dropped anchor, stepped into the launch right then and there, and nobody was able to leave ship until we got it all straightened out.

Lt. McElroy turned out to be one of the finest guys you'd ever want to serve under. His first priority was maintaining morale. He let us have a "still." A couple of the guys from Alabama made moonshine whiskey in our ship's warehouse and that was okay with him. He had me order a generous supply of ethanol for the sick bay and, when morale was down or when we'd been out on the water for nine or ten days, or it was Sunday and nobody had anything particular to do, he'd say, "Okay doc, break out the orange juice!" and we'd pour the ethanol into the orange juice, and I'd take out my accordion. People on shore would hear the music out over the water and, perhaps because of that, they'd kind of flock to our boat; they figured there must be a party. Sometimes, we'd be three miles off of Mexico, where the international boundary is, and pretty soon at night, when the sun was going down and everybody was drinking "orange juice," the Mexican boats would start coming out and offering women and tequila. We were no longer policing the game; we were players. McElroy thought that was great—it was good for morale as far as he was concerned. Those were fun days.

Besides being a generally great guy, occasionally he would do things that were really amusing. At a certain point, a Coast Guard Academy graduate came aboard as an Executive Officer (second in command). Oddly enough, his name was "Pledger," just put a "U" in front and you've got me. Not that Pledger was like me. He was a gung-ho, spit-and-polish kind of guy. With McElroy you could wear anything you wanted, and mostly we wore levis and t-shirts. He didn't care about the uniforms as long as the job got done. Well, Pledger comes on and he wants everybody to spit shine their shoes and wear proper uniforms. Given what we'd been used to, he was wrecking morale. He would invent pointless and unnecessary drills. One day when we were coming in from a patrol, Pledger leapt off of our ship into the water and hollered, "Man overboard!" We had to lower a boat and go out and pick him up. And, of course, the Hospital Corpsman had to go in the rescue boat. When I hauled him up, I thought I'd give him what he was asking for, so I yelled out in mock panic, "This guy isn't breathing—we got to do artificial respiration on him." In those days, as I noted before, you did that by putting the patient on his stomach and pumping on his ribs on the back. We put him over the bench, and I damn near broke his ribcage!

After this ridiculous fiasco, McElroy called the "operations gang" up into his office. This consisted of the hospital corpsman, the yeoman, the radioman, and quarter master. McElroy said, "I don't know how you're going to do it, but you guys have to get rid of Pledger."

"Aye, aye sir!"

Well, the yeoman had a friend in Alaska, so he wrote up an official-looking set of orders for Mr. Pledger, transferring him up there, and sent them to his buddy, and his buddy sent them back down to Pledger. Pledger now had orders from the commandant to go to Alaska, transferring him to a ship coming out of there. He packed up his bag and took off without a peep and, whatever happened, we never heard from him again.

When we were in dock, there was another Coast Guard boat across the dock from us that just made short runs for rescues. If they had to go out when I was on two-hour standby, I'd hop on board with them. Life was great, and I was confirmed that I was going to give medical school a shot.

The ship across the dock had a really good skipper who was also very supportive of me personally. He agreed with McElroy that I shouldn't re-enlist—that I should go ahead and see if I could become a real doctor. That was very fatherly advice. I knew I could get off my ship after two years of sea duty, and that would leave me one more year to fulfill my term of duty.

McElroy got me promotions as fast as he could recommend them and, by the time I left the *Cartigan,* after two years, with him in charge for, oh, eighteen or twenty months, I was First Class Hospital Corpsman. It usually takes five or six years to attain that rank. McElroy felt that I was too smart to stay in the Coast Guard and he advised me not to reenlist. I told him I was thinking of going to medical school. I needed to go some place where I could take general chemistry because I wanted to finish my pre-med in one year after I was discharged rather than two. In order to take qualitative analysis and organic chemistry, you had to have general chemistry first and I didn't have that, so I wanted to go some place where I could take night classes. The two choices were Baltimore and New Orleans, and I got Baltimore.

McElroy was able to arrange it so that I was sent to Baltimore. There they put me in charge of the clinical lab in Curtis Bay Shipyard. I played the piano in strip shows about four nights a week to start saving money for school, and I took chemistry two nights a week. I asked the professor who was teaching the class to watch me closely. I said, "I don't want any bullshit. If you think I can make it through medical school, let me know. If you don't think I can, I want to hear it. I don't want to waste my time if I'm going to be a wash-out." I didn't have any of the math background, but I was able to go up to the blackboard and reason my way through problems that ordinarily required algebra. I wound up with A's from him, and he wrote me a nice letter to wherever I wanted to go.

The way I got to work in strip clubs and jazz clubs in Baltimore is interesting from a musical point of view. I'd just bring my accordion to jazz clubs. Of course accordions are pretty square for playing jazz, to say the least, and the black musicians weren't about to let some white guy come in and replace the piano player. But there was a baritone sax setting on my accordion. Now baritone-sax players were something of a rarity, so I'd come in and start doing baritone sax things on the accordion, and pretty soon I was well-known around Baltimore.

The first jobs I got were with a guy named Little Joe Davis. Little Joe and I played for strip shows a lot. I found out an interesting thing about strippers—many of them were married, and they'd get picked up about 4:00 a.m. by their husbands in a station wagon, sometimes with three or four sleepy kids in the back seat. That really shocked me, because I thought working the strip shows I'd get to have dates with all these strippers!

Actually, I did get to know many of them, and I got to know many prostitutes, too. Prostitution was running rampant in Baltimore in those days. I was able to do some work for public hygiene, undercover as it were. Since I was running the Coast Guard lab, when guys came in with gonorrhea, I could go and find the contact and suggest that they go to the public-health service and get treated. Since I knew most of the girls on the "street" after a few months, it was easy for me. Guys would say, "Well, I know this gal 'Texas Jean,'" and I 'd say, "I know her," and I'd go and tell her she was infected. I got a really good reputation for being "efficient."

Not all of the gigs I got were faking baritone on the accordion. Occasionally, I'd be hired as a pianist. In one strip club where I was working piano, they had an additional lounge upstairs where a black pianist named Charlie played. Charlie and I got to be pretty friendly. We took breaks at different times in the evening, so it was possible for each of us to take time to hear the other play. One night after hours, Charlie said, "I'd love to show you some of the stuff that you can do with your left hand. You got a pretty good right hand, but you could use a little work on your left, so why don't you come on over to my house after work?"

Well, that Saturday night we finished up around 3 o'clock in the morning and I went home with him. I got to meet his wife (she was a blond kindergarten teacher who smoked cigars). We drank a little gin and black coffee and then got down to some serious music business. Charlie taught me to play what you call "walking bass" with my left hand—the kind of bass line you'd hear in most jazz music of the 1950s, either "cool" or "bebop." I had been playing "boogie" and "stride piano" style, which was pretty old-fashioned by that time. It was really very useful to learn this new stuff. Charlie, his wife, and I got along really well, as we came together like this about three or four weeks in a row.

Then one night, I was there and we were playing away, and there's a nasty bang on the front door. We stop playing, Charlie goes to open the door, and it's the police: plainclothes municipal cops. I didn't find out till later they were narcotics guys because, as soon as they saw me, they told me to get out. As you know by now, I don't take kindly to being ordered around by the cops, so I said, "Hey—I'm here learning to play the piano."

"Right. And I'm here for ballet lessons. This ain't no music studio, it's a house of prostitution, and if you don't want to get busted, get the hell out of here!"

They sort of shoved me down the stairs in front of the brownstone—there were eight or ten steps. I tumbled down but managed to stay more or less on my feet; but believe me, I knew I was being shoved. I got in my car and drove around the block a few times; then I came right back and went back in again. This convinced them, no doubt, that I was a "John," so they decided to arrest me, at which point they found out I was a hospital corpsman. This was no help at all. Now they were going to charge me on suspicion of delivering narcotics to a known user who had done time. I had no idea that Charlie had, as it turned out, been a morphine addict and had spent a few years in prison for that.

Well, they took me to the police station in Baltimore and they were going to book me on suspicion of drug dealing as well as frequenting a house of ill repute, but I started raising so much hell about this being "racial prejudice" (I'm not sure what I said, but the less sense I made the crazier I seemed, and the more inconvenience I caused them, which was the point), so they finally called the Coast Guard base and the officer of the day sent a lieutenant over to pick me up and take me back there. The guy who came to collect me turned out to be someone I had helped out by not putting gonorrhea on his chart (so his wife wouldn't find out about it), and he just said, "Where do you want to go?"

I said, "Take me back downtown." And that was my punishment for being at Charley's house.

After that, Charlie and I didn't practice much together anymore because they would always be watching to make sure that I wasn't delivering Coast Guard narcotics to him.

I had a pretty busy year in Baltimore, but I made a lot of money. I worked in the strip shows on the average of four nights a week. I did some sales of Watkins products. It's kind of like a Fuller Brush. I would go around to a neighborhood, and I'd knock on a door, show my wares, and hopefully sell some. Cleaning products mostly. I studied whenever I had a chance. I took my science classes, I ran the Coast Guard Lab, and I saw patients in sick bay.

Once it was clear that I was going to do well in my science courses, I decided to try to get out of the Coast Guard. I applied for early discharge, and I succeeded in getting out about six weeks early so I could go back to what was now called "Wayne State" to finish my pre-med qualifications. This was early September, 1957.

While still in Baltimore, I contacted our family physician back in Detroit, Dr. Rinefort. I wrote him a letter and said that I was interested in becoming a doctor. What school would he suggest? He wrote back, "Well, why don't you go where I went to school?"

It turned out he had attended Kirksville College of Osteopathy and Surgery in Missouri. He was an osteopath. I had no idea what an osteopath was. It didn't make any difference to me. A doctor's a doctor! And they agreed to accept me before I got discharged, providing I finished my pre-med courses with a "B" average. They didn't even interview me. They just accepted me.

At Wayne, I took physics, organic chemistry, and qualitative analysis, and I also took algebra the first quarter so I could do the physics. The second semester I took physics, organic chemistry, and quantitative analysis.

During the year when I was taking pre-med courses I met, courted, and married my first wife Beverly. Here's how it happened.

One afternoon, soon after I got back to St. Clair Shores from the Coast Guard and not more than a week before I was to start classes at Wayne State, my buddy Moe and I were changing the oil of my car in front of my house (Moe had been discharged from the Navy on the same day as I was discharged from the Coast Guard; we were already fraternity brothers from undergraduate days at Wayne). As we were working away on my car, this gorgeous babe comes driving by in an equally gorgeous white 1956 Ford convertible, pulls up two houses down from us, jumps out of the car, waves, and runs inside, as it turned out, to change her clothes and get paraphernalia to start painting her house. She was five foot three. Built like a brick shithouse. Brown hair, brown eyes. Very attractive.

Pretty soon she's outside again, now in jeans and with a casual shirt on, agilely climbing a ladder with paint brush and bucket and going to work on the upper part of her house. Moe and I are observing all this and kidding each other about her when suddenly a Cadillac pulls up. A guy in a business suit gets out, slams the car door, runs up to the ladder, climbs up after her, and challenges her about something or other.

They got into a terrible scrape that lasted a few minutes, after which he climbed down and off he went. She went back to painting her house.

Moe and I are watching this. We're trying to figure how to introduce ourselves.

Finally, I just walked over to the bottom of the ladder and said, "We've got some oil drained from my car. Do you have any weeds you want to kill?"

She said, "No, but there's a tree stump on the lawn I need taken out."

Yes, ma'am! Moe was an engineer, so we managed to use leverage and other engineering principles to get the thing uprooted. Now we were in with her just fine, so we invited her to come with us to a fraternity party that we happened to be going to that evening. The idea was that she would accompany both of us. She agreed.

As the party went on, Moe and I, of course, were vying for her attentions, and I wound up the winner. I took her home and, from there on, it was just—what should I say?—"heavy duty." We got married two months after that. Very quick. Maybe a little more than two months—December 7th. One of the big reasons that we did this was: her mother did not want me in the house. We were arguing about that one day in the living room. It was Beverly's house, but her mother was trying to say to me, 'You can't come in here.' I don't know what she was thinking; maybe she thought if Beverly got hooked up with me, she wouldn't have a place to live, that kind of thing. Once, she threw a hot coffee at the front of my shirt. That pissed me off a lot. Pissed off Beverly too. So we went over and saw my folks, two doors away, and told them, "We want to get married."

My mother was crazy as hell; she just said, "We'll drive you down to Ohio and you can get married there."

Beverly was a legal secretary in Grosse Point. Our first child, Leslie, was born just a week or so before I was to depart for Kirksville, so I had to go to osteopathic medical school by myself in spite of being newly married and a brand new father.

We were living at my mother's house, and I remember when she started going into labor—that was around six o'clock. I was playing the piano at a nightclub in Pontiac, Michigan, to get some money but keeping good track of what was going on. Beverly went to the hospital, ten miles away from where I was playing. I'd call every hour or two during the time she was in labor. I called in one time and they said it's all done. I went to the hospital and she'd already delivered, so I missed that. When she recovered from the birth, Beverly went back to her job with the attorney, and she and Leslie lived temporarily with my mother, stepfather, and grandparents next door in St. Clair Shores.

I never applied to a conventional medical school. There was a guy in Baltimore who used to get me jobs playing piano for rather well-to-do families—house parties and stuff. He was willing to pay my way through Johns Hopkins, but he turned out to be gay, so I didn't do that. I was sure there would be strings attached. I also should say that I saw some of the M.D.s at the hospital in Baltimore do some pretty awful things and, even though I wasn't yet aware that there were alternative ways of practicing medicine, I had some pretty serious misgivings in general about the profession of conventional medicine as I was coming to see it.

For example, in Baltimore, when I was in charge of the laboratory at the sick bay, I was also seeing out-patients. There was a public-health doctor that I was attached to who was very, very weird. Whenever you entered his office, he'd have on one of those magnifiers that doctors used to use. They protrude about three or four inches in front of their glasses. Like a cartoon image of a doctor, his feet up on the desk and often reading an "Archie" comic book, but he never seemed to have time to see the patients! There were a couple of instances that I was aware of, when he made some very serious medical mistakes. Once, he medicated a guy who was really hurt and didn't report it at all and, when they got the patient to the hospital, they gave him an anesthetic and he died immediately from drug interaction. It was just plain slovenly. And I thought, if this is what "real" doctors are like, it doesn't interest me whole lot.

In a sense, I may have been latently developing a view against conventional medicine and therefore was already open to the alternative approach of osteopathy. But the truth is that I didn't know anything about osteopathy at the time, and the fact that Kirksville was osteopathic didn't influence me.

Medical School and First Marriage

As a matter of fact, Kirksville was not just *any* osteopathic college: it turned out to be the *original* osteopathic college. It was founded by the founder of osteopathy himself: Andrew Taylor Still.

Still had been a Civil War surgeon and, during his service, he lost three of his own kids in a severe meningitis epidemic. He got the idea that the drugs administered to kill an infection also harmed people and had in fact killed some of his family, so he started looking for other ways to take care of illness.

Dr. Still came to believe that dislocations of bones or dysfunctions of joints frequently contributed to diseases in the organs—

gall bladder disease or heart disease etc. For instance, the cause of a heart problem might be that the *fourth thoracic vertebra* was "stuck." Let's say you fell out of a tree when you were kid, and the vertebra never did mobilize properly after that. A major nerve to the heart comes out of the segment of the spine where the vertebra is, so that the nerve would be somewhat impinged, or dysfunctional, just because it had an abnormal amount of compression on it. As a result, the vital nourishment that the nerve provides to the heart would be either reduced or cut off, and the heart would become more vulnerable to disease. Still's idea was that if you fixed the problem where the nerve was getting compressed, you would be able to avoid heart disease in the future. He analyzed problems like that for every organ in the body, and his analyses hold up pretty well to this day. He also decided that compromised blood flow to an organ might be responsible for that organ becoming diseased. He came up with the principle that structure is related to function and that the body makes its own medicine.

He started working this system out right after the Civil War. He was kind of a visionary, if you will.

Well, Dr. Still presented his ideas to the American Medical Association and they told him to either desist in this heretical view of the cause of disease or risk forfeiting his license. He chose to continue with what he thought was the truth, and he wound up in Kirksville, Missouri, because there was no resistance there, and that's where he started the first school of osteopathic medicine.

When I arrived in the early 1960s, there were still people in Kirksville who could tell stories about Dr. Still. I remember one such person—a very old black man I met one night after a fraternity party. We were sitting around drinking beer in the basement of the frat house when he came in and joined us. It turned out that he used to drive Dr. Still's carriage for him. This is the wildest thing. He said, "Me and old Doc Still—we'd go out in the carriage and we'd go to a house—houses were miles apart, see—and Doc Still would knock on the door and say 'Is anybody sick in here?' If somebody was sick, Doc Still would go in and treat 'em. And if the person was sick enough, I'd take 'em back to the school where Doc had a clinic and leave 'em there. Doc Still would go ahead on horseback to the next place." The guy with the carriage would drop off the patient and then catch up with Doc Still again. Makin' the rounds. Soliciting patients.

The old man also said that there was a railroad that ran through Kirksville and that, after Doc Still got established, he used to go down to the station and treat people right there on the platform. When he was done, they'd get back on the train and go where they were going!

Anyway, to get back to *my* story. I got good grades in that year of taking physics, "qual" and "quant" and organic chemistry at Wayne State, so I was bound for Kirksville.

However, while I was in Detroit working on my pre-med requirements, a number of very odd things happened. For instance, my stepfather Nick's shop was robbed repeatedly by inmates that he had met when he was doing his time at the Detroit House of Corrections. I presume that he talked a bit too freely about his jewelry store, so some of his prison "buddies" decided to target his shop when they were released from prison.

I'll always remember one of these occasions. I got a phone call from a very weak-sounding Nick to come to the store and help him. When I got there, he was recovering from an encounter, but there was blood on the back of his head. A solitary robber had entered with gun in hand. There was no one else in the store at the time. The robber pointed the weapon at my stepfather and ordered him up against the wall. Nick obeyed and told the gunman to take whatever he wanted, but the thug bashed him on the head with the gun anyway. He blacked out briefly and awakened on the floor with the robber close to his feet, pointing the gun at him and actually pulling the trigger. Fortunately, the pistol jammed and didn't fire. Nick's adrenaline must have kicked in at that point because, in a flash, he threw his heels into the air, projecting his body up on his shoulders and, from that position, clubbed the robber in the groin with his feet. The robber hit the floor. In the meantime, Nick got up, reached for a can of cleaning acid located conveniently on his workbench and gave the fellow's head and neck a rather astringent dousing. With the intruder out of commission, Nick called me. When I arrived, the robber was gone, the police were there, and Nick was still a bit hysterical.

Another time, when an intruder came, Nick was ready with a pistol he now kept under the counter. The robber ran out of the store, hopped into his car, and was off with a screech of rubber. Nick jumped into his own car and gave chase but couldn't catch him.

There were more episodes, but you get the idea. The message was: "If you go to prison, don't blab about your jewelry store!—and especially don't tell them where it is or where you live."

While I'm on the subject of interesting rescue calls, at about this time, the police called asking me to come to a local pharmacy and pick up Grandpa. I went to the address they gave me. As I pulled up, I saw his 1935 Plymouth (a Plymouth was built like a tank in those days) with about half its length sticking out of Golinski's Drug Store. It had smashed through the huge front window and the little stone wall beneath it. Grandpa was ranting about his foot having slipped off the brake and onto the gas pedal. He lost his license.

As I was planning my move to Kirksville, I realized that I was going to need a place to live. I found out they had a trailer court a few minutes from the college, so I decided to find a trailer. I turned to my Uncle Fred, a guy who, you may remember, was not "acceptable" to my grandma or to my mother, but whom I always liked. Fred was a building contractor and he got me a construction trailer—the kind they have out at building sites. I think it was twenty-six feet long, and it cost me three hundred and fifty dollars. The summer before I went out to Kirksville, he helped me figure out how to put in a heating system and a bathtub, so I did all the plumbing and wiring and took it with me to school.

I towed the trailer to Kirksville with our '57 Ford convertible. I went straight to the "All-State Trailer Court." Before I left, I phoned ahead, and the woman who answered said they only allowed "modern" trailers at the trailer court.

I said, "Gee, ma'am, my trailer's really pretty old."

She asked, "Does it have a toilet?"

I said "Yeah."

She said, "Well, that's modern in Kirksville!"

It was Alma all over again; only now, being in school was completely different because I knew what I was doing there.

Driving to Kirksville with a trailer on the back of my car was quite an experience. I'd never done anything like it before. The caboose bumped against the car whenever we were going downhill because I didn't have a good brake hooked up on the trailer, and I had to improvise controlling it by trying to time my speed just right. This was a skill I developed as I traveled, a kind of on-the-job training, as it were. It was a little scary, but I did get to Kirksville in one piece.

The only problem was that all the bumping and jostling jarred my plumbing loose, and the first thing I had to attend to once I got hooked up in the trailer park was re-doing the soldering job on my copper pipes. After all, I did have to conform to the local standards for "a modern trailer!" It took a couple of days to get that job done, and meanwhile I had no plumbing. The day after I arrived, I had to report for a physical examination at the school. Of course, since I didn't have any water, I couldn't take a shower. The doctor in charge of the out-patient clinic system at the school gave me the physical and passed me all right, but then he suggested not so discretely that I go home and take a bath. Oh Jesus, what a way to start!

I must say right here, that there were problems in my marriage with Beverly almost from the get-go, though we did manage to stay together for eleven years—mostly, I suspect, by not having very much to do with each other!

Not all our difficulties were Beverly's fault. Before I left for Kirksville, she had found out the hard way that, before we were married, I had fathered an illegitimate child in Baltimore.

While still in the Coast Guard, I had had an affair with a woman named Nancy. Nancy became pregnant, but she didn't want any help from me. In fact, as soon as she learned of her condition, she left for Miami. This happened early in the spring of 1957, some months before I got out of the service and returned to Detroit. I married Beverly on December 7, 1957. One day in December shortly after we were married, Nancy somehow got hold of our phone number and called when I was away. She spoke to Beverly and announced that I was the father of her newborn boy. I never heard from her again. I don't know actually whether Nancy wanted me to contact her or not. I only know that Beverly never imparted that information if she did. So I have an unrecognized son floating around somewhere. I have no idea what name she used for him. To this day I've never met him, but you can imagine it wasn't a very pleasant way to kick off my marriage with Beverly.

During my first year in Kirksville, I stayed in touch with my new wife as best I could, taking into account no phone in the trailer and the expense of long-distance calls. A little before Christmas I got a telegram saying that she and Leslie were coming from Detroit and I should pick her up at the airport at Kansas city. Well, Kansas City is about a three-and-a-half hour's drive from Kirksville. She was coming in at about noon on a Saturday, and I was to take my first biochemistry exam at nine o'clock that morning.

Biochemistry was to become my main subject in osteopathic medical school, and I was already completely taken with it. There was no way that I could cut this exam. I figured I'd take the test as fast as I could, and Beverly would just have to wait at the airport. Maybe the plane would be late or something. It wasn't, but we met up all right without too much of a fracas. I did finally find my wife and child at the airport, not too many hours late, and I brought them to Kirksville and they stayed with me in this little twenty-six foot trailer for a few weeks. Then she went back to Detroit. Later in the winter they came back again, this time to stay.

The exam itself was no problem. The professor, Dr. Stacey Howell (about whom I'll have plenty to tell) gave us six essay questions, of which we had to answer five. One of them described a dinner a patient would eat—a pork chop, some potatoes, some broccoli, or what have you—then I had to inventory how each piece of food was digested by each enzyme in his stomach. But I was in so much of a hurry that I misread the instruction or else I just miscounted what I had done, and only answered four, though

I swear I left the exam room thinking I had done what I was supposed to. Well, Professor Howell called me in after the grading was done and said, "You're pretty damn arrogant, aren't you?"

I said, "What do you mean?"

He said, "You answered four questions perfectly and then you just left two off because you knew eighty percent was passing."

I had to explain to him the pressure I was under. To this day I have no idea whether or not he believed me.

It was kind of weird, given how important Dr. Howell eventually would become to me. But perhaps our relationship was being tested—tempered—and prepared with absurd obstacles at the beginning.

The next examination I had to take with Dr. Howell a few months later also had irregularities. Suffering from a cold with a bad runny nose, I came to the exam with a box of Kleenex. When I got to know Dr. Howell, I realized that what he did at this point was a just a prank on his part, but at the moment it was terrifying. He confiscated the box of Kleenex and announced to the class that there were probably crib notes in there, so he pulled tissues out one by one and said after each, "Naw, that's okay, naw that's okay" until he had plucked out every damn tissue in the box. When he was done, he told me I could put them back in the box. Then we went ahead with the exam. The test itself was, again, no problem. It was another one of those five out of six essays, and in this one I performed the full round of answers.

At the end of my first year I asked Dr. Howell if I could be a biochemistry lab assistant, and he said, "Sure, that's fine. I'd love to have you."

During Christmas vacation of my first year at Kirksville, my mother and stepfather, Nick, came to visit us. Soon after their arrival, Nick got on my case again about being too lazy to get a job—school was just a way to avoid work. Even though Nick's schooling didn't go past the fourth grade, he was a successful businessman, so what was holding me back at age twenty-five with all my schooling? I ought to be a success at something by now.

I decided to take Nick to the anatomy lab to show him that we medical students did actually work. Dissecting a cadaver was just as laborious as repairing a watch.

When we got to the lab, I unveiled a partially dissected cadaver that I was studying, and Nick agreed that this did indeed look like work, but how much money could I make at it, he wanted to know? Immediately, after asking this last question, he spotted a big, gray "cake" box. It was about fifteen feet long, four feet high, and four feet wide, front to back. It contained a myriad of spare cadaver parts all floating/soaking in a three- to three-and-half-foot deep sea of formaldehyde. He asked me what that "box" was and what was in it. I replied, pretending innocence, "Gosh, Nick, I don't know. Take a look and tell me what it is." Nick went over, lifted the lid, smelled the formaldehyde, saw a few stomachs and livers and heads and arms and legs and spines, all floating in that lovely-smelling fluid, and ran outside and vomited. He never said another word to me about getting a job, but to maintain his pride, he often remarked how looking in that tank cured him of his sinus trouble! Go figure.

I learned to love Nick. In his way, he only wanted to be helpful. About seven or eight years later, he needed to have his gallbladder surgically removed and, like a fool, I scrubbed in as a second assistant at Nick's surgery. It was a mess. Around his gall-bladder and bile ducts were solid masses of adhesions. I got a little light-headed during the surgery, so I must have cared about him. Surgeries otherwise have never bothered me.

While things were going along pretty well academically, there were a few bumps in the road regarding my living situation. As usual, I had found a way of making pocket money doing music. One Friday after Beverly and Leslie had moved in permanently, I was playing for a dance job. It was still wintertime and there was snow everywhere. I came home about one o'clock in the morning to find a classmate named Pat, a Korean Vet, hanging out at our trailer talking to my wife. He was kind of drunk and seemed to be having what today I would recognize as a post-traumatic stress disorder flashback. There happened to be another guy in the trailer park that Pat really didn't like—I never found out why—but Pat really had it in for this guy, and he was swearing up and down that he had to "get" him. He started crawling on his belly through the snow from my trailer, past four other trailers, and finally to the one where this guy was living. Beverly and I were following him and kind of laughing about the whole thing. When he got to the "enemy" trailer (the owner of which was inside asleep), he crawled under it and disconnected the heat tape for the water pipes so that whole water system would freeze up; then he got hold of the jack and lowered the whole trailer at one end by about a foot so that the water would leak and run down the inside and, when the enemy woke up, he'd have an ice pond at the low end of his home.

Now that was all very funny, except that the next day the victim of this winter-night foray went to the trailer-court manager and complained and, of course, all the footprints and body prints lead unambiguously back to my trailer. I was evicted from the court.

(In spite of this misadventure, Pat and I remained friends for a long time. I kept up with his progress. He eventually succeeded in achieving his goal, which was to become a surgeon, though I don't think he ever quite got cured of his post-traumatic stress disorder. He continued to have unusual episodes of weird behavior. I called

---

him one New Year's eve and I talked to his wife. She couldn't find him anywhere and then she called me back the next day; he was in his office on the table, giving himself a vasectomy. Drunker than a skunk. She found him laying there asleep with his hoot'n'anny hanging out, the slits made, and the tubes tied. It was about four or five years later, he died of a stroke.)

When we were evicted from the trailer court, we actually had a month to get out, so I applied for and got accepted into a local housing project for veterans. It was a good deal: it cost $25.75 a month. I was getting $160 a month from the GI bill, so we were doing fairly well. I had saved a considerable amount of the money I had made in Baltimore and, believe it or not, the tuition at Kirksville in those days was $750 a semester (you need a hundred thousand dollars to get through medical school today).

The second year of study at Kirksville included pathology—the study of disease processes. Shortly before summer vacation began, I heard from my mother that my beloved grandfather had liver cancer. He had been diagnosed at Art-Center Osteopathic Hospital in Detroit. Rather than die there, he preferred to come home to the house that he and I had built in the summer of 1949 after my high school graduation. Dr. Rinefort, the man who got me into the Kirksville College of Osteopathy and Surgery, was still our family doctor. He suggested, when I came home for summer vacation, that I should care for Grandpa. I arrived with my wife and two children about a week after Grandpa came home to die. As I watched and cared for his feeble and wasted body, I found out how much I loved him,

During that summer, we stayed at Beverly's house (which she still owned) about three doors away from Grandpa's house. (Remember, after Leslie was born, Beverly stayed with my mother and stepfather because she was going to work and needed them to help take care of Leslie, but she never sold her own house.)

One day, about two weeks after we arrived home, Grandpa asked me for a glass of beer. My recent education in pathology told me not to grant his request, but my heart told me to call Dr. Rinefort and ask what I should do. Dr. Rinefort said to give Grandpa the beer. He might die a day sooner, but he would go a happier man than if I refused him the beer. I poured a glass of his favorite beer and propped him up in his bed. My mother and grandmother were standing behind me, Grandma on her walker. Grandpa took a swallow of the beer, looked right in my eyes, and said, "Johnny, the two most spoiled women in the world are standing right behind you." Immediately his head fell away from me, his body slumped, and he was dead. Neither of the two women ever made any comment.

After my second year at Kirksville, I received a Rockefeller Fellowship to study, teach, and manage the laboratory for Dr. Howell. He was a really wonderful man. In his early sixties, with a great sense of humor, Dr. Howell also had achieved a considerable degree of prominence in his field. He had been a runner-up for a Nobel Prize and is credited with the discovery that enzymes are proteins. Working with him, I learned molecular medicine rather thoroughly. He was very much a physical chemist too, so I became competent in the aspect of chemistry that is based on physics.

Dr. Howell was also known for some famous wisecracks. He's the guy who said, "I don't know why we're worried about the Communists; it's the viruses that are going to get us." He was also way ahead of his time regarding ecology and pollution. He used to say, "Detergents are wonderful. They save housewives a lot of work. And if we keep on dumping them in the Ohio River, the goddamned thing's going to foam up over its banks." But most important, he was a genuine scientist. It is from him that I learned what real inquiry and research are all about.

I wouldn't say that my interest in science itself began in Kirksville—I loved the chemistry class that I took in Baltimore and the physics that I studied at Wayne. However, when I got into doing my fellowship in biochemistry with Dr. Howell, it all came together.

Dr. Howell was a prankster, no doubt about it, and there were many nutty things about him. For one, he talked funny. I used to be able to imitate him pretty well. His initial lecture for every class would be about evolution. He'd begin by stammering out, "Uh, uh, well I know that a lot of you fellows don't believe in evolution. Uh—we are positive now that it's true. You know that little thing on the end of your tail there—that coccyx? Uh—you know that—right? Okay! That used to be a pinwheel." (The students are writing down "pinwheel.") Then he'd say, "And you know all those gas-forming bacteria in your bowels? Well, when you were out there in the water, the gas would blow right out your anus and turn that pinwheel! That was the propeller that got you up on the land. How in the world can you disagree with *that?*" And nobody ever told the next year's class.

He also had a long lecture he'd give on addiction that was a classic. It began, "I don't know why everybody's worried about addiction. Hell! Everybody's addicted. As soon as you're born, you're addicted." Then he'd give an obscure and very technical description of some substance and wind up with, "As soon as you start using this stuff, you can't live without it. Yet it will kill you, ultimately." What was it? Oxygen!

Besides being in his classes, I worked with him during the summers when the school was closed. It was just the two of us.

My own education in osteopathic school was a little unusual because of Howell. Here's what happened. In my freshman year, I fell in love with biochemistry, as I mentioned, so I applied to be a laboratory assistant for my second year and got the job. Then, out of the blue, toward the end of the second semester of my assistantship, Dr. Howell came to me and said, "Upledger, you're doing good work, and I'd like to offer you a fellowship in biochemistry. You will be paid for three years of work, and during those three years you will do two years worth of regular curriculum requirements. You'll take classes two-thirds of the time. One-third of the time, you'll be working for me." They didn't really split it quite that finely, but in essence that's how it turned out. It meant I had to attend this school for five instead of four years.

I took all my regular classes for the third and the fourth year except surgery; I took surgery during my fifth year. During that year, I also worked in biochemistry with Dr. Howell. That left me a little time free, and I used it to precept in a doctor's office.

Dr. Howell taught me a lot about scientific method, as I said. He was one of the original investigators of the antibiotic *lysozyme.* You find it in egg whites; you find it in the tears in your eyes; and now they know that it appears in a lot of different places. He discovered that if you injected a certain form of lysozyme into a rat's *peritoneal cavities,* malignant tumors would often form. He thought that he was on the road to a better understanding of cancer. He really was a runner-up for Nobel Laureate. He's the man who proved that enzymes were proteins. He worked for John Sumner, a one-armed biochemist. He got his Ph.D. under Sumner. In fact, Sumner got the Nobel Prize for the particular piece of work that Dr. Howell turned in for him as his Ph.D. One summer, he had me work on lysozyme. He didn't tell me at the outset the objective of the research. He just said, "I want you to get lysozyme today and isolate it from the egg, okay? Now, you're going to do the same thing tomorrow and the next day. We are going to look at this stuff and analyze the three samples. And they'll be a little different from each other."

After we had the samples, he said, "Now, what's the difference between the samples from those three days? Okay—you've got different eggs, that's one thing. The humidity was (such and such) the first day, the second day (such and such) and the third day (such and such)." He'd go through all the variables and ask a series of questions about why the three were different. Instead of just caring about the result, he got me to look at all the intermediary questions as we were going through the process. I turned out to be very good at that kind of inquiry. To this day, whenever I encounter a new phenomenon, I ask what could have caused it and begin to examine the possibilities.

He was a brilliant man who changed the way that I thought about science. He taught me to be qualitative, not quantitative, not to focus too much on the details. He said, "There's always ten percent in either direction from whatever answer you get, for error. Things are always approximate." He thought it was false security to believe you had the exact number. He told me, "I know that you're going to be an internist; you're going to go out and practice, and you're going to do a great job. I just want you to know that if the laboratory doesn't agree with your physical findings, suspect laboratory error." And, to this day, I do. Dr. Howell taught me you have to remember biochemical individuality. People don't all have the same biochemistry. One person's high blood sugar might be another person's perfect.

Clearly, I got influenced strongly that way. He prepared me for research also. His rule of thumb was: Don't give yourself a goal, but look at what happened today. Then at the end of the day, write down your questions about what happened. Observe things. In the morning, sit down and decide which question you're going to look at next. Stay out of this "controlled experimental design" thing. Experiment and observe your results and then always question them.

The other thing he gave to me that was so brilliant—and you can tell I'm living on this now—he's a guy who used to say, "It's all size, John. Here you are, you're this size. Every cell in you is a microcosm and every atom is a microcosm of the universe. Then here we have a sun and we're the electrons spinning around it."

Not all my teachers at Kirksville were that good; in fact, I remember my surgery teacher was really bad. We called him Hollywood Hal. He did truly come from Hollywood. He was so goddamned arrogant because he had operated on movie stars. He knew me because I wasn't taking his course along with the rest of my class. I had to wait till the last year, and then he took advantage of me two times. He had me be an assistant on a prostate surgery. It was my first assistantship. I was scrubbing up. The nurse came in and said, "You don't have to do that."

I said, "Why not; I'm assisting."

She said, "You don't know Hollywood Hal. You'll see."

They took me in there. The prostate guy is on the table. He's got his legs up in stirrups and they had my hands underneath the sheets. Then they told me to put a finger up his butt. I put my finger up there. Then he said, "I'm using that as my landmark for when I get in there and start taking out the prostate. I don't want to make an incision in the colon, so you just leave your finger there."

I found out later that it was all bullshit, but I was under there for the whole surgery.

Then I didn't take his final exam in surgery. I attended some of the classes, but I couldn't take the exam because the chemistry one was at the same time and I had to be there. He said," I flunked you."

I said, "What do you mean? I'm doing this as part of my fellowship." But he got on my case.

I led about four other guys over to his house, knocked on the door, and said, "Either I get a B or you get your ass kicked." I didn't want to have to take the goddamn class over.

During my fellowship in biochemistry, it wasn't all deep learning lightened by Dr. Howell's sense of humor. There was a certain amount of rather unpleasant biochemical grunt work that occasionally taxed my ability to handle it. One morning, for instance, Dr. Howell said he wanted me to go to the slaughterhouse to pick up some blood for the students in the lab. I drove to what turned out to be a really rural location—a packing house—and announced my errand. I don't know what I had been expecting—probably something like lab officials in white coats taking proper bottles from refrigerators and handing them to me. Well, these guys weren't in white coats, let me tell you. They brought me to an area where they had a live steer on a kind of ramp and started hitting it on the head with a sledgehammer. When it was more or less unconscious, they pushed it out into the middle of a disgusting area—all mud and feces—maybe twenty or twenty-five yards across, and then they handed me a gallon jug, and while I held it up to the steer's throat, they slit the jugular veins and let the blood run into the jug. This was the blood I was to take to the lab for the students to work on.

There were other things that we did that today I would consider quite inhumane. We put rabbits into insulin shock just to demonstrate to students the function of insulin. I would draw blood from a rabbit's ear; we'd test the sugar level; then Dr. Howell would give it a shot of insulin and I'd draw blood and give it the test again to show that insulin makes the sugar level go down. But it's pretty hard to draw blood out of a rabbit's ear, to get the vein right, and, of course, the rabbits suffered. Sometimes they lived; sometimes they died.

We did a similarly barbaric test with chickens. Dr. Howell fed some of them brown rice over a period of time and some of them white rice. The chickens that ate white rice got beriberi. They eventually got wobbly and couldn't walk. Beriberi results from thiamine deficiency, and the thiamine is in the brown husk of the rice. The white has no vitamins in it at all. Dr. Howell made a big point of that: how the rich people in China eat the polished rice and they wind up becoming vitamin deficient, while the poor guys out in the field eat the brown rice and of course stay more healthy. It was an advantage to being poor, health-wise.

During the summer of 1962, between my fourth and fifth years (1962 was the year of my extension), Dr. Howell had me researching brain chemistry. I drove down to a big library in St. Louis and went through everything I could find on neurotransmitters and on how psychotropic drugs functioned. "Miltown" was still in use as the tranquilizer of choice, and Librium was just starting to be prescribed. I became quite conversant with the chemistry of the brain and how it related to these substances. Dr. Howell had me deliver what I had learned at a CME (Continuing Medical Education) presentation to a group of osteopathic physicians. It turned out that this awakened a rather bitter dispute within our own psychiatric department, which was controlled by psychoanalysts who didn't approve of any molecular approach to psychiatric patients. They demanded that I cease and desist teaching this under the school banner. I received an official letter to that effect.

During my fifth school year, I had three afternoons a week free because that year I was just making up for time I lost as Dr. Howell's assistant. I used these to work with a physician in Kirksville named Dr. Gross, who was famous locally as the "lightning bonesetter." He could pop every joint in your body in seven minutes flat. I felt that I was, by now, strong in the molecular aspects of disease, but I hadn't had much experience working with my hands, even though it was my manual work in the Coast Guard as much as anything else that made me want to become a physician. Dr. Gross was happy to have me precept with him mainly because I did understand the molecular aspect of things. He himself didn't. He thought perhaps I would be the guy that would begin to integrate molecular medicine with hands-on medicine. He treated me like a son, and I worked with him solidly for that year.

At a certain point during that time, he went on a vacation and asked me to cover the office while he was gone. I said, "But I don't have a license, and I won't have my degree until I finish this year."

He said, "That doesn't matter. You don't need a license, you can work under mine. You just run the office and treat the patients. You've been working with me for four or five months now, and I trust you. You're the only guy I know that can fix my wife's neck!"

Dr. Gross gave me some general advice about how to run a medical office that I follow to this day. He said, "When a patient comes in, always be yourself. If they don't like you, they'll go somewhere else. You don't have to pretend you're somebody you're not. If you just be yourself and don't try to invent a front to please everybody, your office work will be a lot less stressful."

I really took that to heart. I remember when I opened my first office in Clearwater, Florida, two years later, I had a couple of patients that I just referred to somebody else even though I was broke. His words were echoing in my ears.

He also suggested a certain way of keeping patients' records that always looked sloppy in most people's eyes. He said, "Don't ever write anything of interest that could be subpoenaed! Just put down a lot of general stuff." I was already hip to what he meant from my experience with gonorrhea cases in Baltimore! Dr. Gross used 5x7 cards. He'd have about twenty office visits on each card. I pretty much do the same thing. I put down a couple of words, and that's it.

For one semester during the fourth school year, we had to work in special rural clinics set up by the school, something that medical schools ought to do a lot more of to alleviate the health-care problem. A Dr. Casner at Kirksville devised the project. In northeast Missouri, there were many towns that were just getting smaller and smaller for various reasons. One was that these habitations had developed around the railroads, but the railroads didn't stop there anymore. Since the 1950s the interstate highway system had changed the transport business from railroad to trucking. By the early 1960s, these towns tended to have no more than five or six hundred people in them, and some of them were about the most poverty-stricken places you can imagine. The way Dr. Casner would set a clinic up was to go to a town and offer one on behalf of the Osteopathic College if they would pay half the expense of establishing a site. It might cost altogether $35,000. If the town couldn't afford that, another possible arrangement was that the town would provide the labor to build the clinic, and the college would provide the construction materials and the clinical supplies and services. From these methods we had something like sixteen clinics, and they were all within two hours' drive of Kirksville.

Our clinic days were Monday, Wednesday, and Friday. On these days, we'd arrive at noon and see the patients from the town for one dollar a visit. There would be a couple of doctors on call back at the hospital whom we could contact if we were puzzled about some patient's problem. Also one full D.O. would make rounds and show up towards the end of the day. If we had a tough patient with whom we wanted help, we could get it at that time.

I think this program was wonderful if only because it taught us to get along with townspeople. They had no particular reason to trust us—we had to develop that trust. So you learned a heck of a lot about patient rapport. This served me very well in Florida when I developed my own practice and, later on, opened two free clinics.

I was assigned to a rural clinic at a God-forsaken place called Elmer. There were three of us that got sent out there: Roy Farnaman, Ruth Carter, and myself. I'll never forget our first visit. We had no idea what to expect, what the people would be like, or what conditions we were going to be working under. We were greeted by a local fellow who represented the town and led us into what looked like it once was a bank building—not a big city bank, just a little old town bank. It was situated at about a 5° angle relative to the street, probably due to changes in ground consistency—the foundation was sinking on one side or something. This fellow took us into the building, and the first thing he said was, "Now see this here hole?" There was a rough-looking, roundish hole, about two feet across, in the wood floor. He continued, "I got some plywood here, and we're going to nail it down to cover the hole for you because the snakes'll come in through there if we don't."

My mind went through a series of expletives. Finally I said "Whoa! Okay. Let's do it."

That was our clinic, and we did get it set up. Apparently Elmer hadn't been used to very much medical attention before we arrived. We turned out to be the first participants in the program there. But we took out our gear and spent an hour or so getting organized.

Once we were settled, but not organized, and it was getting to be about one o'clock in the afternoon, we decided we had better go have lunch. We hadn't brought any food with us because we thought there would be a restaurant there, and indeed there was—a strange-looking place across the street from a filling station. We took our seats and Ruth ordered first. "A hamburger with French fries, please."

It's hard to imagine how a waitress could be taken aback by so ordinary a request, but she was. She said, "Do you want your hamburger warm or cold?"

"Excuse me? Well, warm."

"Okay, but it will take a little while."

"Why is that?"

"It's from last night and it's cold. We'll have to heat it up for you."

Then I ordered coffee and she said *that* would take a little time, too. A little guy came out through the restaurant from the kitchen, I swear, with a *bucket,* and I saw him scurry across the street to the gas station, fill up the bucket with water, and bring it back to the restaurant. A couple of minutes later I got my coffee. To tell you the truth, I don't remember whether the coffee was good or bad, but I suspect that my taste buds were not in a state of high expectation at that point. Now that I think of it, I remember that I resolved to order a beer the next time around. The restaurant was apparently inspected by the health department there—well, there was a certificate over the counter that documented the fact. No doubt the inspector was trustworthy, because he himself came from Elmer, and I'm certain he made sure there wasn't any more than roughly the standard allowance of insects and other vermin in the kitchen when he passed the place.

While we were working at the clinic over the course of a few months, a couple of things of note occurred. There was a place called Pickler Park, which was sort of a suburb of Elmer, if you can imagine such a thing. It was inhabited by *really* poor people, even poorer than the population of Elmer. I remember a father coming into the clinic with a couple of kids who were so emaciated and anemic that I couldn't believe it. If, say, a normal hemoglobin count is 14, as I recall, these kids were, like 6 or 7. They were pretty ill. I asked their father what they had been eating, and he said, "Well, you know, we're kind of poor."

"But what are you feeding them?"

He said, "Bread."

"What else?"

"We put ether with the bread."

I asked, "Why do you do that?"

"It makes their stomach numb so they don't hurt when they get hungry."

They'd been living on bread and ether for weeks. My God. I was able to have them hospitalized, but who knows what happened to them after they got out.

I also learned how to do *proctoclysis* in Elmer. I'll explain what this is in a minute. People in rural areas may have no familiarity with ordinary medical procedures and treatments, and they can be just plain scared. Or at least that's the way it was in the early 1960s before the era of TV shows that take you into hospitals and tell you about all kinds of things. It would often happen that you would need to give a patient intravenous feeding for one reason or another, but they'd refuse to let you put a needle in a vein. What you *can* do—and I learned this from other guys who were working out there in the boondocks—is put an enema tube up their rear end and attach a bag of whatever solution you want them to have and run it in real slow. The body will absorb it through the bowel. This is called "proctoclysis."

I learned how to do that in Elmer and Pickler Park because there were people there who would refuse to be hospitalized even with medical conditions as serious as heart attacks. They weren't about to leave their farm. The truth is, hospitalization often wasn't necessary. I just employed proctoclysis to give them a solution of potassium, insulin, and glucose, or whatever I thought was going to be good for their heart. They actually did fine that way. I never had anyone die from that kind of treatment.

Dr. Howell retired in 1963, the same year I graduated. He died about three years later. I had known his wife, Edith, fairly well because I used to be invited over for dinner rather often. When I heard of Dr. Howell's death, I called Edith to offer my condolences but also to ask about a certain pile of handwritten notes that I knew he had been collecting for a book on cosmology. I realized that I was probably the only living human being who could interpret his notes and write his book from them. I said, "You know, Edith, I would be most happy to ghost-write this book for your husband. My name doesn't have to be involved at all. I just would like to do him the honor of putting his book out there."

She said, "Oh John, I'm so sorry."

I said "What do you mean?"

"Well, I was so distraught when he died that I had all of his things destroyed." So that big pile of his handwritten legacy got burned up. That bothered me a good bit because he had some wonderful ideas.

The graduation ceremony at Kirksville was no big deal—we just went through a line and got a diploma. I think I had a tie on. That would have been about the only time I ever wore a tie in Kirksville.

In returning to Detroit, I had to bring my old trailer with me. I had kept it even after I got kicked out of the trailer park. I stored it on a guy's farm for a while and eventually brought it to the Vets' housing barracks and set it up there. It was in good enough shape, I thought, to build into something with which I could haul all my worldly goods back to Detroit on the back of the car and, after graduation, I got it ready to make the journey. It was now pretty much like the back of a big semi truck, even though it was only 26 feet long. My mother and stepfather had come out for my graduation, so they were going to make the trip back to Detroit with me, Beverly, and the kids. We now had Leslie and two sons, John and Mark. Also, Beverly was very pregnant with number four.

I loaded all my stuff onto the now-open trailer—it was a pretty heavy load (most of the weight being books)—but I got it all on. We were about one hundred miles down the road toward Detroit when I heard a huge, unrecognizable sound coming from behind. I stopped and looked. The front and the back of the trailer were resting on the road. The frame of the thing had bent with the weight. Oh my god, I had my mother and stepfather in their car, my very pregnant wife and three kids in our car, and here we were, stuck in the middle of nowhere.

Well, my stepfather, Nick, as it happened, was a Mason—a Shriner—and of course the Shrine is a fraternal organization set up, it seems, to provide assistance under just such situations. He said, "Let me see if I can help ya'."

We were right near some little town in Illinois. He took the car to a gas station, where he found a phone, and came back saying he had located a brother who'd take care of this for us.

"Okay! But what's it gonna cost?"

"He says $200."

So we drove to Detroit, leaving the trailer with the Shriner brother, and I waited about a week, or ten days, without a word, but eventually the guy showed up. There was a price, however, beyond the two hundred bucks. My stepfather used our good fortune as a lever to get me to join the Masons.

I was in the Masons for quite a while. In fact, I went up all the thirty-two degrees, and then when I got into the "Shrine"—at the final stage of initiation—they wanted me to play a bagpipe because they knew I was a musician. That was their mistake. They gave me this bagpipe and said I was going to be playing it with the marching band. I said no I can't do that. The bagpipe is a horrible instrument to me. I hate it. I won't play it. It has no sharps and flats. If you have a good ear for music it'll tear up. It's always playing notes that are a little out of pitch. I like jumping music. But they wouldn't take no for an answer, so I quit the Masons flat. There are some things you just can't compromise, and my ear wouldn't let me play that damn thing.

I had returned home immediately after graduation because I was to do my internship at Detroit Osteopathic Hospital in Highland Park, near downtown. That was to be from July 1, 1963 through June 30, 1964. I had decided to do my internship there because it was known as the "Mecca" in osteopathic medicine. A good friend of mine who had entered medical school with me in Kirksville was now an obstetrical resident there. He recommended it in these terms: "It only pays $125 a month and you get $100 a month housing allowance, but consider it as furthering your education rather than being a low-paid job." Okay.

I naturally expected everything to be just fantastic. Having been a biochemistry teaching fellow, I had rather high expectations regarding what I thought the scientific proficiency of a doctor should be. For instance, I myself could sit down with a pencil and paper and, looking at a blood test that showed a patient's blood potassium to be low, calculate very quickly how much potassium we had to give him to bring him back to a normal range; but none of the doctors in the hospital could do that: they all had to look it up in a little manual that they carried with them. They had either never learned the kind of chemistry I learned from Dr. Howell or they had forgotten it.

Beyond this, it seemed to me that they were making a lot of mistakes in their basic medicine. I told the friend who had recommended the place, "I came here to learn."

He said, "Well you *are* learning—you are learning what you don't want to do!" And that made me feel better, because I was seeing a lot of examples of precisely what I did not want to follow.

Basically, what was disappointing about my internship was that, even though this was nominally an "osteopathic" hospital, nobody was following either the philosophy of osteopathy or the scientific philosophy that I had learned from Dr. Howell. Medicine to the doctors there usually meant looking at a symptom and attempting to obliterate it, period. They seldom looked for the underlying causes.

You can gather from many popular histories of "alternative medicine" that give accounts of osteopathy, chiropractic, and so forth, that, by the middle of the twentieth century, osteopathy had pretty much lost its mandate—it was no longer the practice put forth by Dr. Still to correct the blindness and abusiveness of conventional medicine. In the Detroit Hospital it had *become* conventional medicine.

But Kirksville still had a strong philosophical flavor. It adhered to the original concepts and, as I said, Dr. Howell had taught me always to reflect within myself, "Okay, you see the symptom. Now, why is it happening?"

Detroit Osteopathic Hospital was one of those all-to-common institutions, packed full of patients, where the doctors had all the latest equipment, but where nobody—well, "nobody" is too strong a word—but where very, very few physicians ever bothered to inquire about an ailment's primary cause, which could be several layers beneath the presenting symptoms.

I'll give you an example. I went to Detroit Osteopathic with every intention of becoming an internist because that specialty fits very well with biochemistry. My first rotation was in internal medicine, and it happened to be with the president of the American College of Osteopathic Internal Medicine. First of all, as I alluded to earlier, he didn't know enough biochemistry to be able to do what *I* could do, which was kind of silly. He was dependent upon those little manuals that were, in fact, distributed by drug companies, telling how much the dosage should be. He was relying on somebody else's ability to make a calculation, and I felt it important for a doctor to make his own because every patient is an individual; you can never determine dosage for sure by means of a rule of thumb. Plus, it's really a hell of a thing to be dependent on a drug company to determine the strength of a prescription.

At the hospital, they didn't feel that way at all. They didn't like to think about patients as individuals. They fit people into pigeonholes. You were not supposed to think, "Okay, let's find out why this gall bladder went bad;" or "Let's find out why this uterus is dropping;" or "Why is this person having recurrent bouts of asthma?" Not at all. Rather it was: define the symptom, prescribe treatment on the basis of its category, and on to the next patient as quickly as possible!

Well, about three or four weeks into my internship, the internist that I was working for invited me to do a residency in internal medicine, to begin when I finished my internship. (Don't be confused by the terminology: being an "internist" is specializing in "internal medicine;" being an "intern" in a hospital is the last phase in one's medical training. These are two completely different things.) Becoming an internist was, indeed, exactly what I had been intending to do, as I said, but I was already beginning to question whether or not I really wanted to go through with it.

One day a certain woman came in. Now, the intern always does the admitting physical and takes the history of the patient. This particular woman had a lot of pain in her right, upper abdominal area and in her back. After palpating her back and abdomen, I said to my supervisor, "I would like to do a pelvic examination on her because I really suspect that she's got some kind of a cyst up in the area of the kidney, and I'd like to be able to pinpoint this a little bit better."

He said, "Internal medicine doesn't do pelvic examinations."

I said, "What do you mean?"

He said, "You're on internal medicine, you don't do pelvic examinations. You have a surgeon do it."

I said, "Well, I would like to be able to put together what's in my head with what I'm feeling, so I can be more intelligent about this."

He said, "As long as you're on this service, you won't do that stuff." And I decided right then and there that I did not want to be an internist and be bound by these really foolish restrictions. It was ridiculous that I had to get somebody else to do a part of a physical examination that I was perfectly competent to perform myself.

Then, as I went through the various services, as the year went on, I found that even though this was an osteopathic hospital, nobody was looking at "osteopathic" questions like, "Is there a spinal dysfunction related to a particular organ problem, say, gall bladder or pancreas?" There was none of that. It was all just plain, conventional medicine. (Another thing that was quite noticeable was that the guys that were doing that kind of medicine had egos that would hardly fit inside a large house.)

About five months into my internship, I was pulling night duty. The weather outside was an atrocity—snow, sleet, and sub-zero temperature. I was to learn a lot about death and dying that night. As soon as I checked in, I was paged up to the post-operative floor and greeted by a surgeon and a family physician (they were called "general practitioners" in those days). They were both rather excited and started babbling at me that the patient in room such and such was dying. They had operated to perform a routine bowel resection and found cancer all over the place. They couldn't stop his internal bleeding, so they just sewed him back up and put him on IVs and blood transfusion. The blood was going into his right arm, three IVs were going into his left arm, and there was also one IV in each leg. They wanted me to keep him alive until his wife could see him and a priest could come to administer his last rites. The doctors told me all this and then left in a hurry.

I went in to see the patient. He was a middle-aged laborer of Polish descent. He was slightly conscious as I went in to say hello and, as I was introducing myself, he lost consciousness and his blood pressure was dropping.

I ran out to tell the nurse to get me a couple of vials of aramine. I gave him two CCs of aramine through the IV tubing. He came back to life, smiled and said, "Hello." I went out to call his wife, who (as I found out as soon as she answered the phone) spoke no English. I knew a few words of Polish—enough to get it across to her that I needed to speak to someone in English. The patient's brother came to the phone, and I explained as best I could that the patient could die at any moment. I asked him to please get the wife to the hospital as soon as possible. I gave the room number.

I ran back to the patient's room where I found him once again unconscious. I gave him another two CCs of aramine. He revived, smiled at me, and said words that have since remained indelibly imprinted in my brain. He said, "Thanks, Doc, I almost died, didn't I?"

I said, "Yes. Your wife is on the way. Now I'm going to get you a priest, so hang on, please."

I called three churches before I found a priest who would venture out in the bad weather.

I went back into the room. He was gone again. More aramine. He came back, with essentially the same words. "I almost died that time. Thanks, Doc."

I stayed in the room. In a few minutes the priest arrived. I gave the patient enough aramine so that he would be aware that he was being blessed. He thanked me for that, too. The priest did his thing and left.

Then his wife and brother arrived. More aramine to help him say goodbye to them. He did this and faded again. I thought I would let him go this time, but his wife looked at me with pleading eyes, so I couldn't resist and gave him another round of aramine.

By this time, I was having trouble thinking straight. I went out to the nursing station, and the head nurse looked at me in a very pitying way. She produced a bottle of Southern Comfort and told me to take a shot. I figured she was right, so I did.

My shift ended at 8:00 a.m. According to the charts, he died at 8:40. I learned a lot about how we have the ability to thwart the natural death process and how a guy like him can die gracefully and without fear. He had agreed to stay alive, with the help of the aramine, just to please his wife. What a night!

About halfway through my internship, a situation arose where I was faced with a terrifying choice. A few years earlier, my grandmother fell down in the yard while hanging clothes out to dry. She fractured her hip and had it pinned surgically at a small osteopathic hospital on the east side of Detroit. This accident was, I believe, just before I returned from my first year at Kirksville. When I got home, Grandma was back from the hospital with sutures still present in the surgical site. They looked very "ripe" to the hospital corpsman in me. I called the surgeon, and he asked would I please take them out. I agreed. When I cut the sutures, the incision popped open, and at least a pint of rather rank-smelling yellow puss came pouring out. I called the surgeon again and described what I had seen. Unwilling to tolerate a confrontation on his sloppy work, he said, "Who do you think you are?" and hung up. I went to his hospital and found that his operating room opened onto an alley that was rife with vermin. It was no wonder that Grandma's incision got infected. I tried pointing that out, but there was no talking to the surgeon.

I went back to Grandma and tended her wound. It healed, but she was dependent upon a walker for the rest of her life.

Why do I go into this story now? Can't you guess? During my internship, one night when I was doing night service in the emergency room at Detroit Osteopathic Hospital and I was the only physician awake and present in the emergency room, the very surgeon who had screwed up my grandma's hip and was so rude to me presented in the midst of a heart attack. He was all mine! I could let him go or save him! While I was thinking about letting him go, I did all the right things to keep him alive and got him into bed with oxygen, intravenous polarizing solution, and subcutaneous heparin. We reversed the infarction process, and in a few days he was fine. Today I would say about this episode that my hands are much smarter than my brain.

There were a few more very interesting things that occurred during my internship at Detroit Osteopathic Hospital. This lawyer—let's call him Mr. Jackson—tried to get me to do things for the mafia while I was interning in Detroit. It was hard to turn that one down because I was making $250 each month altogether, with four kids. That's what they paid interns in those days. It was $150 and then $100 for housing if you were married. But I kept my ass clean. He'd call me and say, "Do you know how to do a uterine scraping?"

I'd say, "Yes." He knew I was in obstetrics at the time. I think my wife must have told him.

Then he'd say, "I have a good friend, she's sixteen, and she's pregnant. It's worth $2,500 for you if you'll scrape her out.

I'd say, "No, I can't do that." But that was his method. The first time he connected with me, he wanted to know if I could prescribe or get a hold of some pills that would help his friend make it through a lie detector test in Lansing.

I said, "No, I can't do that."

Then he said, "That one was going to be worth $1,000."

He just kept calling me. Every service he offered that kind of money. After I'd say no, he would sometimes oddly comment, "Good move."

After I finished my internship, he explained. That's how he got stuck with being a mafia lawyer. He took one case for the money, which he knew was crooked; then he was sold to the mafia for the rest of his life—or he'd be dead. In those days, they honored you if you wouldn't do it. After a certain number of times, if you wouldn't cooperate with them, they'd just leave you alone.

There was also a lot of bad and corrupt medicine happening in the hospital itself. One was when a certain Surgeon B removed the wrong breast from a cancer patient by mistake. He covered his rear end by giving the patient the "good news" that the cancer had not spread to the other breast, which he had removed, and now he could remove the affected breast confident of a cure.

Another *faux pas* of Surgeon B occurred when he decided to do biopsies on normal pancreases while performing surgeries for abdominal problems such as cancer of the bowel, etc. I was on his service when he decided to do these pancreatic biopsies. He did three in two days. After the operations, pancreatic juices were preventing closure of the biopsy sites. Pancreatic juices are digestive enzymes that will digest meat in your digestive track and will digest *you* when they get outside of the protective channel that nature has provided.

The post-operative patients were actually digesting their own skin, as the digestive juices obeyed the law of hydraulics that says that a fluid will follow the path of least resistance. I told the smartest internist in the hospital about these three patients. He did two things. First, he educated Surgeon B about the sequelae of pancreatic biopsies. The biopsies stopped immediately. Second, he suggested that I put a tube into the incision on a low suction and pull out the pancreatic juices that were liberated by the biopsy. Since the suction would not be one hundred percent effective and some of the enzymes would continue to leak, he suggested that I use a slow drip of a protein solution, somewhat like Sustagen, which is available in health-food stores, to be digested by the leaking enzymes, which would thereby become neutralized. I followed his suggestions, and the three victims of Surgeon B's ignorance healed over the next week.

The same surgeon at one point had to have a woman readmitted to the hospital three months after he had operated on her hemorrhoids. I was still on Surgeon B's service. It was my job to do the history and physical examination on newly admitted patients. She told me that since her hemorrhoids had been removed, she had been suffering from large-bowel incontinence. She was being hospitalized because Surgeon B had told her that transplanting her bicep muscle into her anus would allow her to develop rectal control again. I thought to myself, "Does this mean that she will be able to control her bowel movement by contracting and relaxing her right bicep muscle?" I thanked God that I finished Surgeon B's service before this poor woman was subjected to further surgery.

Surgeon B wasn't only ignorant and incompetent. He turned out to be quite corrupt. While I was still on his service, he offered to teach me this special procedure for hemorrhoids and to set me up to perform it in my own "little hemorrhoid hospital" at no cost to me. All I had to do was send all the patients that came to my little hospital to him for any further surgery that they might just *happen* to need. I asked what would happen if I sent a patient to another surgeon for treatment. He replied that he would kick me out of my little hemorrhoid hospital and bring in another young doctor who would be more cooperative. Needless to say, I declined.

Surgeon B was not the only physician I encountered during my internship who had no business practicing medicine. I have two very fascinating stories to tell about a rather elderly internist we shall call E. Internist E had a great reputation with older general practitioners of osteopathic medicine. This reputation covered a rather wide expanse of southeastern Michigan and northern Ohio. I was on Internist E's service, which meant I did rounds with him daily when he saw his patients and did all his scut work before and after his rounds. Internist E may have been a fine physician in his day but, during the time I was on his service, he had a rather gross tremor, so I had to do most of his "hands-on" work for him.

At one point we were seeing a sixty-year-old woman whose husband was one of internist E's physician fans. Her husband insisted that Internist E himself should do a speculum examination of his wife's vagina and cervix. It was usually my job to do speculum placements for him because of his tremor. In this case, Internist E was determined to do it himself. With the woman in the proper position, he lunged with the speculum and it went into her anal orifice rather than her vagina. She screamed in pain. Internist E displayed his cool by loudly stating that these damned nurses were always giving him the wrong instruments! He had me insert a fresh but identical speculum which he confidently asserted was the right one.

Here's another very funny story about Internist E that stethoscope users especially will appreciate. Internist E was called to the emergency room to see one of his established patients. He assembled a group of about six or seven interns and one resident to view him in action with an emergency-room patient. When he wanted a stethoscope to listen to the patient's heart and lungs, he borrowed the resident's stethoscope. Matters got complicated owing to the fact that Internist E had forgotten that he had his own stethoscope hanging by the ear pieces around his neck! At the crucial moment, he put the resident's stethoscope to his ears but picked up the listening end of his own instrument and placed it carefully on the patient's chest. He started wavering side to side as he listened to the patient's chest. What he was hearing was a meticulously amplified version of the listening end of the resident's stethoscope going back and forth across the front of his own shirt. With a puzzled but still confident look on his face, he gave the resident back his stethoscope and directed him to auscultate (listen to) the patient's chest and explain his findings to the interns. He walked away, none the wiser.

The poor guy should have been retired, but that didn't happen while I was an intern. In July, 1964, when I finished my internship, Internist E was making his rounds in an electric wheelchair, so whenever he went into a ward, they had to shut down the oxygen to avoid an explosion.

Towards the end of my internship, I arranged to go into practice in Detroit with another physician named Chester McFarland; however, I left Detroit before we got very far into our relationship. I finished my internship on June 30, 1964, as I mentioned, and was ready to enter practice, but Dr. McFarland immediately took a six-week vacation. I covered his office for that period, beginning with the Monday after the Fourth of July. There was no time to form a close relationship with him. Meanwhile, a few of my Rockefeller Fellowship biochemistry students had graduated and were in practice down in Florida. They were interns and practitioners at a rather young osteopathic facility in the Largo-Clearwater area called Suncoast Hospital and were seeking to enlarge their staff. They knew that I had been a good student so they were recruiting me. (I had already passed the Florida state medical boards while I was interning. I had taken these exams mostly to get four or five days off from that very demanding internship! A list of the people who pass the boards is made public. The Suncoast guys had seen that list and recognized my name.)

I received a call from a Suncoast Hospital administrator suggesting that I might like to join their staff. Of course, I told them that I was about to enter practice with Dr. McFarland in Detroit.

They said, "Well, we'll provide air fare, motel room, and a car for you and your wife to come down and check us out. You can stay for a week or ten days as our guests. You can look around at your leisure, and if you still don't want to join us—okay! No harm done."

We took them up on their offer, and at the end of the ten days I said, "Jesus, I don't want to leave this place." So we moved to Florida. It took about a month for us to settle on renting both house and office spaces.

Suncoast Hospital

Florida was wonderful in many ways, and I was very happy to be beginning my own osteopathic medical career in earnest. While I was there, I opened a free clinic for drug addicts; I became a practicing acupuncturist; and I discovered CranioSacral Therapy. But all this in due course.

One of the advantages of working in association with a young hospital was that I was pretty freely able to explore aspects of medicine that most interested me. I was also allowed to invite speakers from various medical fields as part of the CME program. Actually, I engineered this possibility myself because there were certain areas of contemporary medical practice that I really wanted to find out about by meeting the people who were engaged in them.

While I was "chairman of general practice," as we used to call it, at one of the hospital staff meetings I suggested that we needed somebody to be in charge of bringing in various medical authorities from across the country and around the world so that we could have continuing medical education classes right there at the hospital. I knew that if I suggested it, the guys would say, "Well, why don't *you* do it?" They did, and I said, "All right, I will!"

One of the first outsiders I brought in was Dimitrio Sodi-Pallares. He was the leading cardiologist in all of Mexico, and I wanted him to come to us because when I was in, I believe, my third year in Kirksville, he lectured and made a great impression on me. I had resolved to use certain aspects of his methodology for our heart patients. Now that I had my own practice on Clearwater Beach and was tending to three or four heart attacks a week, I was putting what I had learned from him into practice. I had kept my notes on his lecture, and I followed them to a T. I never had a heart attack patient die; they all lived and did very well.

To entice him to visit us, the hospital paid for me to go down to Mexico to see him personally. I spent five days working with him in his laboratory and convinced him to come up and lecture to us. Working in his laboratory was a real joy.

Dr. Sodi-Pallares had developed a treatment called *repolarization*. His idea was that many heart attacks occur not because a blood vessel is occluded, but because there has been a loss of potassium from the inside of the cardiac muscle cells. When the potassium goes out and the sodium comes in, the electro-potential charge across the membrane is reduced. Normally, it's about 100 millivolts. When it gets down to about 75 or 80, the muscle can't contract hard enough to give you a forceful expulsion of blood from the heart ventricle.

His approach was that when somebody is having a heart attack, the first thing should be to repolarize the heart by administering a solution of potassium insulin and glucose intravenously. (This was a technique, you will remember, I was already applying rectally in the Elmer, Missouri, clinic. It was from Dr. Sodi-Pallares that I learned the treatment, though not the rectal method of administering it.) The insulin goes in and carries the glucose with it, and the potassium attaches to the glucose, so it gets into the cell. When the potassium level goes up, the sodium starts excreting from the cell, so the cell recharges and the strength of the heart muscle returns.

If, in fact, repolarization is what is called for, the patient does fine, and very often this is the case. Dr. Sodi-Pallares said that everybody's always looking for the clot that caused the heart attack. Occasionally people would die in the hospital and he'd immediately open their chest and look at the heart, and very frequently he couldn't find a clot but he could see that the muscle tissue was not healthy. When the muscle stops working efficiently, it stops receiving the blood, and then the blood becomes static. If you wait long enough to perform your autopsy, the clot you find is just that static blood, which ultimately coagulates.

Back at the hospital, I thought I'd check this out. I went to our pathologist who performs all of our autopsies, and I asked him, "When you get deceased heart-attack victims, do you always find a clot?"

He said, "You don't always find it but you know it's there, so you put it on the autopsy report as being present anyway."

Hmmn. So much for statistics based on autopsy records!

Another methodological point Dr. Sodi-Pallares made: a lot of times when you get all excited because a patient's having a heart attack, you scare him to death!

Whenever I was called in for a heart attack in a home or motel on Clearwater Beach, I'd call the ambulance, and say, "No siren, no speeding, everything's fine." I'd start the patient off with the repolarizing solution right there, and I'd give him a little heparin. I swear I never had a problem until we installed a cardiac intensive care unit after about four or five years. I had misgivings, but I put two patients in there, trying to go along with the management of the hospital, and they both died. So I never used it again. I never had another patient die of a heart attack.

Dr. Sodi came to Suncoast two years in a row and gave us beautiful lectures regarding these matters.

While I was practicing at Suncoast Hospital, I learned an unexpected lesson from the death of a male patient named Shirley. Shirley was a World War I veteran who originally came to my office with low-back pain, high blood pressure, absent mindedness, some occasional mental confusion, and episodes of anger that had no apparent immediate cause. When I x-rayed his low back and pelvis, I saw some opaque areas in his buttocks on the films. He told me that these were from gold shots that he'd been given when he was in his twenties. He had contracted syphilis during World War I. The Veterans Administration health-care system kept track of him. He maintained a positive blood test for syphilis after the series of gold shots were given. When penicillin came along in the early 1940s, the Veterans Administration gave him a course of treatment with penicillin injections. He continued to carry a positive blood test, but no other symptoms were noted.

To make a long story short, Shirley's back got better with treatment. We kept his blood pressure under control, but his mental deterioration continued. The osteopathic manipulations that I applied mostly to his neck did not help his brain function. This was before I had any inkling of the existence of the craniosacral systems and how you treat them. It was also before CT scans and MRI evaluations. All we had to look with were x-rays. After not too long, Shirley suffered what looked like a stroke. I admitted him to the hospital and he died within a few hours.

I obtained permission for a full autopsy including his head from his widow. I assisted our pathologist in performing it. After opening Shirley's head, we discovered a colony of *spirochetes*—

syphilis-producing organisms—in the forward part of his brain, just above the optic chiasma (where the two major nerves from the eyeballs cross). These syphilis germs were *alive*. We carefully traced them into the left optic nerve, through the nerve, and into the left eyeball, where they had apparently been living since World War I!

What did I learn? Germs are very smart, very resourceful, and they want to go on living just like people do.

I got another very powerful lesson about the world we live in from a patient named Sam. This one was about both the socioeconomic rules that govern our hospitals and our so-called system of justice. Sam was in his mid-sixties. I had been taking care of his quite healthy, ninety-year-old mother for about six months prior to taking him on as a patient. Without an appointment or a phone call, Sam suddenly burst into my Clearwater Beach office in a panic, begging me to help him. I took him into one of my treatment rooms. He immediately dropped his beat-up khaki pants. He had no underwear on. There was an indwelling catheter in his penis and a transparent, blood-filled, catheter bag strapped to his left mid-thigh.

It seems that Sam had been working at a fruit-packing house, moving heavy crates by hand. A few days before he appeared in my office, he had gone to the men's room to relieve his bladder and noticed blood mixed in his urine. He reported this to his supervisor, who sent him to a hospital near the fruit company. Note that he was admitted only because he had Workmen's Compensation coverage to pay the hospital bills.

The hospital staff did several painful laboratory studies on him and took x-rays. During his first night in the hospital, after the poking and prodding of the day before, Sam woke up at about 5:00 a.m. He needed to urinate but could not. In pain, Sam notified the nursing station. They called his doctor who ordered that Sam be catheterized by the male nurse. The doctor would see Sam later in the day. The catheterization was difficult for the male nurse to perform and very painful for Sam. Eventually, the nurse pushed the catheter hard enough and it entered Sam's bladder which finally drained. He experienced some relief. The male nurse left the catheter in place and hooked it up to the bag that was now strapped to Sam's left thigh and which he had so dramatically displayed to me.

When the doctor arrived at about 11 o'clock in the morning, he informed Sam that his prostate gland was hopelessly enlarged and would have to be removed. Sam accepted the doctor's word and began preparing himself for the surgery which was to be performed the following day.

Sam was then visited by one of the office personnel. He was questioned about his own ability to pay for the surgery. Sam had no insurance beyond Workmen's Comp and couldn't pay cash. At 3:00 p.m. he was told that his surgery was canceled and that he was being discharged from the hospital. His prostate problem was not work-related. His Workmen's Compensation insurance did not cover it.

Sam was essentially evicted from his hospital bed with the catheter and bloody urine-filled bag still in place. He stopped at the hospital administrator's office on the way out and showed him the catheter and bag and pleaded for mercy, but to no avail. He came to my office directly from the hospital. I called the Suncoast Hospital administrator, explained the situation, and got him admitted as a pro-bono patient. I phoned one of my surgeon friends, Dr. Reagan (cousin to ex-President Reagan, by the way), who consented to do the surgery. Sam would owe him the money and pay when he could.

By 5:30 p.m., Sam was in bed and scheduled for surgery the next morning with Dr. Reagan using yours truly as first assistant. All went well in terms of recovery. What we found in surgery was later confirmed by the pathologist: Sam had a severely traumatized prostate gland, probably suffered during the poking and prodding at the previous hospital.

After his recovery, Sam decided to sue the original hospital so that Suncoast and Dr. Reagan and I could all be paid. Sam couldn't find an attorney who would take the case, so he decided to become his own attorney. He spent days in the library at Stetson University Law School. He filed all his papers and, after a time, went to trial before a six-person jury. He testified, I testified, the surgeon testified, etc., etc., etc. The jury seemed to be on Sam's side but, for no apparent reason, the judge suddenly dismissed the jury and then dismissed the case against the hospital. Sam went down in defeat.

Sam helped me learn something about our judicial system: UGH!!! Be careful! This justice business may not be all that it's cracked up to be.

Break Up and Divorce

Though my medical practice at Suncoast Hospital was going very well, other aspects of my life were not. It became increasingly clear to me that my primary interest was in medicine, not in making a lot of money. I really wanted to continue to be a student in some sense, and to keep on learning and exploring. Unfortunately, it also became clear that Beverly had married me because she imagined she was going to be a rich doctor's wife. But I wasn't aiming to be a rich doctor. We began to quarrel. We eventually broke up, although it took eleven years of marriage for our difficulties to come to a head.

A couple of things beyond our difference of opinion about how I should conduct my career ended our marriage. One was that by the time I started practicing in Clearwater, we had four kids. In retrospect, I can see how having four kids in seven years would drive any woman nuts. But I was busting my hump trying to support us all, and early on I felt that she wasn't holding up her end. I'd come home from the office and she'd be sleeping on the couch. The kids would be running all over the place. During my internship, I had had her checked by one of the internists because I intuited there was something not quite right with her. He diagnosed that she was suffering from *post-hyperglycemic neurogenic hypoglycemosis*. What's that? High blood sugar, caused by nervousness, alternating with low blood sugar. She had high blood-sugar levels that were followed by low blood-sugar levels, and the low blood sugar made her pass out and fall asleep. But the diagnosis was also that it was "neuorgenic," i.e., emotionally based. She went to a psychiatrist.

Then I found out that she had become a poll watcher for George Wallace when he was running for president—George Wallace, for Christ's sake! And I'm integrated as hell! Boy, did we have it out on that one! I pretty much knew it was over then.

You might think it's surprising that I could have been married for ten years and not know anything about my wife's political attitudes—but it's true! And I think the reason was that when I got married, I was doing pre-med at Wayne University and getting ready to start osteopathic school. I was always busy with my studies and then with the internship. We really didn't get to know each other until after I graduated, finished with Detroit Osteopathic Hospital internship, and began my practice in Florida. That's when we began to see that our views on a lot of things were really quite different. Our first disagreement was about my practice itself, as I mentioned: whether I was going to practice medicine as I saw fit and earn enough money to support us, or whether I was going to make accumulating money my priority so she could have a big swimming pool. Then, when George Wallace ran for president, she let me know how racially bigoted she was. I flipped out on that one. I told her I did not want her to teach my children to be racists. And that was the immediate cause of our split-up.

By this time, I had founded the free clinic—I'll tell you about that in a minute—and she didn't like that because it was taking up time that I could have been using to make money. I suggested that we separate. She could visit her family back in Michigan for a while; I'd bring in a housekeeper for the children. We could try this for a month and see how we got along. Well, she agreed to that on a Friday, and on Tuesday I was served with divorce papers. That was her idea of agreeing! I should've known—she was a legal secretary.

The divorce process took well over a year. It finally went through in 1969. It was one of the messiest divorces you can imagine. She had all kinds of reasons why she couldn't go to court.

As soon as I got divorced from Beverly, I went over and lived with Dianne. She was pretty young, maybe twenty. Here's how I met her: George Coope, one of my doctor friends, called me and said, "I have a gal that I don't get along with—her personality is too rough, but she's damned good in the office and I don't want to hurt her feelings. Would you interview her?"

I had her come over and I hired her on the spot. She had a very high IQ and was very efficient for someone young. George Coope didn't want to have to fire her. She was on my wave-length; she supported my attitude about how to treat patients and meshed with the things I was doing professionally. I was already beginning to experiment in ways that weren't conventional in terms of practice.

I had started the free clinic, and I was working a lot with heroin addicts. When Dianne and I decided we were going to get married, she already knew most of the guys from the clinic—the junkies—and she really liked what we were doing for them. I will never forget this—Dianne and I decided we would drive over to the east coast of Florida, find a notary public, and get married. About ten of the junkies got together for a little send-off. They gave us a present. I shoved it into the glove box; then we drove over, got married. We opened it on the way back, and it was a marijuana thing about a foot long and about an inch around. I thought, "Oh, Jesus, if we ever got stopped by a cop...! I'd be in jail yet."

The Discovery of the CranioSacral Rhythm

Over the next five or six years, my work in Florida expanded and took on several of the aspects that have remained characteristic of it ever since. I started the free clinic, I made the discovery that led to CranioSacral Therapy, I learned and began to practice acupuncture, and my interest in spirituality and psychic awareness was born. The first three are kind of intertwined. Psychic awareness will receive a chapter of its own.

I started the free clinic so I could treat young people with drug addictions in a setting apart from my regular patients. I did my regular practice in my office from around 10:00 a.m. to about 6:00 p.m. After hours, I ran the free clinic, for which I raised funds.

Another founder was a Green Beret medic from the Vietnam War, Butch Anderson. He's now an M.D.—an internist. Butch was there most of the time. A few other dedicated people lived on site and attended it 'round the clock. I was the "license," the guy that organized the thing and "oversaw" what happened. I'd drop in around 8:00 at night for an hour or two to make sure everything was going all right.

Now for the beginnings of CranioSacral Therapy. That will naturally bring us back around to what was going on at the clinic. I've told the story of how I discovered CranioSacral Therapy in my other books, but this is where it all began, so it's worth telling one more time. It began with Delbert. I'll always remember Delbert—he probably was a patient sent from God!

Delbert had a terrible problem. He had a systemic parasitic infection called *echinococcus*. Delbert was the father of a young lady named Judy. I was the family physician of Judy and her husband. I had delivered their baby. One morning, Judy called me and said, "Doc, on the way to the hospital, could you stop and see my Dad? He's on the floor here and he's vomiting blood."

I had never seen her father before, but I said, "Sure, Judy, I'll stop by."

Well, when I arrived there, at first I was pretty angry because there was Dad on the floor all right. He had been vomiting blood, but I could smell booze all over the place. I said, "Why didn't you tell me he was a drunk?"

She said, "He's not a drunk. He just drank some whiskey to ease the pain in his stomach." Not a smart move. Anyway, I took him to the hospital and I found out that he had the *echinococcus*— a parasitic infection, as I mentioned. That's what we diagnosed. He had *echinococcal cysts* in his liver and his brain. I treated him medically and he did pretty well. I discharged him from the hospital after a couple of weeks, but a week or so later, I got another call from the family. He himself would never call, but his wife did. She said, "Delbert can't walk."

I said, "Why not?"

"His feet hurt so bad. The skin is turning all black and it's cracking and it hurts him like the dickens."

I said, "I don't know what that is."

"Well, would you check him and see what you think?"

So I stopped by and took a look at him. I really couldn't tell what this was. Ultimately, I sent him to Gainesville—to the medical school up there. All they were able to tell me was that he was a "constitutional inadequate." That's what I got. Some diagnosis! They also said he had black lung disease—he had been a coal miner. I said, "I know that already. What's the matter with his feet?" No dice!

So I sent him to New Orleans, to the Oxner clinic. Again, no diagnosis. Then to Duke University. No help. Next, I sent him up to the coal miner's hospital in West Virginia. He was covered by his retirement fund. Nothing doing there either, so I said to his family, "I don't have an answer for you guys."

"Doc, would *you* please put him in the hospital once more and see if you can find out what's wrong?"

In he went. At about this time, a new neurosurgeon named James Tyler joined us. I had talked to him a little bit before and thought he was a pretty smart guy. He'd been in general practice for nine years before he did his general surgical residency, and then he'd gone to Japan to study neurosurgery. He'd only been back in the States maybe a year or so. I asked him, "Would you take a look at this guy? I have no idea what's the matter with him."

He examined him and said, "I just have a feeling that there's something wrong up in his neck."

I said to myself, "Uh, oh! Who is this character? The guy must be nuts. What's he talking about?"

He said, "I'd like to do a *cervical myelogram* on him."

Well, I didn't feel good about that because performing a cervical myelogram is not risk-free. If the scalpel slips, you open a pathway to infection in the form of meningitis and/or encephalitis. On the other hand, Delbert didn't feel good about his feet, and he was just about ready to kill himself if he didn't get this black stuff off them pretty soon. I explained the whole thing to the family. I said, "I have no idea whether we'll find anything here or not. The neurosurgeon thinks maybe we will."

They said, "Do it." So we did it. Sure enough he had *plaque* on the posterior aspect of the *dura mater,* about at the level of the third cervical vertebra. The dura mater is a membrane inside the spinal canal. The third cervical vertebra is in the neck. Just as Jim Tyler had predicted, something was wrong in Delbert's neck. A plaque is a deposit that gathers on a surface. It was about the size of a dime and turned out to be a calcium plaque.

Jim said, "I think we should go ahead and remove this plaque."

I said, "What's that got to do with his feet?"

Jim said, "I'm not sure how it works, but in Japan they think along these lines."

I relayed Jim's opinion to the family, and they said, "We'll try anything."

We scheduled surgery, with me assisting Jim. We exposed the dural membrane and saw the plaque. Jim said, "Hold the dura still so I can just scrape the stuff off and we don't cut the dura." But it wouldn't hold still. And that's when I saw the craniosacral system for the first time. And everything in the universe changed then, though it took me a while to catch up to what had happened. I was like Johannes Kepler who had seen the movements of the planets as they were but at first didn't know what he had seen. The dural membrane just kept moving in and out of the operating site. It moved toward me and away from me at a rate of about ten cycles a minute. It wasn't in sync with the breathing and it wasn't pulsing in sync with the cardiac monitor either, so it had to be something else.

And Jim—he's doing *this,* and the anesthesia guy's doing *that,* and the nurses are doing *their* thing, and I kept saying, "Does anybody have any idea what this movement is?"

Nobody wanted to pay attention to my question because they were focused on their surgical tasks, but I was supposed to be holding it still, so I was pretty curious—I was failing at my job! When we were finished with the procedure, I asked everybody again whether they knew what it was. Nobody knew. So that's how I discovered what I eventually realized was the craniosacral rhythm. I wondered a bit about it, I talked to people about it. Nobody seemed to know why this thing would be happening. It was apparently a new phenomenon that I was observing, but there it was. There was no denying its existence.

Shortly after Delbert's operation (which did cure his black feet, by the way), I noticed in an osteopathic medical journal an ad that something called "The Cranial Academy of Osteopathy" was offering a class. I remembered that when I was in osteopathic college in Kirksville, we had to sit and listen, every so often, to a guy from this very same Cranial Academy talk about how skull bones are not locked in place as is asserted by conventional medical wisdom but are capable of motion. I hadn't paid much attention. The Cranial Academy donated money to the school so I behaved and sat and listened; but most everybody considered them to be a bunch of crackpots.

Well, with that kind of preamble, I wasn't well disposed to their ad, but I had begun to speculate to myself that there was some

kind of hydraulic pressure inside the spinal canal that was causing the dural membrane to pulse, though nobody seemed to know
anything about it. When I saw the ad, I thought, "Gee, maybe
they're talking about what I saw during the surgery." (I must admit
it also occurred to me that I could get continuing medical education credits for attending. We were supposed to get fifty credits of
CME for the osteopathic society anyway, and this could give me
forty.) So the ad, in fact, grabbed me for many reasons.

The course was to be given in Louisville, Kentucky. I'm not
certain of the precise date. I wish I could tell you. It was about
1972 or 1973. It was probably six or eight months after I first saw
the movement of the dura mater in the surgery on Delbert. The
course consisted of a wonderful lecture on the anatomy of the skull.
It was absolutely beautiful. And then we went to the tables. One
of the instructors put her hands on my head, and I could feel my
head bones moving all over the place. She wasn't doing anything
to cause them to move but they were moving. I could just feel it.
She said, "Put your hands on mine." I did, and then she said to
put my hands on my own head. It was no more than thirty seconds before I realized it was the hydraulic force inside that was
causing the motion. From there on, for me it was just a matter of
looking at the details. A lifetime of details.

By the time I left the class, I had very good ideas of my own
about how to account for the movement of the cranial bones, but
I hadn't succeeded in engaging the interest of my instructors. The
people at the Cranial Academy had very mysterious concepts about
what was making the bones move. Truth-be-told, they didn't have
a clue as to what it really was. They didn't even know what they
were doing. Their story was that an energy from God was coming down into their hands and shifting the cranium around. They
said the bone that drives it all is the *sphenoid* because the sphenoid

spans the cranium from one side to the other and rocks back and forth. The energy from God is pumping the bone and that sets all the other bones in motion. The whole system was supposed to move just like a set of gears being moved by God. I tried to suggest to a couple of them that perhaps the cause of the movement was cerebrospinal fluid pressure rising and falling inside, but they would have none of it. They said in so many words, "If you're not going to be with us on this, then shut up—get out!"

So that's pretty much how it was. They were a very sectarian group—and very religiously based. What was the religion? Their own! You better believe it, brother! God came down through their hands and made it happen. I wanted to provide a scientific basis for it, but they didn't like that at all. Their anatomy was beautiful, however, and the experience enabled me to develop the idea that the rise and fall of the cerebrospinal fluid in the compartment formed by the dura mater was driving this whole system.

Now, you mustn't think that when I experienced the pulsation of the dura matter in the Delbert case, I was combining what I saw surgically with something that I already knew from osteopathic practice. I didn't know anything about what was called cranial osteopathy at the time I saw Delbert. My only exposure to cranial osteopathy in school was from the Cranial Academy people, as I mentioned. Most of our faculty didn't really believe in it. It had originally become a part of osteopathy through the work of a student of Still's at Kirksville by the name of William G. Sutherland, but it was unusual to find it practiced in present-day osteopathy.

A few words about Sutherland. In the first decades of the twentieth century, he began to investigate the movement of the cranial bones. According to conventional medical knowledge, the cranial bones are locked rigid, but Sutherland found that they move. The therapy he developed based on this perception was cranial osteopathy, though it had become marginal, as I said. Nonetheless, practitioners of cranial osteopathy were still around and were creating confusion within the profession. The people who believed in it were considered even by many osteopaths to be a bunch of weirdos. When I took my research position a few years later at Michigan State, one of the things I was asked (off the record) to investigate was the validity of cranial osteopathy. The dean of the school said, in effect, "You're a good scientist. Please. Find out if this stuff has a scientific basis. If it doesn't, we'll junk it and disown these guys. If it does, we'll expand it and develop it properly into a scientifically legitimate discipline." In fact, that issue was central to my being recruited at Michigan State.

At most osteopathic colleges in other parts of the country, students were not being taught any cranial osteopathy at all. In order to learn it, you had either to go to the Cranial Academy or to another institution, the Sutherland Cranial Teaching Foundation. The same people ran both places.

When Sutherland put forward his concept about the movement of the cranial bones, even the American Osteopathic Association (AOA) was very uneasy about it. Sutherland feared that his idea could be abandoned at any time, so he formed two organizations. One was the Cranial Academy, which was reluctantly recognized by the AOA; the other was the Sutherland Cranial Teaching Foundation, a private foundation beyond its reach. The idea was that the latter would carry the banner should the Cranial Academy fall into ill repute.

Sutherland himself actually experienced the cranial rhythm. He intentionally put himself in a position to feel it. He started out looking at the skulls on display in the Anatomy Department at Kirkville. What struck him was that the sutures between the different cranial bones seemed to have evolved as they had structurally for a purpose, and that purpose looked to him as if it should be motion. He started fooling around with his own cranial bones and trying to feel if they could move. Eventually, he outfitted himself with a football helmet to fit his skull closely; there were various screw devices in the helmet that were directly in contact with his head. He found that the effects of tightening specific areas of this helmet could alter his sensations and moods: he could give himself a headache by tightening one screw and make himself manic with another, and so on and so forth. I'm not sure when exactly he started feeling the cranial rhythm, whether it was before or after the football helmet (it's been some time since I read his book), but he did feel it, and he taught it. He also experienced *stillpoint induction,* the stopping of the cranial rhythm so the system can readjust; but none of us in school and none of us practicing conventional osteopathy *à la* Dr. Still knew very much about what Sutherland had done.

Today there are osteopaths other than those trained at the Upledger Institute who teach cranial movement. I taught it at Michigan State when I was there, and I believe a lot of schools are starting to teach it and are calling it CranioSacral Therapy just as we do, and some of them are even using my original textbook.

Anyway, let me tell you how *our* CranioSacral Therapy developed after Delbert. I came back from the Cranial Academy and told Jim Tyler about what I had experienced. By this time, we were pretty good friends and we began thinking together about the therapeutic possibilities of working with the cranial rhythm. One day Jim asked me, "Do you think we could use it to help my office girl's son's ears?"

"What's the matter with them?" I asked.

"Well, he's had three or four tympanotomies. [Tympanotomy

is a procedure where you pierce the eardrum and put in a tube to relieve pressure. It is commonly applied in cases of chronic or repeated middle-ear infections in children.] They put the tubes in, and the pressure was relieved. Later on the tubes came out spontaneously. A little later the pressure went back up, and they had to do it again, and this cycle went 'round again and again."

I said, "I don't know—let's try."

I worked on the boy. I figured out how his temporal bones [the bones that encase middle and inner ears as well as the ear canals] ought to move, and I adjusted them. That was the first treatment that I ever gave outside of fooling around in the Cranial Academy class. My first one. And his ears got better. He didn't need the tympanotomy ever again. As a matter of fact, he had been scheduled for one the following week and it was cancelled. I was thinking, "This is wild! There's really something in this!" Then Jim and I started to talk about how dural tubes can glide up and down in the spinal canal. It was really nice having a neurosurgeon to share this stuff with rather than some cuckoo bird who says, "God's putting energy in my hands." But don't jump on my bandwagon too quickly. As you will see, even big bad John came to have a much more cosmic view of energy before the final score was in.

Jim now started to send me headache cases. He had already been referring people to me for acupuncture. (I'll talk about how I became an "acupuncturist" in a little while.) I started doing cranial work for headaches and was very successful.

The first case in which I used cranial work instead of the requested acupuncture was a World War II veteran. He had neglected to use his ear plugs when standing next to one of the large cannons on his battleship when it fired. He suffered from a constant ringing in his ears and moderate to severe head pains ever since this incident. I worked on his temporal bones with manual Cranio-

Sacral manipulation. His symptoms disappeared in one session. When he told Dr. Tyler what I had done, Dr. Tyler was pleasantly surprised. The patient remained symptom-free.

Pretty soon we were talking about how, when the membranes between the cranial bones are strained, there is an abnormal pull on the dura in one direction or another.

One day Jim asked me, "Why don't you 'scrub' [assist in surgery] with me on a couple of neurosurgical cases—head cases—and you can treat them the next day? Since you'll be there during the surgery, you'll see exactly what's going on inside, and then the next day you can work on the patient a little bit, and we'll see if it helps."

I probably did eight or ten cases like this, after which he remarked, "John, this is miraculous. I'm only getting about half of the morbidity I usually get. The patients are out of bed the next day and everything is working better." Upon reflection, we realized that it was probably because we were enhancing the flow of fluids in the cranium and getting rid of degrading blood cells. This was helping nutrients get in and washing away debris by normalizing the tension patterns in the dural membrane. Because I was scrubbing with him and seeing what he was doing inside the patient's head—what he cut, what he sewed—I could be very intelligent about what I was doing.

The word got out on the circuit that I was working in this way, and, of course, what was interesting about it was that much of the osteopathic profession wanted these guys in the Cranial Academy to all die and stop being an embarrassment. Now comes Upledger, Mr. Science, Mr. Biochemist, doing this stuff with the neurosurgeon and having success. So, really, when they asked me to go to Michigan State, one of the things they wanted me to do was either to prove that cranial osteopathy works or prove that it doesn't, as I noted before. If we could prove it had a scientific basis, then we'd make it a scientific thing, and if we couldn't, we'd get rid of it once and for all. Well, by now I was certain that the cranial bones moved and that it was our evolving *pressurestat* model that made them move. My theory was just a clarification of the idea about hydraulic pressure from cerebrospinal fluid that had occurred to me almost from the beginning—the idea that I presented to the Cranial Academy and that almost made them puke! Heresy! Get out of here! But today there are osteopaths and many others all around the world who accept the fact of the cranial rhythm and our pressurestat model for how it works.

The Free Clinic

Another important aspect of my early practice was my work with acupuncture. I began to explore acupuncture in 1968. My experience with it grew directly out of my work at the free clinic. Here's the story of how we started the clinic.

Not long after I started practice, I was serving as family physician for an Italian family. One day the momma came in all crying and said, "Will you see my Tony?"

I asked, "What's the matter?"

"My Tony is addicted to the heroin."

I said, "I don't know anything about heroin addiction."

She said, "Naw, but you helpa me, you helpa my husband, you gonna helpa Tony maybe. Please! Please! Please!"

"Okay, have Tony come in."

Tony came in. I said, "Tony, I don't know anything about heroin addiction. You know a helluva lot about it. If you really want to get clean, you can suggest to me how we might do it and, if I approve of what *I* have to do, we'll do it, and if I can't do it the way you suggest, then you'll have to think of another way."

Well, Tony *did* know about his addiction and he *did* want to get clean, so Tony and I sat down and worked out a program. Tony had a lot of input into it, and I think that's why it was successful. We used a diminishing dose of Dilaudid over about a week. Dilaudid is an old thing that we used to use on post-op cases. It's a morphine derivative that kids on the street were using. It was not supposed to be prescribed. I did check with my attorney and he said that, as long as you're on a reducing dosage, it's perfectly legal for you to administer it. I started him off on Dilaudid—three pills a day for two days, two pills a day for two days, and one pill a day for two days. That was okay, and Tony got clean.

Pretty soon I had Tony's two friends coming to my office, and they brought friends of theirs, and before long, every day at noon hour, I had half-a-dozen or so heroin addicts sitting in the waiting room with my regular patients staring at them. It wasn't working. You can't intermingle these two groups.

This is when the Federal narcs came down to see me. One of them said, "I understand you've been prescribing Diliaudid for known addicts."

I said "Yeah, I guess you could say that's what I've been doing." So he said "We're going to take your narcotics license away from you if you continue to do that."

I said, "Wait, I had my attorney check this out and I'm legal."

He said "Your narcotics license is a privilege, not a right, and I'll pull it from you."

I thought, 'Holy mackerel.' So what I did to get out of this was that I spread the word with the kids that were using Diliaudid that we didn't need it any more. We had Dr. John's new super pills, a replacement drug. I had the pharmacist next door stuff a mixture in red capsules: a little bit of Telin (which has a non-narcotic pain killer) and a little bit of Phenadrin (which is anti-allergy). I'd give the street guys two of those and tell them it was more powerful than the other stuff. My helpers were giving them the same spiel. It was a placebo, except it did have some more mild drugs in it. The addicts did fine. Now I've got phony pills and a B12 shot and both of them worked for getting off of heroin. Which tells me that addiction is in the mind.

However, in the end, that first addict Tony almost got me. I received a call from the sheriff in Hillsboro County, Tampa. He said they had an addict in a cell who had committed himself to Lexington, Kentucky, where the Federal narcotics hospital was. They were going to hold him in the cell until it was time to ship him up there. Trouble is: he's going crazy. He's banging his head on the bars—he wants to know can you give him some of that Dilaudid stuff that you've been giving to the other kids?

I said, "No, I can't, the narcs told me that I can't."

The guy sad, "This kid's going to die!"

I said, "I'm sorry, I can't do it. I can send you some of my super pills, but I can't give you any Dilaudid. Then I said, "I'll call my narc and find out." I phoned this agent out of Miami who happened also to be named Tony, and I said, "Tony, this is Upledger; listen, the sheriff in Hillsboro County has a guy in jail who's going to go to Lexington to get cured and he's asking me if I can give him some Dilaudid to help him settle down. He thinks he's going to die in his cell the way he's acting."

Tony says, "You better not; I'll take your number."

I said, "What do you mean? The kid's going to die!"

He said, "I don't care; it's better off if he dies." Then he gave me this spiel—he said, "I think we ought to put all the addicts on an island off the coast and give them all the heroin that they can shoot, so they'll overdose and all die. That would be good as far as I'm concerned.

I thought, 'Boy, what an attitude for a Federal Narcotics agent.'

As things happened—and I've learned to understand that they *will* happen this way—Butch Anderson, the Green Beret I mentioned before, got a hold of me. He said, "I understand you're treating heroin addicts."

I said, "More than I can handle."

He said, "I've got a bunch of buddies that are strung out, too. Maybe we can get together and start a free clinic."

"All right, that's a good idea."

By this time, I had expanded my practice a bit and was house physician for the local Sheraton Hotel. It had a nice nightclub, so I talked them into setting up a fund-raising dinner for us. I sent out invitations to all the people I knew at twenty-five dollars a plate. We raised about three thousand dollars. With that money, we opened the clinic. Butch became the resident manager and I was the overseer, as I said before.

I enjoyed working with heroin addicts because, once you pop them open, they're really nice folks inside. The ones we were getting, for the most part, weren't real slum types. They were junior-college kids that had gotten strung out at a party or something and didn't know how to get off of it.

It's not all that difficult to help people who really want to overcome their addiction. Dealing with their legal problems is another matter. I will always remember how I felt when the kids who had been busted came in to get off of heroin and were *successful*, only to be sentenced to do prison time at their sentencing hearing. Randy was one of those kids. While awaiting sentencing after his conviction, Randy got clean and started a small furniture-building business. He spent his free time out on the street trying to help other addicts get clean. He was sentenced to ten years in prison in spite of his good work.

Then there was Bob. At the age seventeen, Bob got nabbed for flying drugs into the USA from Mexico. His girlfriend, Wilma, was pregnant. They were both heroin users. They came to our free clinic and got clean. One day while Bob was awaiting sentencing, his attorney asked Bob for five one hundred dollar bills for the sentencing judge to keep him out of jail. I went to court with Bob. He was allowed to go free. Bob whispered to me that the judge was one of his drug customers.

Darlene was about five months pregnant when she came to the free clinic. She was using PCP and almost every other psycho-active drug that she could get on the street. She never messed with heroin. She was having problems with blood clotting. Her platelet count was very low. She was bleeding under the skin, in her eye ground (under her conjunctiva and retinae), and internally. I hos-pitalized her at Suncoast Hospital, where I was on staff. They waived her charges. She improved. When discharged, she had no place to go, so we took her into our home and she did house-keeping work in return. She delivered, much to my surprise, a nor-mal, baby girl on Christmas Eve, in the hospital. She keeps in touch with me. Her daughter is grown now. Darlene is happily married and does volunteer work in a local hospital.

    I could tell stories about free-clinic happenings forever, but I'm sure you get the drift.

After a while, I became well-known in the area for my work with addicted kids, and I was very much appreciated in the commu-nity; but being appreciated by the community is not the same thing as getting official support. Quite the contrary. The police, for instance, were not interested in my ability to restore addicts to being normal citizens. They viewed them as criminals, and they wanted to use us as a source of information to catch them.

The State's attorney at that time was trying to get a referendum passed to assign tax money to fight drugs. And here were Butch Anderson and I seeing, I don't know how many, addicts (because we intentionally didn't keep track of how many guys we treated), but I'm sure we were dealing, after a while, with at least thirty addicts at a time. It probably took only a few weeks for each one to get them clean. In any case, the State's attorney office subpoenaed our records once and got a couple of names and went out and arrested the kids. Here these kids were trying to get back on track only to wind up in jail. So we started making our records unintelligible to anybody who subpoenaed and read them, just as Dr. Gross had advised some years before. We'd say stuff like, "George is in, doin' better, continue Rx," and then sign it.

We did get a little bit of help from a particular police officer. At one point, I treated a vice-squad cop who had gotten a case of gonorrhea. He came into the clinic and asked if I would treat him without letting his wife know and, of course, I knew this story before from my time in Baltimore. I agreed, and in gratitude he became something like a "mole" for us into the police system so that we always knew when the police were watching us. For instance, he came in one day and said they were tapping the clinic's phone! Another time they sent in a couple of guys who in fact were vice-squad cops, pretending to have bad withdrawal symptoms. They wanted to trap me into prescribing something illegal, but of course I didn't because I'd been tipped off by my "mole."

We finally did put an end to the phone taps. One day my man

called me at my office and said that they had the taps on the free clinic. I thought about what to do. I listened a couple of times, and I could hear the little click that signified that they were listening in. I went home and called the clinic and talked to a gal named Nicki who was our free-clinic assistant manager. I said, "Nicki, I just heard the strangest thing out on the street."

"What's that?"

"Well, it seems that the biggest pusher—the biggest importer of heroine in this part of the country—is the Sheriff himself!"

My mole called me the next day and said, "I don't know what you did, but they've taken the tap off, and somehow I don't think you'll have to worry about it any more."

Besides phone taps and sting operations, they did everything they could just to harass me. I got arrested about six times—nothing for which they ever preferred charges—but if I was driving two miles over the speed limit, they'd grab me. It seemed like every cop in Florida knew my car. I'd get hauled into the police station for one thing after another. I got wise to it very quickly and came up with various ways of handling it. For instance, I'd demand my one phone call at the police station and make sure that they heard that I was calling a reporter at the *St. Petersburg Times*. They'd grab the phone and kick me out of the station before I said a word. They knew the free clinic was getting really good press from that paper. I was getting a really good reputation for treating narcotics addicts, and they didn't want the public thinking that the police were picking on me.

(Once I did stay over night in jail because, instead of calling the *St. Petersburg Times* I ordered a pizza. And they didn't like that at all.)

They really were out to get me, though. One time while I was running my own jazz club (I'll tell that story a little later), I went into a little place called "The Court House Bar" to listen to the band because I was thinking about hiring it as the next group. I parked my car in a vacant lot right across the street from the bar where cars parked legally all the time. It just so happened that I was the only one there that night. I didn't think much about it. This was a Tuesday night and business must have been down. When I came out after about an hour, there was a tow truck about to haul off my car. It already had the rear end up in the air. I ran out screaming: "Hey! Wait a minute! Wait a minute! What are you doin'?"

"Well, look here—see that sign?"

Sure enough, there was a No-Parking-Violators-Will-Be Towed-Away sign attached to a pole. It was a brand new sign. They had literally put it up since I had gone into the bar. Had they actually gone to all this trouble just for *me*? It was hard to believe it. But here it was, about 11 o'clock at night, and I swear there was no sign when I parked my car there earlier.

The tow-truck driver said, "I got to take your car to the police station." He let me ride with him in the truck.

At the station, I had an inspiration. I said, "Okay, who here's got a license for the narcotics that are in my trunk?"

Silence.

I said, "All right. I got demerol in there and I've got a license for it. But you took my car, and you took my stuff, so it looks to me like you're stealing narcotics." And they threw me out of the station.

———

Acupuncture

All in all, we weathered our problems with the police pretty well. The clinic thrived, and it was through it that I got into acupuncture. Not very long after we opened up, Butch attended a meeting of the Free Clinic Association in San Francisco. He came back with a little book called *Acupuncture Anesthesia* with a picture of Asian people on the front. The book had instructions for inserting needles to reduce pain anywhere in the body. I said, "This is crap, Butch."

He said, "Hey, wait a minute. You're the one who's supposed to be open-minded. Why don't we just try it?"

We went back and forth a little bit, and eventually I said, "Okay, we'll try it."

I used to close my office on Thursday afternoons, so one Thursday after hours, I brought three of the most difficult pain patients I had into the clinic. One was a prostatic cancer patient with bone metastases, a limited time to live, and hurting like hell. Another was a woman with an alcohol-related liver problem. We'd had her in the hospital, dried her out, took out her gall bladder, which was full of stones, and cleared out her hepatic duct, but she was still hurting a lot in her upper-right abdominal quadrant. The third guy had acute rheumatoid arthritis, and I had been unable to bring him down and control him with anything. I brought in these three people and introduced them to Butch and his little book that showed you where to put the needles.

I used for the task a bunch of twenty-five gauge hypodermic needles (that is, small ones), and I went around sticking nine needles in the people's bodies where the booklet indicated. Needle locations were the same for everyone. Clearly, I was not inspiring much confidence, so there was little chance that this was going to be a psychosomatic cure! Anyway, within twenty minutes of the last needle insertion, all three of them were pain-free. WOW! That was like getting hit in the head with a sledgehammer. I'm thinking, "There is something here I don't know anything about!"

I had them come back a couple of times, and each time I was able to get the pain to go away.

Since this seemed more effective than pain medication, I tried to work out a way for each of them to use needles without having to come into the clinic every time. The wife of the guy with the prostatic cancer and the bone metastasis was a typist at the hospital. I showed her where to put the needles. She started inserting them in her husband every morning. He never had any more pain and died in a couple of months without morphine or other analgesics.

The man with rheumatoid arthritis—well, he didn't *want* his pain to go away! He was controlling his family with his pain. That became very clear. The acupuncture was bringing him relief, so he quit coming.

The lady with the liver problem was the most interesting. I don't know what was wrong with her to this day, but she kept having pain in the area of the liver as well as bile in her urine (bilirubinuria). We finally got it under control with the needles. I don't know how I figured it out, but after about three treatments using the nine-needle protocol, I got it so that a single needle insertion would take care of her pain and her bilirubinuria, but that one needle had to stay in a long time—longer than a session at the clinic. I had to devise a way for her to have it in at home and not have to take it out as she went about her day.

I began by putting a needle in and leaving it there sort of sideways so it could lie flat. I smeared antibiotic cream over it and then just placed a band-aid over that. But this turned out to be too irritating, so I improvised a method for stimulating the acupuncture point without using a needle at all. I put a silk suture through the skin. I placed the stitch right through the acupuncture point. And then—you know those little chains you get on old-fashioned bathtub plugs? Well, I tied one of those to the suture. Any time she was in pain, she could pull on the chain, and it would stimulate the acupuncture point.

Inside of six weeks—no more bilirubinuria, no more pain, no more suture. She was fine, and she stayed fine for years.

Here is one more early acupuncture case.

Harold had been a prison guard at Sing Sing in New York. He was also an electrician and a plumber. Harold was in his early seventies, and he came in for bellyaches and minor things like that. He was a regular patient without any serious medical problems but, at a certain point, he started having attacks where he couldn't breathe. The first time, he went to the emergency room, but after that I thought it best to hospitalize him. I kept checking his heart. The heart rhythm was irregular, but it was okay as long as I got it back on track by working on him manually. It looked to me like he was having what we call a "cardiac asthma." That means there's an asthmatic situation, an allergic reaction, though in his case it probably wasn't a true allergy, just something his body couldn't handle. I hospitalized him four or five times for that and finally turned him over to the cardiologists. They installed an oxygen tent in his home, put him on digitalis and other drugs—something to prevent fibrillation, a steroid to prevent the asthmatic attacks— all of which had minor side effects. In short, the whole treatment began to dominate his life. After a week or so of this, he came in to see me at the office and said, "John, I just don't want to live like this. If I got to do all this stuff, I want to die. Screw it."

I knew he meant it. He was that kind of a guy. But because he had gotten to know me, he knew I was an experimenter and, in particular, he had heard about my dabbling in acupuncture. I'd only been into it for a few months when he asked about it. I said, "Gee Hal, I don't know what acupuncture can do for you."

He replied rather plausibly, "These heart guys don't know what they can do either, and they haven't been able to cure me yet. I'll stick with you."

So I took his pulses. I learned that method of diagnosis from Felix Mann's book. More about him later. You know in acupuncture you feel the pulse along the meridians of each of the organ systems to read its condition. I was just learning to do that. His heart pulse was good, his lung pulse good, but what was not so good was his kidney pulse. He had almost no kidney pulse at all, which in acupuncture means that his kidney system was probably the primary cause of the whole problem.

I pulled out my acupuncture book and I put a needle in every point I could find that was supposed to stimulate the kidney. I wound up putting about twelve or thirteen needles in this guy. I used his bladder meridian, I used the water cross-over points for a lot of the other meridians, and I used stimulation and alarm points on the kidney. That all came out of Felix Mann's book.

I put the needles in at about three o'clock in the afternoon and left them in for a little while. When I took them out, I said, "Harold, I want you to collect all your urine for the next twenty-four hours and bring it to me tomorrow." I thought this might indicate something. I really don't know what I expected to find.

Well, he came in the next afternoon with a *gallon jug* that was almost full of urine! There were about ten people sitting in the waiting room and he stormed in and shouted, "Look at this, you son of a bitch! You had me up all night pissing."

I wanted to tell him to quiet down, but hey! He was my friend. I thought of Dr. Gross's advice, so I just let it pass. I thought, "Here I am, folks, if you can't handle it, go somewhere else!"

His urine was normal. He just had to get rid of a lot of fluid. I think what happened was that I stimulated his kidney so much that he detoxed whatever was causing the trouble. I have no idea what that was.

Harold was fine after that. I didn't have to treat him with kidney needles a second time. He never had another attack. The only further treatment I performed was whenever he knew he was going to be unusually exposed to atmospheric toxins—if he was going to pick somebody up at the airport or he knew he was going to have to entertain someone whose perfume bothered him—I'd needle the anti-allergy points in his ears. He never had to go to the emergency room or be hospitalized again for his cardiac asthma. He had a herniated a disk later on, and he went through the surgery with no heart problem at all.

That's how I got started in acupuncture. Once I gained some confidence in using needles, I thought, "Hey, we've got all these heroin addicts at the clinic. Let's see if we can treat heroin addiction this way." I came across a little information—I don't even know where I got it—but the Japanese were talking about injecting a drop of vitamin B_{12} intradermally in the lung point of the ear, which is also the "addiction point." The claim was that this could help withdrawal basically by diminishing the desire for the drug. And it did, so we started expanding on that. Heroin addicts, for instance, will often have lung problems. They become infected by pathogenic emboli. If they live out on the street (which was true of a few of the cases we had), they experienced a lot of exposure to bad weather and so on—so I learned how to treat the respiratory system. The next most common problem was with their GI tract, so I learned how to treat that—all with the needles.

Acupuncture was beautiful because you could get the needles (as I mentioned, we were using hypodermic needles) for a penny apiece, which was good because we were operating financially on fundraising from the community.

I need to emphasize that I did this all by reading it out of that book and going from there. It was quite a while before I ever attended a class on acupuncture. In fact, it wasn't that easy to find one in those days. Before I took my first course, we estimate I had already administered about two-thousand treatments to a large number of people.

Eventually I did take a course—with a Professor Yahama, a Japanese guy. He gave a two-day course up in Gainesville, Florida, but he didn't tell me a thing I hadn't already found out for myself. He gave a long lecture on the theory of acupuncture. Then he put patients in the gymnasium up on tables—there were about twenty of them—and he went around putting in the needles. "Pain gone?"

"Yes, yes, yes."

Then he'd take the needles out. Finally, one guy had the nerve to ask, "Well, how do you know where to put the needles?"

"Aah—this is a big family secret. You come to my office in Maryland, pay two-thousand five hundred dollars—one week I teach you."

Finally, an anesthesiologist named Frank Warren founded the National Acupuncture Research Society. I attended many of his weekends. They were usually three-day—Friday, Saturday, Sunday—things. I did about two-hundred-and-fifty hours of that stuff. And that's all.

But back to my story. When I saw the needles work in my office that first time, I knew there was something there. I got hold of a catalog that Butch had brought back from the Free Clinic Association along with *Acupuncture Anesthesia* and found that it listed books on acupuncture that you could order. I saw that a guy named Felix Mann—a British internist—had written four of them. I thought, "I'm going to get these because he might talk a language

I can understand." And he did. He took acupuncture and put it in Western medical terminology so that a Western doctor could comprehend it easily. You didn't have to believe in "evil wind" and all that stuff. And, really, I learned how to do acupuncture using his rationale. One single book contained his prescriptions for combinations of acupuncture points to "needle" for various problems. In general, he had a nice approach. I learned a lot from him. He was particularly good at providing concepts for Chinese images and metaphors; for instance, pain is "fire" in Chinese; an "exit" is where the energy comes out of a meridian; a "source" is a two-way valve. I don't know just how much pain I was able to treat as a result of these translations, but it was a lot. I just figured out, "Well, okay! I want the pain to come out the exit of the meridian and I want the source to be open because I don't know whether energy should go in or come out," so I'll use "the fire, exit, and source points" on all the meridians that go through the painful areas, and lo and behold: the pain does go away! And usually it doesn't come back. My attitude was, *"It's* a little crazy, but *I'm* not crazy." And that's basically the way I got started with it.

I'm not sure exactly what it is about me that allows me to be open when something like acupuncture hits me. This occurs even though there is some initial skepticism. I just go ahead and pursue it. When something strange happens, instead of running away from it, I become intrigued by it. I suspect it's because I feel more secure than other people. I don't *need* to understand something before I take an interest in it. I'm not afraid of looking into the unknown. In fact, I relish it. I think that, in general, it's a question of having no fear. Once again, I go right back to my mother. She taught me how not to be afraid. I do not allow myself to be afraid. When I was little, I could not afford it because I knew if I was afraid, I would make noise and, if I made noise, I would be punished. At least that's as good a guess as any. But maybe that lesson from my mother was only a reflection of some deeper karma I was carrying.

I think we are put on earth together with specific other people to learn specific lessons. I believe that each of us is an individual aspect of a single group soul. I'm going to write in the next chapter about how I "got spiritual," and I'll have some more to say about this. The psychic Harriet Jerome, who turned me around one-hundred-and-eighty degrees on the question of spirituality, once told me, "A lot of times your soul or your spirit needs to evolve to another level. And we come to earth to get a lesson." I challenged her on this and said, "Well, if everybody is a soul before they are born and each comes down and gets into a body, how do you account for the rapid expansion of the population of the earth?"

She said, "It's because a single soul can occupy several bodies." Now, she didn't talk about my mother at this point, but using her rationale that a single soul can become several interacting persons on earth—I really think that my mother and I are of the same soul. And I think that my father is too. And my grandfather.

Psychic Awareness
and Spirituality

Harriet Jerome

I've been saying all along that I feel that each of the people in my family contributed in an important way to my becoming who I am. You can see that I mean this in something more than the ordinary psychological sense wherein we are formed by our environment and influenced by our parents. I believe that my mother, my father, my grandfather, my grandmother, and my half-sister Phyllis came together on earth for a definite purpose that really has to do with my work. So much of what I am today and what I have accomplished has sprung from abilities I developed while connected with these people. I think probably we're all from the same spirit.

I also feel that I have received spiritual lessons all through my life, some of them very precise and clear. The first lesson of this sort was what happened when the Coast Guard captain's steward couldn't get up off the floor. All I did was hold his leg lightly with both hands and ask inwardly for help. Help really came! I could feel the change in his energy in the tissue of his leg.

I owe my ideas about all of this to my friendship, for a brief period, with an extraordinary "little old lady" psychic, Harriet

---

Jerome. I think of my meeting with Harriet as "how I got spiritual"—how I, once and for all, stopped being a skeptic about things that science can't explain—and how I came to accept that my life is really being directed by spiritual "guides" that are *not* part of my ordinary personality.

Harriet demonstrated for me that information was indeed coming to me from something like previous existences. I began to believe in past lives because that information was so vivid and so correct. Also, spirits would enter Harriet and speak through her to me. I accepted all of this stuff.

How I got involved with Harriet is a bit of a story. I had been in private osteopathic medical practice in Clearwater, Florida for about three years when I fulfilled an old dream: I opened my own jazz club. I'd played jazz piano in all kinds of places since before I was a teenager, as you know very well by now. Now, one of the things of which most jazz musicians are quite certain is that they know how to run a jazz club better than the boss—just ask any jazz man! What we think makes for a really great club is for us to be completely free to play the music we want to play, the way we want to play it; but the owners are always saying, "The people aren't responding to what you're doing. You have to play tunes the people can recognize, and don't take so many long, improvised solos, etc., etc." So we play things that are more commercial, in more conventional styles, in order to keep our jobs. In other words, we play without always putting our souls into it. And it does keep the customers coming and the orders for booze flowing; but we always think in our heart of hearts that, if we could only be allowed to do our own creative thing, it would draw a big crowd. And the truth is, when this does happen, it does draw a crowd—a crowd of real jazz buffs—people who might only drink one beer the whole night! And that doesn't make much money for the house.

We can pack the house, but the income is zilch!

Anyway, I had been in medical practice for about three years when I got an offer in the mail from some finance company saying, in effect, "We've investigated your potential and you qualify for a $25,000 loan." It started me thinking. I really didn't imagine it would actually happen, but I began making inquiries. I had an attorney-friend whom I'd been treating and who was sending patients to me. He also happened to be a jazz musician—a drummer. I told him, "I know where I can lay my hands on some money. If you hear of a club with a liquor license for sale—let me know. Maybe I can buy it."

Well, I really didn't think he would take me all that seriously, but, in a couple of weeks, he came up with a club, complete with liquor license, that I could purchase for $50,000. It had two hundred seats. It was a redneck, pool-hall dump, but I thought, "We could fix this place up and turn it into a real swinging joint." So I stuck my neck out and went for it.

Well, it was a hard job. We had to re-do the whole dump. And, of course, when it was ready to open, I had to find someone to run it because I didn't intend to abandon my medical practice. I offered it to a friend of mine who had run a restaurant up in Chicago. I said, "Look. You take over. You run the club and handle the finances from here on out. I'll own it, but you pay the mortgage and keep the profits. Whatever you make is yours. I'll have my name on the deed. I'll book the musicians (and reserve the right to sit in when convenient and appropriate)." He accepted the offer, but after a few months, he quit. I guess all that great jazz was too much for him!

Next, I brought in a guy named "Big Gordon." He was well-known around town. I didn't learn how old he was until a little later. It turned out he was twenty-six, and he was on his sixth wife at the time! But he was a smart fellow, and I felt he could manage the club. How I met him was a little strange. One night, he was dragged into my office with a .22 bullet in his head! The question was, would I take it out without calling the police? I didn't know what Big Gordon was up to, or what the circumstances were, and I knew better than to ask. I just opened up the hole a little more and took the bullet out with a pair of forceps. It had not penetrated the inner plate of the skull bone. The bullet was lodged in the bone marrow.

Big Gordon became my club manager and bartender, and things went along pretty well. He was an excellent manager, and we were building up a good business; but one day he came in and said, "Hey boss! I hate to tell you this, but you'd better start looking for a new manager."

I said, "Why?"

"Well, I went to this psychic lady and she told me that a couple of guys in suits are going to come in here and they're going to offer me a job for $25,000 a year and I'm going to have a Lincoln car to drive around in, an expense account, and I'm going to be wearing a suit all the time. And I'm going to take it!" Well, okay! I laughed and didn't think any more about it. About two weeks later, I walked into the club, and here are two guys all dressed up in formal business attire, looking really out of place in this club—it's a very casual scene. They were sitting at the bar talking to Gordon. After a little while, they left and Gordon said, "Well boss, I told ya."

I said, "Whaddya mean?"

He said, "Well, they offered me $25,000 a year, I'll have an expense account, I'll drive a big Lincoln car, I'll go to the airport and pick up people and take them to some land development thing." (It turned out to be the Royal Palm Beach Settlement of West Palm Beach.) And that was it. I thought, "Wow! What a raving coincidence," because I was still a complete skeptic on this stuff. Anyway, he was gone, and I had to think a little bit about what happened because the odds of its being pure chance were probably astronomical. I didn't dwell on it myself, but everybody that had anything to do with the club couldn't stop talking about it.

By the way, that jazz club ended up being something of a tragedy. It didn't last too long. After we lost Big Gordon to his fate, I got another guy. I went to the hotel across from my office on Clearwater Beach and the manager said, "My nephew Jimmy could run it for you." He didn't tell me Jimmy was a felon. Had just gotten out. I hired his nephew and he was doing a bang-up job until all of a sudden the liquor guys came in and said, You got a guy named James McGinley working here?"

I said, "Yeah?"

They said, "He can't work here any more."

I said, "Why?"

They said, "He's on parole. He's not supposed to be around these places."

So the club kept on running. I'd usually go over at ten o'clock at night, play the piano for a couple hours with a group. Things were cool. Then all of a sudden, we have a fire. The place burns, not all the way down, just guts. Up on the roof they found the driver's license and wallet of a cook that I had just fired up. Where I come from, that's called arson. But in any case, now I'm thinking we've got to remodel. I got a bid from a buddy with a construction company. He says, "We can do it for X dollars," and so I submitted that to the insurance company.

The agent at the insurance company said, "No, we've got a letter here from the city that said we have to bulldoze and start over."

I said "What?!"

They had said they would pay for the remodeling, but the city had said they had to bulldoze. So I just forgot the whole thing. I let it sit there. I didn't know what to do with it.

Then an attorney came to see me and said, "I've got an offer here that will give you $300,000 if you will turn this into a narcotics treatment center."

I asked, "Who is my benefactor?"

The answer: "I can't tell you, it's anonymous."

Coming from Detroit and having seen sundry gangsters, I said, "If you can't tell me who it is, I don't know that I want to do it."

He said, "Well, if you decide you want to do it, you can have $300,000 to get it started."

I took aside a couple of my junkies who were clean and I told them, "Get out on the street and find out who the hell's sending this money in."

Sure enough, they came back and confirmed, "It's mafia money." The state's attorney at that time wanted to get a referendum passed to give him extra revenue to chase down addicts. Meanwhile I was acquiring quite a reputation, getting articles in the newspaper probably once a week about the free clinic, about successfully treating addicts. But if the attorney puts out a referendum after I've started a $300,000 unit, the referendum probably won't pass because people will say, "Why should we pay for that with our taxes when this guy's already got a successful thing going?" So that was the whole thing in a nutshell, and I turned it all down.

Anyway, after we lost Big Gordon, my wife Dianne and her best friend, Gerry, who was one of my office nurses, decided they wanted to see the psychic lady that had predicted Gordon's new job. I said, "Come on, Dianne, don't fall for this stuff. She'll just want to get money from you." Well, I couldn't talk them out of it, so they went to see this psychic lady, and it was really weird to listen to Dianne talk about what happened on their visit.

Dianne's appointment was for 4:00 in the afternoon. Dianne's son from a former marriage, Rob, was living with us. I was going to take him to his YMCA swim class and then go to the hospital to make my rounds. I had four or five patients to see there. Then I was going to pick him up at the YMCA after he'd be done swimming. At about 4:10 — something like that — I dropped him off at the Y. Dianne said that at about 4:20 the psychic suddenly interrupted herself and said, "Oh, you poor dear, your husband's in the hospital." And then: "Oh, it's okay, he's a doctor — he's seeing his patients."

Well, hmm?!

I got through with my rounds a little early and had about twenty minutes to wait before I had to pick up Rob, so I went into a bowling alley next door to the YMCA and ordered a draft beer. I didn't really want it but, you know, you have to do something, so I ordered a beer and sat there. That would have been, maybe, 5:15.

At about that time, the psychic interrupted herself again and said, "Oh, your husband's so silly — he's drinking a beer and he doesn't really want it." Oh my god! Now I'm trying to figure out ways she could know that. I actually started imagining that the psychic had hired a private investigator to follow me, but how the hell could he know I didn't really want that beer? You can see that I wasn't giving in easily. My skepticism was threatened but still intact.

Now Gerry, the nurse that accompanied Dianne to the psychic lady, had a husband who was a Korean War veteran. He had left her very shortly before this whole occurrence with the psychic. The psychic told her, "Your husband left you — he's going to divorce you — but don't take him off your medical insurance yet. He's going to run up a big hospital bill very soon. You'll be responsible for it as long as you're still married."

165

Well, he was on the insurance that she had through my office, so we left him on. Then, lo and behold, he got into a car accident, spent four days in intensive care, and died.

Now I was beginning to wonder what was going on, so I called up this Harriet Jerome myself and told her I wanted an appointment. In those days, I kept my office closed on Mondays because that gave me a long weekend. I asked for an appointment at 11:00 on a Monday morning. She said, "Yes, that'd be fine."

Then I said, "Would you like a name?"

She said, "No."

If she's trying to figure out a way to con me out of a lot of money, how does she do this? So I said, "How do you know I'll be there?"

She said, "Oh, it's my business to know those things, dear."

Well, that was on a Thursday, so I had a few days to consider this. I worked it over in my mind every which way but didn't come up with anything definite about it, so I just decided to go in with an open attitude and see. She told me she lived in downtown St. Petersburg, and I would have to go around the back of the house along a dirt alleyway and then up to the back door to get in. On Monday I was wearing some old, paint-stained clothes, and my car at the time was a little Austin-Healy Sprite, so I certainly didn't look like I was a rich doctor—not a likely target if money was the object. I went up and knocked on the back door. It was a little screen door, not locked. A very nice-looking, cherubic lady answered my knock. She had white hair piled up on her head. She wore an apron and was about fifty pounds overweight—everybody's grandmother.

I said, "I'm here to see Mrs. Jerome," and she said, "I know, dear. You're an osteopathic doctor and my shoulder's been hurting me all morning. Would you please come in and fix it and then we'll have our session." Oh, my God!

Well, I followed her into the kitchen. I had her sit down in a chair and I started feeling the vertebrae in her upper back. She said, "Dear, don't bother with that—just put your hands on my shoulders." I put my hands on her shoulders. Now I'm doing what *she's* telling *me*. She said, "Oh my dear, you're too tired. Bluebell? Would you come out and help him?" And I swear on a stack of Bibles, or Korans, or Cabbalas, or whatever you want, the pantry door flew open and there was a noise like WHOOOOOSH. My hand got hot—it was my left hand—her left shoulder started to vibrate, and, in a minute, her shoulder felt better, and that was that! In that minute, I went from being a skeptic to being a complete believer. Call me whatever you want to call me. Harriet and I became good friends.

Who was Bluebell? A cat? Nope. Nothing! Nothing at all! It was like a puff of air!

Harriet had made lunch for us. Soup and sandwiches. She said, "I'd like you to come several times and we can discuss things."

I said, "Fine." So I visited her every Monday at about 11:30. She never asked for money. She wouldn't take it when I offered it. She had a collection basket there, but she wouldn't let me put anything in it. She took five dollars from both Dianne and Gerry, but she wouldn't take any money from me. I went every Monday—maybe twelve times—and we had a little lunch. Over lunch, she would just sit there and tell me about myself: what I was doing, what I was going to do, and the answers to every question I could dream of regarding the spirit world and that kind of thing. She'd talk about the fact that most psychics are fraudulent. Most of them have a little bit of telepathic ability and they look at you and decide— well, he's got some kids so I'll say "Okay, how are the children?"

and the client would say, "Oh my, how'd you know about that?" And she said that on a bad day she would have to resort to telepathy. But on a good day, with a good person like myself, she would let the spirits come right in.

She said that very few psychics are willing to let the spirits come into their body and use it, but she was. We'd be sitting there talking, and all of a sudden she'd stiffen and start talking German, for instance. Then she'd come out of it and say, "Do you know what that was about?" and I'd say, "No."

I remember the first time she did that, it *was* German. We were having our soup. When I was a child, German was spoken in our house a little bit but I never learned it. I can recognize it as German, but that's all I can do. Well, after she finished talking, all of a sudden she came back and relaxed. She said, "Does the name Mary Wall mean anything to you?"

"Yeah, I said, that was my father's mother's maiden name." I only knew that because I had seen his birth certificate and his death certificate, as I mentioned before. I remembered that she was a little old lady when I was very young. My father was in his mid-fifties when I was born. I remember going to a house in Mt. Clemens, Michigan. She wore a long, black dress that went all the way down to her ankles, and she had shoes that laced way up like boots. She smelled of urine.

Anyway, Harriet said, "Mary Wall tells you that you're going to go to a place where it's cold and there's water behind your house. Be careful. Don't get your feet wet or you'll catch a cold." Well, I wasn't even *thinking* about moving north to a place where it might be cold like that at the time. But then, about eight years later, we moved to Michigan. I bought a house that in fact had marshland out in back of it. One day when my boys and I were walking on the ice that covered it, the ice turned out to be too thin and I fell right through into the water up to my knees. As I stood there flabbergasted, suddenly I remembered Harriet's, or rather Mary Wall's, warning!

During one of our sessions, Harriet said, "You know, you've got two doctors who are arguing about who's going to influence you the most."

I said, "Whadya mean?"

She said, "Well, there's a tan-skinned one—looks Polynesian—and then there's another one over there—his name is Henry White." At that time I was already a bit into acupuncture, so I said, "I can tell you now that it's going to be the tan-skinned guy that's influencing me because I'm doing a lot of acupuncture. He must be Asiatic."

She said, "No, it's going to be the other man."

"Oh really?"

"Yes, he's got a very powerful hold on you and he's going to teach you how to use your hands more. He doesn't approve of the needles. He wants you to use your hands."

The name Henry White sounded vaguely familiar, but at first I couldn't place it. Later on in our session, I recalled that when I took my biochemistry fellowship, for an office they gave me a library annex room that had no windows—just a door and a light bulb hanging from the ceiling—but I was totally surrounded by old books. The walls were bookshelves. One day I happened upon a set of class notes in an old notebook that belonged to someone named Henry White. His name was written on the front of the book, and, oddly, what I remember of its contents was some notes about McBurney's point—the point that's sensitive when you've got appendicitis that I had learned about years before in the Coast Guard. In addition, he said that the tip of the twelfth rib on the right was always tender in appendicitis. This proved to be true as I practiced and gained experience. Anyway, it seemed strange that

Harriet should know the name Henry White. As we continued to talk, I remembered that there had been something weird about that book: after I finished reading it, all of a sudden it disappeared! I mean, I put it on my desk, and the next day it was gone. I didn't think that anyone could have gotten into that room in the meantime. I thought that I had the only key. Harriet said, "A strong spirit like that spirit that's over you has the ability to materialize and de-materialize. And he wanted you to read this."

I went along with things like that, though I asked her every question that occurred to me. One question that puzzled me a lot was the one I mentioned before: if every spirit comes down and is in a body, and the spirits were all up there before, then how do you explain the earth's population explosion?

When I asked her about this, she replied, "Oh dear, a spirit can occupy ten, twenty, or one-hundred bodies if it wishes. They come down and they occupy these bodies, and that will provide an educational process or experience for the soul that owns all these spirits. That's how you learn your lessons and that's how spirit is allowed to advance."

She used "spirit" and "soul" pretty much interchangeably, but she thought about spirit as being more earthbound and soul as being higher, but it was just a different name as it got closer to earth, that's all. It was the same energetic thing. I started looking at things that way; and my own experience with my family, as I said before, makes me believe that it's the case.

She rarely spoke about herself, and she never told me anything about how she discovered her own powers. To tell you the truth, I didn't even think about asking her. Maybe the second or third time we were together, she told me that she was diabetic. We were eating, and I said, "How much insulin do you take?"

She said, "Well, it's different every day."

"Do you test your blood?"

"No!"

"What kind of calorie intake are you on?"

She said, "That doesn't matter."

"But how do you know how much insulin you need?"

"Well, every day Bluebell tells me."

She never talked about "bad" spirits; she talked about "mischievous" spirits. She said that there were spirits who had goodness inside of them but were angry about things and would do things that were kind of spiteful. She wouldn't let me believe that there actually are evil spirits. She would not accept that at all. She said, "That's just not true. If you have a mischievous spirit around you, just say, 'Get out of here.'" She herself would do that once in a while. She'd let spirits come into her body and, when one didn't feel right, she'd say, "Get out of here! You have no business here— go on!" It was as if she were taking a broom and whisking it away.

One day she said, "Okay, I think we're finished."

I said, "Thank you so much."

She said, "That's all right—I have three more to go after you and then *I* can get out of here." That was my introduction to spirituality, and I've been open to inexplicable phenomena ever since!

CranioSacral Therapy, Emotion, Memories, and Spirituality

There is another side to the question of spirituality that I want to take up before I get to my life in academia. It has less to do with inexplicable phenomena and more to do with what often happens to one's spirit in the practice of CranioSacral Therapy and what its spiritual significance or relevance may be. It wasn't anything

Harriet and I talked about, but I think it was implicit in everything we did. The practice of CranioSacral Therapy creates an empathy with the patient's being, and the growth of that empathy itself has spiritual meaning. Of course, what happens is specific to each therapist. CST can remain on the level of a structural adjustment, or the practitioner can advance to the point where his or her patients will start getting SomatoEmotional releases. When this happens, the therapist may become ultimately open to what I call "spiritual acceptance." SomatoEmotional releases show that a condition or an injury or a circumstance can put an energy into a person's body that stays there and plays havoc with their life, so to speak. Some people think of these as releases of merely physical energy, but others can see that much more is involved. In either case, if a therapist accepts the idea that the body can retain energy that the brain doesn't process, this amounts to what I call "tissue memory" and often leads to acceptance of spiritual phenomena.

When you have spiritual acceptance in your belief system, what happens is that you just begin to work intuitively and trust it. Many people, myself included, believe that actual spirits are guiding them; other people prefer to say it's just energy and if we were advanced enough in physics, we would understand how it works. I really don't care how they think about it. What really matters is acceptance and trust in the phenomena themselves. But for me, it seems that I have really found some spirits—or they have found me. I consider them spirit "guides" who kind of look over me all the time. There are times when I'll wake up in the morning and start doing something, and I don't know where what I'm doing came from. This happens particularly with books I write or lectures I'm going to give. Before I go to bed, I just "ask" for whatever guidance might be available and, in the morning, my mind will be full of ideas. In regard to lectures, even if I'm going to talk in front of audiences of four- or five-hundred hypercritical people, all I prepare might be an opening sentence or two, and from there on I just wing it. And it comes out fine. I've never had a time when people haven't loved what I've done. And I don't even bother organizing it in my mind. I just trust that it will happen. It comes from my guides. Quite often they speak through my vocal apparatus.

There's another truly strange and interesting spiritual phenomenon that has to do with these spiritual "guides"—well, one aspect of it perhaps isn't so unusual, but what springs from it is truly bizarre. In dialoguing with a patient's illnesses, often their innate self-healing ability will become personified as what I call the "Inner Physician"—the whole story of the Inner Physician is told in my book, *The Inner Physician and You.* This part of the story is indeed very interesting and important and does not stretch one's credulity very much. But in about 1984, the "Inner Physician" phenomenon started taking a really strange twist. Beings that were definitely not personifications of the patient's personality started speaking through them. Perfectly ordinary people, in effect, "channeled" beings that had come to speak to *me!* Not only that. The same entity appeared through the channeling of different patients! They came to tell different parts of a single, coherent story, different chapters of which, as it were, were revealed by different patients. If you are interested in the details about these stories, you can read about them in my book *SomatoEmotional Release.* But I will just say here that there is no question in my mind that the beings who were speaking through my patients were, in fact, "guides" of mine. They themselves said that they were creatures of pure vibrational energy. They took on exotic names like CAUTHUS, EUPHEMUS, and SOUL OF EGYPT for our amusement and our reference, but they recognized each other without names by the quality of their vibrations. They said that they were connected to me from deep in my past. During one three-week period, a strange story about my having been a precocious boy-healer in ancient Greece of the fourth century b.c. emerged from three different patients who did not know each other at all. Apparently, I had been murdered by jealous physicians! Fragments of this story were referred to by three different guides speaking through these three different patients. Apparently, competition among medical professionals was no less fierce in ancient times than it is today. The enmity of these beings against me seems to have outlived its historical circumstances. All three of these patients told me to beware. A few of these assassins are presently incarnate and would like to kill me.

These guides appeared frequently for a while and then just stopped coming. It seems to me that things like that are given to me rather intensively for a while, and then, after I accept both the fact that they are happening and what their message is, they stop happening as frequently. Or it becomes much more subtle.

I think it was 1997 when I experienced two very interesting initiations to a new guide who turned out to have a rather well-known identity. I was finishing a SomatoEmotional Release with Imagery and Dialogue session during an advanced class, when suddenly there came from out of the mouth of one of the students with whom I was working a request from one of *her* guides to speak with me. I agreed, and the student's voice changed. It said that he was going to become my protector guide. I said that I was very flattered and agreed that he would be a most welcome protector. I asked by what name he would like to be addressed, and he said, "You can call me Pete."

I immediately asked, "Is that short for St. Peter?" Why I thought this, I have no idea.

He answered, "Yes."

I thought very little about this conversation until several months later when I had a second experience that supported St. Peter's presence as my protector guide. I had just finished an advanced class with ten Japanese students. The class had gone very well with the help of four excellent interpreters. On the last afternoon, at the close of the fifth day of class, the students asked if they could treat me. I agreed. As they all got their hands on me, I quickly zoned out into alpha and theta states. At some point, I became aware that I was being lifted from the table and placed on the carpeted floor. To me the experience felt like I was out of the reach of gravity—that I was essentially weightless. I floated off the table and very gently and easily settled onto the floor where the treatment continued. I have very little memory of its explicit content.

The next day at the airport in Tokyo, the organizer of the class, Koiche, asked permission to describe to me what the students saw during my treatment session. All of this conversation with Koiche was through an interpreter. Koiche said, "As they lifted you from the table, the image of a very large warrior man appeared to us all holding his sword on high. He simply watched very closely what we were doing with you. When you were safely resting on the floor, the warrior man smiled and put his sword in its sheath."

Then Koiche looked at me and said, "Do you know St. Peter?" Koiche did not know who St. Peter was, but it certainly rang a bell with me!

"Pete" and I began to converse with each other almost daily after that. I began to feel his protector presence as a constant sensation. One morning, after having totally accepted Pete as my protector guide, I made a strange request of him. It was about 4:00 a.m. and we were awakened by a formidable group of woodpeckers, noisily pecking on our wooden eaves. We had not previously been aware of any woodpeckers in our neighborhood. The pecking noise was humongous. It occurred to me to ask Pete if he could chase them away. He replied that he had never done anything like this before, but he would try. I thanked him, and within a couple of minutes the pecking noise stopped. I thanked Pete again and went back to sleep. At about 5:30 a.m., the pecking noise returned. I informed Pete that the woodpeckers were back. Once again the pecking noise stopped, this time in seconds. I thanked Pete again, and we have not had a woodpecker visitation since.

For me, St. Peter is very real. He protects me from hecklers and from the police when I am nonconsciously speeding, and he protects the Institute. I thank him daily for his presence and help.

Though the guides have manifested in these rather spectacular ways, for the most part they are more frequently present to me in the sense that I just get a feeling that they are there. It's not something I need to prove to myself or want to argue about with anybody. It's just my feeling. It works for me. And if it works and I'm being successful, why should I critique it?

The upshot of the phenomena of the guides and their strange stories is that I have come to firmly believe in multiple lifetimes, and this has given me a way to understand my own family background. I understand that I had the experiences I had as a child for good reasons. This seems so important that I want to spell it out again at the risk of repeating myself. I've come to the firm belief that my father, mother, I myself, my half-sister Phyllis, my grandfather, and I'm not sure about my grandmother, are all of the same soul. My mother was put here to make me tough—so I wouldn't fold under pain and fear. My father came along to teach me to become compassionate and diplomatic—whatever I have in that area, he gave to me. My sister and my grandmother taught me love, and my grandfather taught me to be practical. All of those qualities were developed in me so that I'd be able to do what I'm doing now. If I weren't practical, there'd be no Upledger Institute, no 80,000 people trained in CST. If I didn't understand love, or if I weren't tuned in to love, none of the healing would be working. And if my mother hadn't made me strong enough to tell people to go to hell when they get on my case, I wouldn't be able to work so freely, so openly and, if you will, unconventionally.

It's very comfortable for me to think that we were all part— or extensions of—the same soul, and that we interacted as we did in order to accomplish what we are actually accomplishing. I think Harriet's views have influenced me very strongly in that way. They have kept me from feeling vengeful when I have been maligned, wronged, or interfered with, and her views protected me from harboring long-term anger. I seldom, if ever, carry a grudge. I will get mad as hell for ten minutes, and then it's gone. I think it's good to ventilate my adrenals. That's my concession to the physiological aspect of it. You can kill your body if you hold it in, so I believe in expressing anger—but then it's gone, it's *gone!* I think that the things that make me—or anyone—angry are probably put there in order to help one grow—to mature and understand what all of these interactions are about.

I also think it was really good to understand that the boundary line between good and evil is very blurred. I don't accept moral polarity—and that attitude is from Harriet. She put that into words for me. I accept that some people haven't matured enough to let go of their anger or their need for vengeance. But that doesn't make them evil people. It means that they're stuck in anger, and I've often found that you can help them get through that. Harriet put me on a very open road.

Another thing Harriet did for me was show me—she never

said it in so many words—that there's a lot going on in the world that we can't explain scientifically. If you need to explain it scientifically, you're going to be stuck in the same rut for the next thousand years! If you can accept the concept that things usually go along in an ordinary way, but that occasionally miracles or inexplicable things do occur—if you can just accept that that's the way the cosmos is put together—then you're okay. I'm quite comfortable with doing things with people therapeutically, for instance, even when I don't completely understand how what's happening really works. I am extremely comfortable with the idea of blending in with the energy of a patient, with their spirit, if you will. I don't use the word "spirit" too much with patients because it scares a lot of people, but I blend in with their energy and then do what that energy tells me to do. Usually that blending is just what they need to have happen. I become the tool that that spirit can use. Often the spirit knows very well what needs to be done but doesn't have the physical capacity to work with some particular bodily structure. I become a kind of spiritual mechanic: it's a nuts and bolts kind of thing. The spirit can show the mechanic what has to be done.

Though I accept things science can't explain, I still have use and respect for science. After all, the Cranial Academy people were all for a "spiritual" interpretation of what they experienced, but for me what mattered was just the fact that it was happening, and then I looked for a scientific explanation for it. Maybe "God" was just their way of experiencing it, though it made them rigid because they thought that all you needed was God. They didn't ever think the fluid rising and falling was moving the system.

My views about all this actually change all the time. I think I'm progressing. But, in retrospect, I realize that after I first saw the cranial system working during Delbert's surgery, *something* prevented me from abandoning the idea that occurred to me at once: that there was a hydraulic system at work in there. I just kept it in mind. And then, I was *led* somehow to take the course at the Cranial Academy to learn something quite concrete about something that I had been taught to disrespect. I learned techniques that I applied in my practice. I'm not talking about techniques in the sense of "this technique for that problem"—rather the techniques the Cranial Academy people taught about the movement of the cranial bones allowed me to train my hands to feel new things that I could then integrate into my comprehension of what was going on.

Gradually, I realized that I was feeling energy and spirit, as opposed to something merely physical. First, I came back from the Cranial Academy and was able to feel the cranial rhythm. Actually, the first time I went to the table at the Cranial Academy, I could feel it. Soon after I came back, remember, Dr. Tyler, my neurosurgeon friend, had me work on his office nurse's child, and I took care of his ear problem. I just reasoned it through, as I mentioned before. Then, Dr. Tyler had me working on his craniotomy cases, so I learned to feel the rhythm beautifully. I became very confident in what I was feeling because I was very clear about what was happening physiologically and anatomically. Then he sent me a couple of serious headache cases and said, "Why don't you start scrubbing with me on a regular basis and work on the patients the next day." That turned out fine, and I began to have the confidence to explore more and more.

Dr. Tyler turned me loose on patients whose systems had been significantly tampered with surgically. I began to be able to "see," as it were, from a distance, the cerebro-spinal fluid going down the spinal canal inside the dural tube. I mean, when I put my hands on a patient's head, I could sense the craniosacral rhythm, but I d also sense if there were any restrictions to the movement further down the spine. There's a very fine line between experiencing the movement of the cerebrospinal fluid at a distance and sensing what you might call spirit or energy. In any case, I started putting those subtle perceptions into practice. I'd have patients lie down, and I'd work on their neck a little bit. I didn't care what they came in for—if it was heart disease or whatever. But I integrated working whatever the presenting problems were with the cranial rhythm and my awareness of restrictions to the flow of fluid. I started doing this with everybody.

Then, one day, I had my hands on a patient's head and was trying to sense how far down his dural tube I could feel the pulse. All of a sudden, down at the lumbar-thoracic junction, I felt an obstruction. The energy was being diverted to the right, into the liver. Suddenly, I had a perfect picture—right out of *CIBA* (the atlas of anatomy by Frank H. Netter). The picture was of *passive congestion of the liver*. I hospitalized the patient because he was in congestive heart failure, and it turned out to be because of a liver problem. I hung on to the idea that I had accurately *perceived* something when I felt that energy's deviation.

In general, in doing CST, beyond experiencing the pulse, I found that I am able to sense compressions and restrictions all along the spine. I am able to sense where they are, and I sometimes can send fluid through there to remove the restrictions.

Years ago, I developed a technique for training students to develop their ability to perceive restrictions at a distance. Again, this sensitivity has a spiritual dimension. You are feeling what is really going on at the very core of person's physical being. Where else than at the core do you look for spirit?

I taught, first of all, that basically all you have to do is close your eyes and send energy down the spine, and it will bounce back at a restriction. It's almost like using a sonar. I learned about sonar in the Coast Guard. Sonar is the technology that a ship will employ in wartime, say, to scan for enemy submarines. It's an energy that is sent out like a radio wave. It bounces off an object and comes back to you, and how long it takes to go out and come back tells you how far away that object is.

Another way to feel the restriction is to pull on the membrane in the spinal canal slightly and feel where it's attached and isn't gliding easily. The membrane should be able to glide freely for a centimeter or two along the tube of the spinal column. I taught students how to increase their sensitivity when I was at Michigan State University. I would take a strip of Saranwrap, maybe six feet long, and put it on a very slick table top. I would blindfold the student and then take something like a quarter and drop it on the Saranwrap. Then I had them pull it, just a little bit, maybe an inch or two, and then reach out with their finger and try to touch the quarter. After a few tries, they'd get pretty good at sensing how far away the quarter was by detecting the slight tension in the Saranwrap. After they learned to find a quarter, I replaced it with a dime, and just kept using lighter and lighter objects.

I can't tell you where that piece of proprioception comes from, but I think it's inherent in most people. It's just like when you hear a sound coming, and you automatically turn to the source of the sound. It's that kind of thing.

I continued developing my ability to diagnose by sensing down the spinal canal that way. Wherever I sensed a deviation, I would look further. It might take me, say, to the left kidney. It was as if it were following a nerve path, but that isn't quite right. It's more of an energetic path. I *played* with that. Being in regular practice and working in the hospital gave me a good chance to follow up my explorations with conventional diagnostic procedures to see if what

I was perceiving was objectively true. My practice was always to evaluate patients with my hands first and then to validate my diagnosis by physical tests. My diagnoses were usually confirmed.

What happened next was a lesson that taught me that I could actually diagnose clairvoyantly, if you will. One day, I probably had already seen fifty or fifty-five patients in the office. It was around 9:30 p.m. and I was getting ready to leave, but Gerry said, "There's another patient down in room three." Room three was at the end of the hall. On the way down, I didn't look at the chart to see who it was or what the complaint was, but as I walked, I just knew it was a woman, that she was overweight, and that she had gall-bladder trouble. I just *knew* it. When I got to room three, I opened the door and there she was—fair, fat, forty, female, and with all the signs of a gall-bladder problem. After that happened once, I honored it, and it just kept on happening.

I use it all the time now. But I don't use it unless I also *touch*. That seems to be the most comfortable way for me. When I put my hands on a patient, I pretty much know what's wrong with them within five or ten seconds. Now, you can say some of that is precognition; you can say some of that is, maybe, the characteristic of the energy I'm feeling in a patient; but I prefer not to define it. I just use it. I don't try to make it happen. It seems that it doesn't work as well when you put cerebral intention into it. I just kind of create the possibility and let it happen. And if I *question* it skeptically, *forget* it.

My experience is that if I question what the guides give me, they'll say, well, to hell with him, and for a month or so, I won't get any help at all. It's an insult to them to question them, so I don't belabor things that happen, as long as they are working.

I think that at least fifty percent of our CranioSacral therapists have received the same gifts as I have. Your abilities develop as you fine-tune your sensitivity to the system. When you get to a certain level of subtlety, things of a spiritual nature start coming in. A lot of our therapists think that they come directly through the cranial system. I don't necessarily think that. I think that they just come in. They could come in from anywhere, and the main thing is to accept them when they come.

There is a certain feel that indicates when an intuition of this sort is true, when it's valid, though the biggest problem is how to separate out your thought process from what is coming in intuitively. I'm not sure that "intuitively" is the proper word for it, but you can use it, because it implies that you are not making an intellectual decision about it. What you learn is that what comes in "intuitively" is not your own thought process. Once you can distinguish that, you're on pretty solid ground.

Of course, there will always be people who say, "What the hell are you talking about?" Not long ago, I was lecturing to a few hundred M.D.s about these kinds of things because they wanted to stretch themselves a bit, and the analogy I used was the phenomenon of gravity. I said, "If you can't use something unless you understand it, then scrape yourself off the ceiling!" We don't understand gravity to this day! For three hundred years, we've had the hottest shots in physics trying to clarify what makes gravity work. They can describe its functioning perfectly, but they don't know why or how it happens. Yet one of the biggest criticisms I get from the conventional medical community is: "You don't know why or how your therapy works, so how can you be doing it?" Answer: "Because the results are good, and I trust that."

Years later I was on the Advisory Committee to the Office of Alternative Medicine at the National Institutes of Health (NIH). I was elected to the committee to help figure out which types of alternative medicine were effective and which were not. And the argument that came up all the time, mainly with the administration of the committee, was that they required scientific, double-blind research for everything, whereas those of us on the committee were clinicians, and we were happy with studies of clinical outcome: if the patient or patients were better, that was enough for us. I got tired of wasting my time chasing after proofs of what I knew to be true when there were too many sick people to deal with. Who cares about the parameters of proof; it is the parameters of treatment and results that are important. That's a hallmark of my work, and I still feel that way.

There's a contemporary psychiatrist named Judy Orloff who has written a book about being able to sense things about patients even over the telephone. She has a conversation and does a diagnostic interview in her mind before she sees the patient. What distinguishes my practice from hers is that she's *trying* to do it and I'm not thinking about it at all. I honor intuition when it happens, and the more I honor it, the *more* it happens. But the whole point seems to be not to insist on a method, even a "spiritual" method, but just to be open to what's happening and go with it.

The Spirit of Play

I think I realized pretty quickly that I could sense energy anywhere in the body, not only at the cranial bones. The craniosacral rhythm can be picked up all over the body. I came back from the Cranial Academy with the craniosacral rhythm and started by working with that. But then I'd put my hands on the sacrum and I could feel rhythm down there, too. So then I would take one hand and put it up on the patient's head and I'd feel, yep, it's the same rhythm!

You know, in my training in osteopathy I was taught physical diagnosis. I did a lot of exploration of people's bodies with my hands. But even before my formal training, I had experience with "hands on" healing: the Coast Guard steward's leg. I found out then that when I just put my hand on the ailing limb, it made the limb okay. The main lesson was that I didn't have to force anything. If you start poking and prodding, putting *force* into finding out what's going on, all that you will experience will be the patient's ability to defend against your force. If you just let your hand rest there, that will tell you what's going on. The problem will come out to meet your hand.

When you're an osteopath, you see a lot of people come in with bad backs. From early on, I always made it a point to hold the patient's ankles and put a little traction on each side to see if the sacrum's locked up, to see if I got as much play from both sides. This isn't a common practice among osteopaths, but I learned it fairly quickly. You put a little traction on it. If the right side doesn't come as far as the left side, then it's the right sacroiliac that's a problem. It just seemed that this was the obvious thing to do. How did I know to do this?

I think that one of the keys both to scientific exploration and spiritual openness is a certain spirit of play. A successful microbiologist once said that the reason she was so good was because her work was fun. Devising scientific experiments was a kind of game for me, played just to see what would happen. The body knows everything that's wrong and, if you're able to tune in to it, it will tell you what it is. Working with a patient can be an exploratory game. That's really how CST developed—by touching, feeling, exploring, playing with the rhythm. When I could feel that the rhythm was restricted on one side and not the other, for instance, it suggested to me that the fascia or the innervation was compromised and wouldn't allow the innate driving force to move the rhythm. The craniosacral system doesn't put out a high driving force; it puts out a light force, so you have to be very light to sense it. A heavy, anxious attitude will make it impossible to feel.

Now the Cranial Academy guys said the feeling of the rhythm throughout the body was caused by the cerebrospinal fluid going down the nerve roots. Well, that's not true at all. There's plenty of work that shows that the cerebrospinal fluid stops where the meningeal sleeves are attached at the intervertebral foramina. As far as I'm concerned, what happens—and I think this is correct—is that the fluid pressure rises and falls ever so gently inside the skull, and it penetrates in between the brain neurons. This is now a proven fact. The fluid pressure in the interstitial spaces probably stimulates the motor nerve system very gently so that you get a slight contraction and relaxation of the musculature. These muscle activities produce a very gentle pumping action that moves body fluids—interstitial body fluids particularly. If you accept this thesis, then all you have to do is impose a little restriction in the fascial compliance (given how gentle the urging that's coming from the central nervous system is) to stop the fluid movement. Where you feel it stop, that's where you look. That's just one of those things I woke up with in my head. As I've said before, I do a lot of that.

It isn't that I have dreams where I receive special messages or anything like that, even though I am good at dreaming—I'm a big dreamer! But dreaming for me is a kind of entertainment, a kind of play, a way of staying light in spirit or of confronting difficulties with a positive attitude.

By the way, this approach to dreaming is another thing I learned in the Coast Guard. On the ship, my bunk was right next to the "sonar cage." The sonar cage is where the machinery is, and it makes a constant racket. I had to learn to sleep with the sonar gear going and the light on. My bunk hung from the grillwork and swung with the movement of the ship. I learned how to build dream stories around all these sensations. I became very good at it. Sometimes I'd have to wake up in the middle of a dream to take a watch or attend to some problem or other. I'd be up on the bridge for a few hours. When I was done, I'd come back down, jump in the bunk, and pick up the dream story right where I left off. I wanted to know how it came out!

My Coast Guard vessel had bunk beds, as I mentioned. The mattresses weren't very thick, but you didn't have much space above you to the next bunk. Usually the bunks were stacked three or four tiers high. When you first came aboard ship, of course, you got the lousiest bunk. I got one up on the top, way over on the side of the ship, so when the ship rolled, my bunk heaved back and forth and up and down. My bunk was about seven feet up, and I had to climb up the other bunks to get there. As soon as a better bunk opened up—it was a middle bunk actually—I grabbed it, but now I was near the sonar. Only a screen separated me from the cage. I traded motion for noise.

When I started to get a little seasick, I just thought about a roller coaster. When I was a kid, I used to love the roller coaster. There was an amusement park about two miles away from our house, so we'd walk up there and I'd ride the roller coaster like crazy. When the ship rolled, I just reminded myself that I used to have to pay twenty-five cents to ride a roller coaster, but this was free! After I thought of that, the ship's rolling never bothered me again. The noise didn't bother me. Nothing bothered me. I built my dreams around whatever was going on around me.

Maybe the cranial system and its therapy represent another path into the same mind-body mechanism as dreaming.

Life in Academia

Biomechanics

After working for eleven years in private practice in Florida, I took the aforementioned job at Michigan State University. Michigan State had started a department of what they called "Biomechanics," and they invited me to come on as a clinical researcher. The complete title of the institution I joined was Michigan State University, College of Osteopathic Medicine, Department of Biomechanics. The osteopathic college was originally an independent institution in Pontiac, Michigan, but eventually it was adopted by Michigan State, which is in East Lansing.

Our department was one of the very first dedicated to the study of Biomechanics. In fact, I think they came up with the name "biomechanics" because they needed to lend their work an air of legitimacy. The leaders of the department wanted to study whether spinal manipulation and the other original osteopathic practices Dr. Still had initiated were actually effective. They needed a name that would identify their project and give it a scientific sound without prejudicing their outcome. They came up with "Biomechanics," a very neutral term: the mechanics of the body. It was also an apt name, since they did have bona fide physicists in the department. I wound up heading the team that investigated what was traditionally called "cranial osteopathy" but which I myself had been developing independently with Dr. Tyler. I became something of a leader in the department. They didn't invite me particularly to be a leader. They invited me because of my background in biochemistry. They thought I'd be able to talk the language of the Ph.D.'s with whom I'd be working. Out of twenty-seven people, there were only four other clinicians besides myself. They had all primarily been involved with manipulative practices, so I was the only one who came with conventional medical experience in addition to scientific background. They also knew I was involved in acupuncture, and that I was doing "weird stuff" with patients' heads!

I was, of course, already working with healing energy and, in fact, it was by my challenging the faculty to take an interest in it that things really got interesting for me at Michigan State. I claimed that an energy transference occurs between myself and the patient and that it should be possible to measure it. After I presented the idea at two consecutive staff meetings as a potential area for investigation and was ignored, I suggested that the Ph.D.'s weren't smart enough to measure the kind of energy transference that I was describing. An Israeli biophysicist named Zvi Karni picked up the gauntlet. He said, "You're crazy as hell and I'll prove it to you." We argued a little bit, and then he started attending my sessions with patients.

I was allowing myself to be as creative as I wanted in my treatment sessions. Most of my patients had been referred by the State as Workman's Compensation cases. I was a "Professor of Biomechanics" so they referred them to me for evaluation and treatment. They all had physical injuries. I would work on the patients, and

Dr. Karni would observe. Sometimes he'd get quite carried away. He'd say, "Why did you know to pick up that leg?" Or "Why did you know to work with his head?" By this time, I was, of course, exploring what would soon become "CranioSacral Therapy" to see what it could do for various kinds of injuries. What Karni and I came to agree upon was that I didn't know what I was doing! He decided it was his job to keep asking questions until I focused enough so I could tell him.

After observing me work on patients for a while, Dr. Karni decided that we should monitor the whole-body electrical potential of the patient while I was doing "hands-on" treatment. We agreed to think of the patient's body as a bag of electrically conductive material, with the skin as an insulator. Within this electrically conductive substance were millions or billions of electrical generators and batteries. The major sources of production of electrical power were in the brain and heart, so we kept our measuring electrodes on the lower extremities away from the those organs.

For readers who are interested in the technical details, the way we took these measurements was as follows: Dr. Karni constructed what he called a "modified Wheatstone Bridge," to add positive and negative voltage deflection algebraically before presenting these charges on the polygraph. We recorded cardiac electrical activity and pulmonary activity concurrently. The pulmonary actions were measured by the placement of a strain gauge that was connected to circumferentially-placed, nonstretch, band materials at the level of the lower thorax, just above the respiratory diaphragm. All measurements we recorded were presented on a polygraph machine.

We worked together in this manner for a couple of months, and it made me realize how little I really understood about what was going on, even though I was getting good results. I think a lot of people work that way. In any case, Karni discovered that if I found exactly the right position in the body by, say, picking up a foot or a leg or by getting a release through what we eventually called the "craniosacral system," the electrical potential of the whole body would drop; the baseline would get real smooth, between two and five millivolts below what the average might be. When that happened on his meter, he knew that I had found the right position to give relief to that body. We called finding and holding a position in that way, "Position and Hold."

"Position and Hold" is a phrase that I picked up from a practitioner named Larry Jones. He worked with a system that isn't directly related to cranial work. Let's say you've hurt your shoulder doing some exercise. Larry would move your arm until he found a position in which it hurt very little. Usually, if you have a damaged shoulder, knee, or whatever, you can find a position where there's minimal pain. Once he found that position, he would feel around for a point where pressure would take the pain away completely. He would hold you there and, after a few minutes, he would release it, and usually you'd feel better. That's where the phrase "position and hold" comes from. I adopted it and used it in cranial work. For example, if one of the skull bones is not moving properly, I'll find a proper position for it. In this case pain is not the issue. The right position will cause the craniosacral rhythm to stop pulsing. I just hold it there until the pulsation returns. When the pulsation returns, the restriction of the bone motion will have been corrected.

It may have taken us a while to find out how I was doing all this, but we understood ultimately that every time the electrical potential dropped, the craniosacral rhythm stopped. That is how I started consciously using rhythm cessation as my guide to knowing exactly where I should position the body. The changes in electrical potential consistently correlated with the stopping of the craniosacral rhythm. When the craniosacral rhythm started up again, the electrical potential started to move up again, but it never went up as high as the original baseline, and it had much less "static" in it—it was more smooth-waved. If the smooth wave appeared in the electrical measurement and I got a nice rhythm coming back, the patient invariably felt better. But that in itself did not have to be a subjective yardstick. If, when I released my position, the meter went back to bouncing around and the cranio-sacral rhythm felt raggedy, then I knew I hadn't waited long enough or something else hadn't worked properly.

Now the next question was, how could we find out what made what we were doing work like this? Dr. Karni and I spent a lot of time drinking coffee and talking about it, and we ultimately came up with the model of the energy cyst. The energy cyst model explains what happens when the body experiences a physical trauma. When I hit a body with a hammer, let's say, the traumatic energy enters the body at the point of contact. How far does the force go in? It goes in as far as its momentum will carry it against the viscosity of the tissue it's penetrating. Then it stops. We the-orized that the force enters in quantum parcels, that is, in discrete bundles of energy. Say you hit me on the arm. The duration of the blow might be one hundredth of a second but, during that time, my arm might be moving, so there's a movement of the tissue where the blow is received. Say that, during one hundredth of a second, ten quanta go in. Each of these quanta will have its own pathway into, or through, my arm. If my body moves forcefully in a way that bends during that time, each pathway will bend a little bit. Karni's idea was that when energy enters and bends, it can't come back out along the same trajectory it went in. Consequently, your body does one of two things. It either dissipates the energy inter-nally—and in that case you get a normal healing process—or it can't dissipate it, so it "walls it off" and creates what Elmer Green from the Menninger Institute later called an energy cyst. (I'll tell you about Elmer in a minute.)

At the time, Karni called the cyst an "area of increased entropy." He said, "What you're doing is providing energy that is comparable to 'Schrödinger's information' for the area of increased entropy." After the trauma, this disorganized energy is always beating away at the walls that are trying to contain it. In therapy, the therapist tries to find exactly the right position of the body. That would be a position that repeats the original position of the trauma and allows the trapped energy to find its way out. Later on, we recognized that I was also working with the increased entropy when I "put" energy into a patient. The energy I put in is organized, as opposed to the disorganized energy of the trauma. In the presence of the fresh, organized energy, the entropic forces reorganize. "That's life," as Sinatra said.

In addition to measuring electrical potential, we used a thermograph to gauge the temperature at the points of traumatic entry, and we would see as much as two-degrees-centigrade increase in skin temperature when this energy was exiting.

I began to realize that, often when energy cysts are released— when the energy comes out—there is also an emotion that releases with it. I began to think about this as the emotion involved in the injury. For instance, you hit me with a hammer and I get mad or I'm frightened or whatever. The emotion itself gets locked into the cyst at the same time as the energy of the injury. In other words, *the tissue must remember* that injury. Perhaps the energy of the injury has a certain "signature" that it acquires from that emotion. This gives you the kind of emotional release that occurs when the energy cyst is reorganized or released.

There was also a lot of politics and interpersonal stuff going on in that department at Michigan State; some of it was good, some of it wasn't. I was on a curriculum committee, and the very same Dr. Korr who had been my physiology professor when I did my learning at Kirksville was chairman of the department under which biochemistry was a subdivision. He was my boss when I took the fellowship, although I didn't have much to do with him. When I went to Michigan State, we started the same day together, and our offices were right next to each other. He said, "How could a guy with a brain like yours slip by me? I should have noticed you."

There was a reason he didn't notice me. Back then a couple of fraternity guys told me, "Be careful, John, when you take Korr's physiology class. If he gets to know you and he likes you, you'll get a good grade. If he doesn't like you, purely subjectively he'll give you a lousy grade."

I told Dr. Korr, "I grew up in Detroit, and I have a lot of street time in, so I know how to be invisible. And I didn't want you to know who I was."

He said, "Boy, you're good at it because here you are, a student of mine working for me, and I barely recognize you."

We got to be good friends. One day he said, "We've got all these classes on respiratory disease, cardiovascular, gastrointestinal diseases, etc., and not one of them have osteopathic manipulation concepts in the curriculum. They're all just conventional medicine. Yet this is an osteopathic college at Michigan State."

I should mention that State also had a standard allopathic college and a veterinary college too. The allopathy and osteopathy were both in the same building. Being in biomechanics, I was in fact a professor for both colleges.

We had a meeting one day with eighteen attendees, maybe fifteen of them on the curriculum committee, and we started going through all the classes. The first clinical course we hit was on respiratory disease. I said, "What we got to do here is differentiate this from conventional medicine. We can do conventional medicine, but we also want to do rib mobilization and enhance all the things that enable a patient to breathe deeply, loosen the muscles, and so on."

The guy across the table from me was the chairman of family medicine, and he said, "Dr. Upledger, we spend a lot of time and effort showing doctors how not to be quacks. Now you're talking about quackism getting into this class and teaching our students to be quacks again."

I said, "You're crazy; you don't understand the neurophysiology of the lungs and the rib cage."

We argued that back and forth and finally he got personal; I can't remember exactly what he said, but in front of sixteen other faculty I replied, "I'll tell you what: let's you and I go out in the hall, and one of us will be able to come back in. Whichever one comes back in, that's the one that will influence the curriculum in the class." He never said another word to me. I was there at least seven more years—I'd see him in the hall, I'd say, "Hi, Jim," and he'd just keep walking straight ahead.

It was so funny because that's essentially the way I would have handled it when I was eighteen years old—let's go outside and settle this thing! That's the kind of guy I was at Michigan State.

At the time, I thought, 'I'll probably get fired'—but no! In fact the next day I was in my office and the dean came in and said, "John, that was really wonderful what you did; we don't want you to think that anybody is down on you. Just control your temper a little better. Your ideas are beautiful!"

They were beautiful also because I had a major grant to research autism. I was bringing in more money than my salary, so my voice was valued.

Work at the Menninger Foundation

The perception of tissue memory arose more from working with autistic children and my residency at the Menninger Foundation than in my work with Dr. Karni because he didn't think about it this way very much. The Menninger Foundation is extremely well known and has great authority in medical research. The research at Menninger happened while I was at Michigan State. I was able to work there because of Elmer Green, who was the director of "psychophysiological research." He operated under that title and in that position for well over thirty years. Elmer Green and his wife, Alice, wrote the first book on biofeedback. In fact, they gave biofeedback its name. He's probably ninety by now, but he still writes quite a bit. He's the founder of the International Society for the Study of Subtle Energy and Energy Medicine: ISSSEEM. I looked up to Elmer because when I started at Michigan State, I had already read his book on biofeedback and was fascinated by it. I wanted to meet him and began to wonder how to connect with this "director of psychophysiological research."

Another researcher at Menninger, Pat Norris, Ph.D. (Elmer Green's daughter), tried to show that nervous tissue is not the only cell matrix that has memory. From my work with Dr. Karni, I was starting to understand how energy and emotion are, at the very least, inseparable, if not, in fact, identical. I also began to see how energies and emotions are stored in tissues, independent of any record by the nervous system.

I think that the tissue-memory work has never been published under the auspices of Menninger because Elmer and Pat were too radical for the other people there and, as it happened, so was I. When I first connected with Menninger, I was able to give classes to the whole staff, but eventually Elmer became something of a *persona non grata* for supporting what we were doing and being taken up by it. Of course, he was able to stay there and did so until just a few years ago, but he never could get their full support for his work in these oddball areas.

I will always remember the first time I taught a course for the psychiatric staff. It was a five-day thing, and I did it before I had developed the concept of SomatoEmotional Release into a specific program. I gave a compact, five-day version of what today we call CranioSacral Therapy One and Two. I loaded the class with science, by which I mean I had slides of tissue and lots of technical material. When I was finished with my presentation, the chief of psychiatry said, "Doctor, this is very impressive. You have really overwhelmed us. And your science is beautiful. But you know, a psychiatrist isn't supposed to touch a patient because he wouldn't be able to keep up his objectivity if he did that, and so, I'm afraid we can't use your therapy here." Those were the terms of the dismissal of CST. But the psychophysiology lab refused to accept the dismissal. I was invited back a dozen times but always outside the psychiatric department. I talked to pediatric nurses, I talked to regular nurses, and I did a lot of work with the research department under the psychophysiology labs, but I never did get into the psychiatric department again.

How did Elmer Green and I happen to get together in the first place? I kind of finagled that. I was really hooked on biofeedback, and I wanted to meet Elmer, who, as I said, was the founder. My undergraduate degree was in psychology, and I had dabbled a bit in hypnosis. Now, at Michigan State, I was in charge of some of the "continuing medical education" programs for the Michigan State Osteopathic College, as part of my faculty duties. That, in effect, meant I could bring in almost any kind of speaker that I wanted.

The budget was okay too. In my early years there, we had a nice place in Pontiac, Michigan—a nice-sized facility for these programs—so I basically brought in people that I thought I would enjoy hearing. I wanted to hear Elmer Green, so I called him at Menninger and said, "Would you come and give a biofeedback program for a whole afternoon to a group of osteopathic general practitioners?" I thought perhaps I would offer him an opportunity to get biofeedback into some of their offices. Well, he jumped at it. So what I did then—this is something I guess I learned from my years on the streets of Detroit—I scheduled myself in the program for 10:00 o'clock and him at 11:00. He had to be there to hear me. I spoke about the craniosacral system and about our work with autistic kids. (I'll talk about that in a minute.) Elmer got completely turned on. He said, "How'd you like to come out to Menninger and give a class?"

I said, "That would be wonderful." The Dean at Michigan State was beside himself with ecstasy because to bust open the Menninger Foundation was really big time. Elmer liked me right away because of what I was doing. For him, I was integrating hard science with stuff that was a little bit beyond. He thought that was wonderful. We got along great. And it has proven to be a valuable and enduring association.

I lectured with him at ISSSEEM (the subtle energy institute) in Boulder in June, 2001. (Incidentally, a couple of years ago, I received the Elmer and Alice Green Award For Excellence in Medicine.)

Work with Autistic Children

By the time I connected with Menninger, I was in possession of the rudiments of the idea of energy cyst release and was beginning to connect it with emotions. What really helped me see the role of emotion clearly was my work with autistic kids. In 1977, I got a research contract from the National Institute of Mental Health through the State of Michigan to spend some time at a center for autism, and I worked there for three years. The first year, we weren't supposed to *treat* children—just observe and evaluate. The second year, we could treat. I had quite a cadre of graduate students from Michigan State with me. By then we'd been working with the same kids for a while—even evaluation involved "hands-on" work—so they were getting used to us and were fairly cooperative. I would have maybe five students with me for a session. Typically, I would have one student put a hand under the sacrum, one student on each arm and one on each leg. I worked at the child's head. I don't really have any idea why I was doing it this way. I wanted these students to get some "hands-on" experience. But why I placed them exactly as I did—I don't know. Could this be the guides? Who knows?

Anyway, we found out certain things about the kids: if we *decompressed* them front to back, their self-abuse would usually stop. They would stop chewing their wrists and banging their heads and things like that. Incidentally, I should tell you that we also discovered that their heads were, in fact, *very* compressed and that it was a membranous kind of compression. I would say that in autism, a big contributing factor is that the cranial membranes lose their ability to expand as the brain and the skull are trying to grow. Something's happening to denature them. It could be a vaccine reaction; it could be a viral infection; it could be any kind of toxicity that causes a change in the biochemistry of the dural membrane. When we discovered this kind of compression, we took its lead and performed anterior-posterior decompression. The resulting relief from self-abuse was very obvious.

The next thing that we tried was to decompress their heads laterally—side to side—but that wasn't so easy. How do you get a hold of the two temporal bones (the bones on the sides of the skull)? One morning I woke up with the idea of pulling on their ears! The ears are attached to the temporal bones and they make great handles. So I started playing around working on the ears, but as I pulled them, I still couldn't get the temporal bones to glide laterally. Then the students started saying things like, "John, this leg wants to move. I don't know what to do." I've got to be the professor, so I'd just say, "Follow it, follow it." What happened was, the child would start assuming all sorts of positions, because the student was following the motions he/she felt the child wanted to make. Then, all of a sudden, the child might have a tremendous emotional breakthrough. I don't mean an emotional breakthrough like remembering something—but you could just feel this tremendous emotional energy come out of him or her. This happened any number of times with different children. As this "emotional energy" released, the temporal bones decompressed internally.

After the children had emotional and temporal bone releases of this sort, they became more sociable. They would hug; they would kiss; they would play with each other. They would rather play with another child than a pillow. This didn't mean they were *cured* of their autism, but we did see significant behavioral change. It tied together for me somehow with the concept of energy cysts from Karni, though now we were observing energy phenomena that were in whole bodies. These energies were not necessarily put in by a trauma and weren't walled off in a cyst. There was an abnormal energy in these children that was causing them to be a certain way and, when that energy was released, their behavior changed. That's how far I got with that piece of the puzzle at that time.

I said that I didn't consider this to be a cure for autism. Perhaps I should explain. A cure is something I think of as being permanent. Now this is how I saw autism. I thought the kids were autistic because the membranes in the head—the *dura mater*—had been altered biochemically and were unable to expand as the child's brain grew, so what we had to do was use external force to expand them. But you can only get so much expansion and, when the growing brain catches up with the space and has trouble with continued growth, the child becomes autistic again, so then you have to re-expand. This means that you have to keep helping them expand until they stop growing. I started trying to teach parents how to treat their own children so they wouldn't have to live near a therapist. Because what was true of autism was true for any number of other conditions, I started training lay people to perform CST treatments on their dysfunctional children at home.

The autistic child classically chews on his wrist, sometimes all the way down to the tendon, and pushes on the roof of his mouth. He stomps around and talks to toys, but he won't talk to a person and, if his mother tries to pick him up, he screams and pushes her away. Autistic children don't want anything to do with another person. But when we were able to decompress their heads in the front-to-back position, they stop hurting themselves. When they get relief from their head being decompressed, they stop doing that.

But we were still having trouble getting the kids to socialize well. We needed to decompress their skulls laterally; before we had only done front-to-back decompression. So I said to myself, the good Lord put this ear in here with a big canal that goes halfway through the temporal bone and goes all the way to the center, to the petrous. So you can just pull on the outside of the ear gently, and if you get the temporal bones to release, the kid becomes loving and social. He just suddenly becomes a nice person. It's astonishing.

I mentioned that the dural membranes of autistic children are biochemically abnormal. Are they that way from birth? Who knows? I don't pretend to know what causes it or how it develops. One doesn't have to have answers to these questions to see that the situation we were witnessing was very, very interesting. Here's a little boy who is totally autistic, and you get him into a certain bodily position, you hold that position, and then you start to feel energy radiating from his body. His whole body gets hot. It lasts for four, five, ten minutes. Then he just kind of relaxes and, after a minute or two, he gets up and gives you a kiss!

Another one. I don't like the word 'autism.' I don't like a child to be stamped autistic because that automatically means he or she is going to have certain things happening to them in the educational system and, in fact, all over the place, that are going to *make them autistic*. The power of suggestion makes them autistic. I have proof on this one. This was a little boy in New York that was delivered about seven years ago now. He was diagnosed as being a Downs Syndrome child. The parents said, "No, we won't let that word happen." Within ten days after delivery, they were down here, and I started working with their son every three months for a couple of years. They'd bring him in for three or four days initially, and again in three months, then every six months; now it's every year. Today, this Downs child who is officially retarded is in the top ten percent in reading in New York State. The parents would not let the word "Downs" or "retarded" be said to him. The suggestion didn't take, and he's a happy boy who reads like crazy. He comes and lies on the table, holds up his storybooks, and narrates them to me like an all-star. I have to admit, the mother is wonderful and the father is a trumpet player. That's probably why he's so enlightened.

I worked with these children at about the time that I was finishing the work with Dr. Karni. I suspect that the spirit guides decided, "Okay, he's agonized enough about this, so we'll give him another piece of the puzzle."

More Lessons

Once I had learned what I was able to learn from the autistic children, another piece of the puzzle was indeed placed before me. The psychiatric department at Michigan State University referred a patient to me who had a very interesting history. She'd been in psychotherapy for six or seven years. She had no children, no pregnancies, but was suffering from severe PMS. When she was just twenty-eight years old, her husband had convinced her to undergo a hysterectomy, I guess because he found her premenstrual syndrome hard to handle. In those days you could get an elective hysterectomy if you wanted it. She wanted it because she wanted to keep her husband, but he divorced her six months after she had her hysterectomy anyway. Now she hated men and ultimately ended up seeing a psychiatrist. Her operation had occurred seven or eight years before she was referred to me. Since that time, she had been suffering from severe, incapacitating headaches and low back pain, so eventually the psychiatrists sent her to me.

They had been playing with her all this time before it occurred to them that something might be wrong with her structurally.

They thought of me, remember, as a "structural" person. I'm a "biomechanics" professor. That's what I am. I was probing in all kinds of directions beyond structural issues, but nobody was bothering me because I was bringing in research funding. I'm sure they're also saying to themselves, "He's expanding the boundaries of biomechanics significantly." In any case, I was supposed to be an expert in structural problems, so this woman was sent in my direction.

The woman was thirty-six or thirty-seven at this time. I put her on the table and the structural aspects of her problem were pretty easy to discern. She had a left sacroiliac that was wrecked, and she had compression at the base of her skull. I corrected the sacroiliac and the upper cervical compression. She felt great. She thought I was a genius. Psychiatry said, "Watch out, she hates men." That was understandable. But she didn't hate me. I had fixed her.

In two weeks she wanted another appointment. She called and said that the pain was only fifty percent of what it had been, but it was clearly returning. I had her come in, and I did pretty much the same things I had done on her first visit, but this time it didn't help. She screamed and yelled at me. She told me I hated women and that's why I didn't make a real effort to try to help her this time. I'm thinking, "Okay, go see your psychiatrist. It's not my problem." But then she said, "Can I come back?" I said, "Well, sure."

The next time she came in, I had a graduate student with me named Dan Bensky, who has since written a couple books on acupuncture. I put her on the table and began checking out her left sacroiliac. I had my hand under her left buttocks, and I lifted her leg so that it was sort of in the *lithotomy* position—the position you put a woman in when you're examining her gynecologically. This usually involves placing the patient's legs in gynecological "stirrups" to hold them in place during the examination. The stirrups are up in the air about two feet above the level of her body and off to the sides. They hold a woman in a position so that the vaginal area is exposed—you deliver a baby in that position.

I was working on the left side with my hand under the sacrum. The other hand was on her left knee and her leg was elevated so that her left thigh was essentially vertical. On the left side of the table, there was a chair on which she had put her purse. It is important to understand that her hysterectomy had been a vaginal hysterectomy. I didn't know that at the time. But all of a sudden —WHACK!!!—at the back of my head. She had grabbed her purse from the chair and whammed me with it!

I said, "What the hell?"

She said, "I'm sorry, Doctor Upledger. That wasn't you that I was hitting. It's the resident during my hysterectomy. He's leaning on my leg and causing my back to go bad." Well, she had flipped right back to the time of her surgery! "He's causing my back trouble. He's hurting my back. He's twisting. He's doing damage. He's leaning on my leg."

She just went on and on like that, and she really wanted me to believe that he was doing this on purpose, wrecking her back! I got into a long conversation with her. I said, "Surgical residents work long hours—fourteen hours a day—at least six days a week. The poor guy is so tired he probably doesn't realize that he's leaning on you." I'm going on trying to placate her, but she ain't buyin' it, so I said, "Well, it strikes me that if you want to continue to be angry, you're going to continue to have back pain. You can't let go of it if you're still angry."

"Okay." And her back softened.

I thought, WOW! A body position put her back into the reality of her surgery, even though she had been under general anesthetic at the time. I figured I was about through when all of a sudden her head started going back, her neck extending backwards. I recognized what that was: It looked like the position when you're intubating (receiving a tube down your throat to breathe through). I said, "What's going on?"

She said, "This doctor's trying to strangle me. He's trying to suffocate me, choke me. He's putting something down my throat."

I said, "That's the anesthesia guy. He's got to do that for you."

"No, he doesn't. He doesn't have to do that."

"Yes, he does. You don't want to feel the pain of the surgery. It's routine."

She said, "Well, he's saying something."

"Can you tell me what he's saying?"

She said, "The surgeon just said, 'It's kind of strange for a woman in her late twenties to have an *elective* hysterectomy.'

"The anesthesia guy says, 'Well, it's not so bad. She's losing the baby carriage, but she's keeping the playpen.'"

She was furious, and no doubt quite justifiably so. I gave her another long lecture—this one about how anesthesia guys take you to the brink of death, and then they hold you there, and then they revive you and keep you from dying, and that's how they spend their professional lives. They have to be a little bit callous about things; otherwise, they would have so much empathy that they wouldn't be able to do their job.

She didn't give a rat's ass about that. What was important to her was that he didn't respect her. She knew this because of what he said. I said, "Okay. It's been eight years and you can keep that anger; but if you keep that anger, you're going to keep your headaches. If you let go of the anger, you can let go of the headaches."

"Is that right?"

"Yes."

Whew! You could just feel her soften up. Okay. So now she's done. At this point, she returned to normal consciousness and she said, in a soft, surprised voice, "Oh, hello."

Now I'm wondering what the hell's going on here? This time *I* said, "Well, come back in a week."

She said "Yeah," and Bensky said, "I've got to be here."

She came back in a week. No backaches, no headaches, and she hadn't been back to see her psychiatrist or psychotherapist. She said, "I've been irritable and cross and nervous, but I haven't had any pains."

I said "Okay."

Before she came, I made an arrangement with Bensky. I said, "Dan, when she gets on the table, you pick up one leg, I'll pick up the other leg. We'll put her in the lithotomy position and see what happens." It took four seconds and she's WHOOOH. She's under anesthesia. I said, "What's going on?"

"They're taking out my uterus."

She described—honest to God—in precise terms, a tugging on the various fascias and so on. She didn't use technical language, but she described the whole procedure very accurately. I've been in on enough vaginal hysterectomies to know that what she was saying was very authentic.

Then she said, "Now they're taking my uterus and putting it in this pan, and the surgeon is stepping back, and the resident is coming in, and the surgeon is saying, 'Now make the repair.' He put in nine stitches." She counted them. She could feel each one penetrate; it didn't hurt her, but she could feel it. He put in the nine stitches, and then the surgeon came over and took a look, and he said, "That's a pretty sloppy job you did, but we really don't have time to correct it, so I guess it'll have to do," or words to that effect.

So now she's furious again. Well, I gave her a story about how it's the surgeon's job to decimate the ego of the resident, otherwise he won't work for slave wages. She ain't buyin' any of that stuff, so I said, once again, "Well, if you choose to keep this anger, you're going to stay frustrated and angry; if you can let go of it, your irritability will go away—and now's the time to do it."

She just calmed right down, and after that she was fine. She didn't hate men anymore. She turned out so well that I had her come to my classes once every semester and talk about why doctors should mind what they say when a patient's under anesthesia.

Direction of Energy

Let's get back to biomechanics. I want to write a bit more about how the department was set up and about my role within it. My identity as a professor gave me an official area of research, so I was able to experiment and work as I wished without anyone getting on my case. In fact, they never got on my case at all. Never. I probably had more license than anybody else.

The department went like this: Under the Dean of the Osteopathic College was the Chairman of the Department of Biomechanics. The Dean was Myron Megan, a D.O. During my years there, there were three different chairpersons, but the one that was really good to me and that I interacted with the most was Bob Little. He was a Ph.D. in mechanical engineering, and he eventually became very interested in my work.

When Bob Little first became chairman, he looked rather askance at me because I was already doing stuff that was off the mechanical-engineering chart; but he changed his attitude rather quickly when I was able to treat a problem of his.

He came in to see me one day shortly after he arrived there.

Bob's avocation was running. He had a bad bruise on his right heel and was unable to run. I was still researching acupuncture at the time, so I suggested that we try that approach. I put a needle in his *left* heel at exactly the spot that was sore on the *right*. I knew by this time that if there is a pain on one side, and I put a needle in the corresponding site on the other side, it would block the pain. Within seconds he was banging his sore heel on the floor without discomfort. He couldn't believe it. Then I needled his sore heal. He was out running the next day. Suddenly, I was transformed from being *"persona suspecta"* to "Hey—this guy's all right!"

Now, Bob had lost an eye somehow and wore a glass eye. Shortly after I worked on his heel, he developed an infection in his eye socket. He'd been going to the eye doctor and getting antibiotics, but nothing was working, so one day he asked me if I could do some of that "magic stuff" that I did on his heel. I decided to employ the technique that I now call *"Direction of Energy."* I made a "V" with two fingers and positioned the glass eye in the center of the "V" so that I had a finger above and a finger below. Then I found the right place on the back of his head, directly behind the opposite eye, and I directed energy diagonally through the head and to the infected eye socket with my other hand. I just imagined energy shooting from my fingers where I touched the back of his head, passing through the head, and coming out through the infected socket. Within about three or four minutes, the eye socket stopped hurting, and the next day the pus was all gone. He wondered, "Maybe, the antibiotics started working all of a sudden!"

I said, "Could be!" But after that, I could do anything I wanted in that department. I got support from him for almost any direction I wanted to go in. I still think very fondly of Bob Little. We became really good friends. I remember one day he said something to me that has actually become a maxim for my practice. I was wondering about energy and the kind of movement in tissue that you feel when healing is occurring. He said, "Well, John, everything is always in motion. The difference is—if it's a block of granite, the motion is just so slow that we can't see it. The less dense things are, the more rapidly they are able to move." Now for a mechanical engineer to say this to me just blew me away. And I have really kept that in my mind and applied it again and again in working with bones, ligaments, and the solid aspects of other living tissue.

There were five clinicians and twenty-two Ph.D.'s in the department. When I got there, the department was about three years old. I was the only clinician who had had anything other than "manipulative" experience, as I mentioned before. I was the only one in the department that had practiced medicine, done surgery, and other ordinary medical things. The other four clinicians were all "backcrackers." The dean's idea was to bring in people who had developed unusual concepts from their clinical experience. By the time I was recruited, they certainly knew that I had concepts that qualified, because I had been doing this stuff with Jim Tyler who was, of course, a neurosurgeon, and we had written up a couple of articles. They had been rejected by the mainstream medical journals and scientific periodicals, but I'm sure that talk about what we were doing had reached him. (As a rule, my articles would eventually get placed in alternative medical journals. The *Journal of the American Osteopathic Association* published some of my stuff. Their editors went out on a limb once in a while.)

Every Wednesday, we had a general meeting of the department staff. My job on Wednesday—and that of the other clinicians as well—was to stand up in front of everybody—all the Ph.D's (they had degrees in everything from psychology to bioengineering to physics; there were anatomists, physiologists—everything) and tell them what I saw in my practice that was unusual. Ideally, someone would say, "I think I can help you investigate that. Let's see if we can find out what it was about." What we were doing, basically, was interrogating anecdotes. In this environment, in principle, I could do anything I wanted to, but sometimes I would describe what I was interested in and just get blank stares. Nobody would stop me from doing what I wanted, but arousing actual interest was another matter.

The story of how Dr. Karni and I got hooked up together and then figured out what was really going on when I "directed energy" is a bit humorous and worth telling in detail, though I told it in outline before. At one of our Wednesday meetings, I said that I was beginning to get the idea that when I'm doing cranial work, I am exchanging energy with the patients. I said I wanted to start measuring it. The first time I presented this notion, everybody was very quiet. It seemed like nobody was interested. I just let it go. The next Wednesday, I brought it up again. Again, no response; so I said, "Well, you know, it strikes me that this is really happening and, if you guys knew what you were doing, you wouldn't be afraid to try to investigate it. But right now it looks to me like nobody is smart enough to figure out how one might proceed."

Svi Karni was a little Israeli guy in the back, and he said, "Well, I tell you what. I'm going to go with you, and I'm going to practice with you, and I'm going to investigate with you, and I'm going to prove that you're crazy!" Dr. Karni began coming to my sessions with patients and, though we never agreed that I was crazy, it became pretty clear—remember—that I didn't really know very precisely what I was doing.

Karni developed a procedure. First, he would measure the total electrical potential of the body of a patient. When I placed a hand on that body and started *"intentioning"* to do something, he would read the meter again. He found that I was indeed changing the reading. Then we began to work with an opaque screen between us so he couldn't see what I was doing and I couldn't read the meters. We had four meters attached to the patient, one measuring respiratory activity, a cardiograph monitor, and one electrical potential measuring circuit on each leg.

When I put my hand on somebody and then "intended to," let's say, cause a bone in the skull to move in a certain direction or allow the craniosacral rhythm to stop at a still point, the electrical potential of the patient's body would change. Before I started, the electrical potential of the legs would be bouncing up and down, but when I found exactly the right spot and felt the cranial rhythm stop—the stopping of the craniosacral rhythm was what I had come to call the "significance detector"—there would be about a five millivolt drop in the electrical potential as measured on the legs, and it would stay there until I would feel the craniosacral rhythm start again. I had learned to take this cessation of the craniosacral rhythm as a signal that I had found a good position. When it started up again, I knew that I had held the position long enough. At that point, the electrical potential would begin to climb. It would never go back as high as it was before, but it would go, say, halfway back. For instance, if initially there was a range of variation of ten millivolts up and down, then, after bottoming out, it might come back up about five millivolts and make a nice, smooth waveform. At that point, both of us knew *at the same time* that the patient was better, even though we weren't in communication because of the screen. I knew the craniosacral rhythm had started again, and he knew that electrical potential had appeared as a smooth waveform. This was the first objective verification that the craniosacral rhythm really existed, that I was indeed manipulating it, and that it had significance for the well-being of the patient.

Now we went further. We began to experiment with my direct-ing energy from one hand to another through some part of the body because I wanted something on the far side to move or release. The same change in electrical potential would occur. As long as I continued to send and direct energy, the electrical potential might go up a little and remain nice and rhythmical rather than all jagged. So now we were able to document "Direction of Energy."

In general, the phenomenon of "Direction of Energy" implies that we are all actually born with the ability to conduct energy from one hand to the other. This is like Polarity Therapy, but Polar-ity therapists usually say that one hand is always positive, the other is always negative; with Direction of Energy, it doesn't have to do with the polarity of the hands. The energy does pass in one direc-tion from one hand to another, but not because the hands are oppo-sitely charged. All you have to do is intend to move the energy. It doesn't necessarily even have to be limited to the hands. I've directed energy out of my chest into my hand and gotten positive results. Sometimes, if both my hands are busy, I'll use my forehead and direct energy through there. All I'm saying is that every human being has this therapeutic energy within them, and all they have to do is "intention" it, and it will do what needs to be done. As Dr. Karni once put it, "Most patients have self-healing abilities and merely need facilitation. You're just kicking stones out of the road for patients to heal themselves."

Now, that takes me right to a present project of ours that I'll talk about a bit more later: we're teaching kindergarten kids and first graders to use their healing energy, and they're having great success! All they have to do is put one hand on each side of a sore place on the body of their little buddy or their teacher or whomever and "think happy thoughts," and it takes the pain away.

After working with Karni, I started using Kirlian photography to confirm further what we were investigating. I began to *see* the exchange of energy, which again showed me that, indeed, I *can* project energy out into a patient. (Kirlian photography is a technique for making photographs [without a camera] of otherwise invisible patterns of energy. The radiant energy around an object is projected directly onto a photo-sensitive emulsion. Probably, the Kirlian effect is caused by electrons emitted from the object activating the photographic plate in much the same way that light does.) If you set up a "sending" hand and a "receiving" hand; that is, if you decide which hand will be sending and which hand will be receiving, you can send the energy through a traumatized or lesioned area. My rule is simply that the hand that is nearest to the lesion when placed on the skin's surface is the hand towards which I'll send the energy, because I want to pass my energy through the body and get the problem out of the body by the shortest possible route, as with Bob Little's eye socket. The surface exit point is always the one that is closest to the lesion/problem within the body.

Lessons Learned and More to Come

As far as I'm concerned, these were the major "lessons" for me up to this point during my stay in Michigan: the energy cyst concept that I developed with Karni; what the autistic kids showed me; what I learned from the woman with the hysterectomy; and the principles of Direction of Energy. But there was more to follow. Along comes a guy from the Department of Psychiatry, where our hysterectomy patient had been getting her treatment. This psychologist had been struck by the fact that his patient didn't need any more psychotherapy after her treatments with me. The psychiatrists as a group thought that this was pretty remarkable. The particular psychologist's name was Jim Noble. Jim came to me, and I started treating *him*—I forget what his complaint was—but one day he said, "You know, when you're working on me, I experience very vivid visual images. Why don't we try to dialogue with them?" Why don't we indeed!

That was the beginning of what we now call "Therapeutic Image and Dialogue." We have expanded that immeasurably. And I've been "dialoguing" with images of everything that comes along ever since!

All of these "lessons" occurred within a very short period— really no more than a year. That's why I get so suspicious that it was all a "set-up." I mean, I feel that the spirit guides were involved. It is as if they were saying, "Okay—he's ready. Now we'll hit him with the whole shebang." My job is to not reject but to keep up with what they put in front of me and just try to understand what it's about.

I got very taken up with dialoguing. At that time, my wife Dianne was very interested in it, and we talked a lot about it. Jim Noble and I explored it quite a bit with each other, and then I started letting my grad students work on me, and I started working on them. Dialoguing with images naturally developed first into a kind of hypnotic state and finally into the exploration of past-life regression.

During my biochemistry fellowship, I had taken a night course in hypnotherapy from a psychiatrist named Frank Caffin. He gave ten of us one night a week of instruction. I learned to do some hypnotherapy, and that evolved into doing regressions, back past childhood into ... well, whatever was there. The results were very, very dramatic. It was really wild. We would do the regression and start acting out scenes from previous existences. In one session,

I found that I had been a slave on a slave ship, so the students "chained" me down, and I got to fight it out with my "captors." Eventually, we realized we didn't have to literally go through all that violent physical stuff. One could image it, and it would suffice. The body didn't have to *do* it as long as it had the chance to *express* it.

At about this point, I started getting invitations to speak as a result of what I had done at Menninger, going to different places around the country and teaching courses, so I had to come up with a name for the basic process that I was teaching. That's how the term "SomatoEmotional Release" came along. I wanted to differentiate what I was doing from psychosomatic medicine. We were using the body to get to the emotion and help it release. This was something very different from saying that the mind is making the body sick. I knew that there would be a lot of confusion about it otherwise, so we coined the phrase "SomatoEmotional Release" and it just grew—it almost took on a life of its own.

Really and truly, I was in an ideal position to explore the phenomena that these "lessons" had unveiled for me because nobody at Michigan State University, nobody at all, was telling me what to do. Once in a while, the department chairman would ask me not to talk too much about some particular thing, but I got such good grant money, the majority of it coming from the National Institute of Mental Health via the State of Michigan, that I became extremely acceptable in the eyes of the department. It even got to the point where I had my own separate bank account, and the chairman at times borrowed money out of my research income to finance his visiting professors in areas that weren't involved with what I was doing.

People ask me how past-life regression and the contact with the guides changed me personally. The truth is, I don't know. I can't say. I wasn't observing what I was doing. I was completely involved with being in what was happening. I wasn't watching it "from above." What I can tell you is that I was—"obsessed" is probably too strong a word—but I was certainly taken up with it. What happened in my personal life with Dianne, however, was that eventually past-life regressions broke us apart. Here's how:

By 1980, I was into it up to my hips and it started scaring Dianne. I had encouraged her to go to the university to get her degree, and she did—a bachelor's in psychology. Then I encouraged her to enter a masters program. When she got into the masters program, they were teaching her stuff that rendered what I was doing unacceptable. That's when we started fighting. We finally split up because she wanted to go the conventional route and, clearly, I'm not very conventional.

Psychology departments aside, there actually are ways to reconcile an interest in past lives with a conventional interest in psychology, but these weren't available for Dianne, and in truth, for myself—I don't buy them! For instance, some therapists who do regressions have the view that it doesn't matter if the regressions are literally true. "Past lives" are just fantasies that can be analyzed for their relation to the patient's present life. Well, that's certainly a way to get there but, to me, these therapists are really just covering their rear-ends! I'm a little more literal. Let's say that I won't bend that far in order to please society or conform to scientific consensus. And by the way, it isn't that we don't have a test for when a regression is real. We have the craniosacral rhythm to help us. When something is true, the rhythm will come to a quick stop. It's the same significance detector that helps us when we do our version of "position and hold." The significance detector will tell us when anything is really significant. It's true, of course, that you can make up a story that might be very significant but, by and large, escape fantasies will be weeded out.

Actually, I think Valerie Hunt has come up with the best idea for understanding regressions. She calls these other lives *"lifehoods,"* whether they come from one's own past existences or from somewhere else. Valerie Hunt is a wonderful Professor Emeritus from UCLA. She's become a good friend, and we've treated each other. Valerie says that instead of thinking of these phenomena as one's own past lives, one can think that there's a whole cosmos full of lifehoods—complete individual life stories, as it were. Something, some power, decides that if I were to experience a certain lifehood right now, it would teach me a lesson that I need. It wouldn't necessarily have to be my own lifehood—it could be anybody's that was appropriate. That's the way Valerie sees it, and I accept that; I think that that's probably true. I think that we've got trillions of lifehoods floating around. In our work called *"Brain Speaks,"* I teach that a special organ in the brain called the centrum decides which lifehood you need or which one you can accept at any given time. You can buy that or not. I don't care.

Brain Speaks

Brain Speaks is a course that I am teaching right now. The students dialogue with various areas of the brain. When I was working with autistic children, I started to realize that frequently the kids' mothers had been listening to Bruno Bettelheim and blaming themselves for their children's autism. A nun who, at the time, had been working with us as a student suggested that we write a little booklet for these parents so that they would understand the physical basis of their children's problem and stop blaming themselves. Together, we did it. Later, after moving to Florida, I made an instructional video to broaden the information in the booklet and make it more comprehensible.

The video was pretty good, but one day as I watched it, I thought, damn, this is so complicated—I really ought to write a booklet to accompany the video. That booklet eventually turned into my book, *A Brain Is Born*. It's about three-hundred pages long. I cover brain formation from the fertilization of the egg all the way into early adulthood; I also show the ways that something can go wrong and cause paralysis or cerebral palsy or whatever. (I'm getting a little ahead of myself—because this has more to do with what I am doing now in Florida than with what happened in Michigan—but it is a natural part of the story, so I want to keep writing about it here.)

In compiling that book, I realized that if I read five authorities on the part of the brain called the amygdala, say, I'd get at least three different opinions about its functions. Well, by this time, I'd been dialoging with livers and hearts and all kinds of muscles and pains and tumors, but I had never tried to dialogue with brain parts. Something clicked and I just said to myself, "Hey look. If you can talk to a liver, why can't you talk to an amygdala or a cerebellum?" I started thinking about that and then one morning, I woke up and I said to myself, "Okay, let's try it."

It so happened that, at the time, I was conducting an Intensive Program and, as I keep telling everybody, the guides just set it up for me! There was a Jamaican lady as a patient in the program who had had a head injury and had lost her short-term memory. She could start walking to the door of the room and, by the time she got there, she'd have forgotten where she was going. Well, I thought, short-term memory probably comes from the hippocampus. When it was my turn to treat this person—she'd been worked on inten-sively for a couple of days so she was nice and mellowed out for me—I just put my hands on her head and said, "Do you mind if I talk to your brain?"

She said, "No."

I said, "Will you just repeat whatever words come through with-out censoring or editing anything? Just let your brain speak through your voice, please."

"Sure."

I said, "Okay, brain, is there a part of you that's ailing?"

"Oh yes, yes, yes—*I* am!"

I said, "Well, who are you? Are you Hippocampus?"

"Yes, I am."

I said, "Well, what's wrong with you, are you damaged?"

"No, I'm not damaged, I'm just totally confused!"

I said, "What happened?"

"Well, there was a big blow somewhere, there was a big smash, and my energies are running in all kinds of directions now."

So I just put one of my hands on the front, and one on the back, of her head, and I started "intentioning" smooth energy going through, sort of like combing it out, if you will. The voice of the hippocampus said, "Okay, that's good, that's wonderful. Do what you're doing. That's starting to straighten things out."

I worked on her for about twenty-five minutes in this way, and her memory came back. She got up off the table and she was nor-mal. That was my first experience with speaking directly to the brain and some of its parts.

Not long after that, I decided I would start a class called *"Brain Speaks."* In *Brain Speaks,* we interview all kinds of brain parts and, if the authorities can't agree regarding what the function of one of them is, I can talk to the part directly and it can tell me what it does. I don't need the authorities. When you want to know something, why not go to the source?

Now, in that class, one of the parts I have them talk to is the centrum, which I mentioned before. The centrum is a singular, little pyramidal piece that sits up on top of the two hippocampi. There is one hippocampus on each side of the brain. The centrum is just a tiny pyramid, maybe an inch high, but it sends up something like a virtual antenna that elevates through the top of the cranium. The centrum itself is a physical part of the brain, but the antenna is pure energy that shoots up about eight inches and pulls in all kinds of stuff—basically energy loaded with information. The antenna brings it down into the centrum, and the centrum sorts it out and sends it to places in the brain and body where it can be interpreted.* Some of that information consists of the lifehoods that Valerie Hunt talks about. Once they are drawn in, they are deposited for storage in the medulla and are carried in little bi-layered, lipid capsules. When the cerebellum or centrum decides it's time for someone to receive a "lesson," the appropriate lifehood will be discharged, and the person may experience it as a SomatoEmotional Release, as a past-life experience, or whatever.

The centrum is a material part of the brain, as I noted. It isn't considered very significant by conventional medicine. It's given about one paragraph in *Gray's Anatomy*. It's been almost totally disregarded, as the pineal body was until recent years. Actually, the pineal body is apparently subservient to the centrum.

---

*I've recently written a book called *Cell Talk* that includes what we've discovered from dialoguing with brains. I've done about nine *Brain Speaks* workshops up to the present.

Cellular Consciousness and Talking to Cells

Having talked to various organs and physiological systems, I finally got down to talking directly to cells. I began doing that initially in the context of working with the immune system. I found out that I could talk to cells in the immune system and get them to attack specific things like tumors and infections. I finally decided I would write a textbook on this and, as I was doing so, I realized that I had to deal with the question of *cellular consciousness* and even *molecular consciousness*. Regarding the latter, as far as I'm concerned, protein molecules are extremely intelligent. They present an aggregate consciousness that contributes to the total cell's consciousness. The tissues to which the cells contribute will have the aggregate consciousness of its cells, and so on, up the line. By getting all the way down into dialoguing with proteins, we're able to correct cellular dysfunctions; we're able to awaken stem cells—and I know all the garbage going down about stem cells—but I've been able to put my finger on bone marrow and talk to stem cells and then get them over to repair a liver, for example, just by asking them to do it. There's no need to move in external stem cells. You just need to dialogue with your own ones and get it done.

In *Cell Talk*, I want people, first of all, to grasp my consciousness concept. Then I get pretty scientific, with a section on cell biology. Next, I go into stem cells, and from there to *Brain Speaks*, then to immune cells and how to deal with the whole immune system on a dialogical basis. Finally, I speak of auto-immune disease, cancer, and apoptosis (cellular suicide). At the end, I tie it all together and provide the therapist with a whole variety of approaches to dialoguing.

I have several really extraordinary cases that I'm working on right now that involve these questions, but I'll save them for later.

————

Past Life Regression

Now let's return to the past-life material. Sometimes, the regression takes one back to a violent death where the energy of that event actually seems to carry over into the present life and stops there, almost as in an energy cyst.

I began to understand that your problem today might be something you brought with you from a past life (or lifehood). What I saw—and this is something that I really already knew—was that when I take you back into a past life (when, for example, somebody stabbed you in the back or a cannonball hit you in the belly, or whatever it might have been), we can take you to the moment just prior to that event and relive the experience. As you're dying, we have your spirit come forward and, instead of letting it depart immediately, we cleanse it of all of its injury and then have it enter into its new body. I've played that game many times. All of our therapists have been taught how to do this, and I think that most of them use this approach as it seems indicated. It's probably the next really big thing—the comprehension that energy is capable of moving from lifetime to lifetime and creating similar situations.

In both energy-cyst work and cellular memory, the central radical discovery is that information from past experience is retained by the physical body. In other words, energy itself passes through what seems to be a nonphysical dimension; but actually, it's not nonphysical at all. The way I see it, energy is just very thin matter. Matter is very dense energy. Matter and energy are on a continuum. Particles of energy, if you want to speak of particles, or even

————

waves, are continually becoming matter, and matter is continually becoming energy. Both energy and matter carry information with them, so you've constantly got information being exchanged between very fine energy and very dense matter, back and forth, back and forth, back and forth. Energy moves from lifetime to lifetime, and information does too, and it is possible to learn from that information by as simple a process as just talking with it! (I am not saying, of course, that cells and molecules speak English. I am saying that words are energy too, other forms of the same thing. That's why cells respond. They respond to the true energetic component of our talk with a similar-frequency energetic component of their own.)

An important principle that I've evolved is that, therapeutically, I don't want to take your involvement with your past life away from you until we find out whether it does in fact harbor a lesson to be learned. Maybe that cannonball that you're bringing with you from your previous death is there for a reason. Or maybe it's there because your life was interrupted and you weren't ready to end it. Or maybe you've now learned the lesson connected to it but don't know how to get rid of the cannonball! All of those possibilities have to be explored. That's generally true about symptoms wherever they come from: they have to be released at the right time—only when their role in your life is understood.

Very, Very Quiet (once again . . .)

Way back at the beginning of my years at Michigan State, I was practicing and exploring without really understanding what was going on, as I have confessed before; but this willingness to explore new territory without even a hypothesis as to what was happening has continued to be my trademark approach. I am simply willing to go wherever the phenomena take me. I have always been a pretty good observer, and I just go along with what I observe.

For the most part, I never wrote up what was happening while I was doing it. Writing and reporting came later. There's some of that in the "SomatoEmotional Release" book—several case studies. But that was later. At the time it was going on, I didn't attempt to bring any attention to it. I didn't want to. Once again, this reticence came from what my mother taught me. In Michigan, I knew that what I was doing was, truth be told, way out of the realm of "biomechanics." Even though I very quickly won the approval of the dean, I also knew that I did not at all have the approval of the psychiatry department, but I didn't want that fact to interfere with my work. My main concern was to maintain my freedom. And things were quite clear. There was an understanding between the dean, the department chairman, and myself, that as long as I didn't make waves, I could do any damn thing I wanted. I kept that agreement. I kept quiet about the more "far out" aspects of my work. I didn't tell people not to talk about it, but I myself didn't make a fuss. I tried to make the students believe that it was just run-of-the-mill stuff. I was researching acupuncture and acupuncture points and meridians and doing Kirlian photography, and all of this fell under the general rubric of biophysics and biomechanics. But this was just a smokescreen. I think I did pretty well with it. Nobody really knew how far out I was.

Leaving Academia

The only point where I really took a stand finally resulted in my leaving Michigan State, but it had nothing to do with anything "far out" at all. A report from the Director of Special Education for the county indicated that one in twenty kids in the State of Michigan had a learning disability or a brain dysfunction. It was clear to me that school kids with learning disabilities could be helped by craniosacral examination and treatment at least fifty percent of the time. I felt we needed to supply treatment, but all I got was official resistance. I made the case that you don't know on which day of a kid's life the fact that he can't read will create a scar on his psyche that's going to be hell to pay. I said I wanted to be able to provide treatment as soon as a learning disability was diagnosed—today or tomorrow but not the day after. I proposed to set up a night class for non-osteopaths and nonmedical students to teach nurses and PT's to do basic craniosacral work. The dean and the curriculum committee okayed the class; however, the American Osteopathic Association was more than a little bit upset about this. "This is an osteopathic college and you're an osteopath and you're going to be giving away 'trade secrets'" was their informal message.

I was shocked, but I kept my cool. I said, "Okay, but I still think the kids are more important than territoriality." The American Osteopathic Association backed off and the University approved. They let me do a night class for people at a post-graduate level—people who already had a graduate degree that made them a therapist of some kind or other. This included special-ed teachers. That first class had about thirty-five people in it, and I found out that, in a quarter, I could teach them to do a craniosacral system evaluation. That was my original intent: to evaluate the kids and see which ones could benefit.

Well, that went fine. Now everybody was interested, so I talked the Provost's office into letting me have another quarter to teach them some simple techniques to take care of the most obvious kinds of problems. And that worked fine. Now they gave me a clinic. I had them bring the kids into the clinic and some of the people I'd trained worked with them. Pretty soon a lot of non-licensed people were making evaluations and doing basic treatment. Then, one day, I got the word from the American Osteopathic Association to the effect that I shouldn't be doing this; I shouldn't be teaching non-osteopaths to do osteopathic treatment. I said, "This is hardly osteopathic treatment. This is something that was designed right here in this department and just because I'm an osteopath doesn't make everything I do osteopathic. Christ! I screw in light bulbs. Is that osteopathic work now?" I kind of got feisty with them.

It never came to me officially, but they managed to let me know that if I proceeded with this, they would take away my membership in the American Osteopathic Association and, of course, that would be the end of my professorship. When push came to shove, I informed them that I'd be happy to go to court on that one; I'd be happy to let the public know that the American Osteopathic Association would withhold potential help from school kids because they wanted to keep their territory safe. They backed down and never gave me any more trouble.

Unfortunately, another obstacle developed that I couldn't deal with so easily: the tax base in Michigan deteriorated because of the plight of the automobile industry in the area. Funding was cut, and the program was discontinued. That's when I left. Everyone looked at me as though I had lost my mind. I was a full professor with tenure. What else could I want?

The Birth
of the Upledger Institute

When I left my post at Michigan State, I came to Palm Beach and eventually set up the Upledger Institute. That was the next phase in my dialogue with the universe. The Institute was founded pretty far along a chain of events that began with my connecting with Elmer Green at Menninger. Here's how it unfolded and led me to Palm Beach.

About a year before the end of my time at Michigan State University, Elmer had me teaching at Menninger. I was giving a class in hands-on Craniosacral Therapy (what would be a CST One and Two combined at the Institute today). One day, Elmer took me aside and, pointing to one of the students in the class, asked, "What do you think of that guy over there?"

I said, "Well, he's got good hands, but he doesn't know a thing about anatomy."

"That's because he's a minister. His name is Hal Rosenkrantz. Why don't you see if you can help him make better use of those good hands?"

I thought about it a little, and then I sat down with a note pad and wrote out for him a ten-step protocol. He could perform this protocol on friends, etc., without any risk of harm, and his hands would be in training by doing it. (It's actually the protocol that we still teach our CST students.)

A month later, I got a call from him. He was all in a panic. He said, "I've been doing your ten steps on my friend. He's got a diagnosis of spinal S-T-E-N-O-S-I-S." (Stenosis is a narrowing of a duct or a canal.) His arms were all numb."

"Spinal stenosis?"

"Yeah."

I said, "Nothing in the protocol is going to hurt that."

He said, "No, that's not it. He's getting better, and now they're not going to do the surgery. What the hell can I do?"

I said, "Praise God, brother. You've got success and you're in a panic about it!"

He kept on following the protocol and getting good results with this patient and others. It turned out that Hal ran a church down here in Palm Beach. It was the local branch of an organization called "Unity Church."

Unity Church is an international thing. To be a member of a Unity congregation, you can have any kind of religious preference you want, as long as you have some sort of faith; so there are people of the Jewish persuasion, people of the Catholic persuasion, and so forth. Unity fills the void for anybody who has gotten a little sick of the rigors of a really tight religious organization.

The Palm Beach congregation had a very nice, large church building and about four thousand members. In fact, Hal had come to the Menninger class by invitation of Elmer Green, as Elmer had helped Hal set up a biofeedback clinic at his Unity Church in West Palm Beach. Now there was the possibility of a Cranio-Sacral Therapy clinic at the same church.

Once Hal had gained confidence in the protocol I gave him, he said to me, "How would you like to come down and do a Sunday morning sermon at my church?"

I said, "Jesus, I haven't been to church in fifteen years."

He said, "I'm sorry. Just come down and give them a lecture. The topic of the lecture could be 'Taking Responsibility For Your Own Health'." I couldn't resist that.

He said, "We'll split whatever comes in the collection box. Okay?"

"Whatever."

So I went down to West Palm Beach and gave them that lecture. Then I did an afternoon workshop and showed them a little bit about basic craniosacral work. It was a precursor to our current ShareCare workshop. ShareCare really began by teaching techniques to the parents of kids we were treating, as I told you before—brain dysfunction kids. But then we realized that almost anybody, not just parents of sick kids, could benefit from learning how to use their hands in a therapeutic way or a helping way. So ShareCare was started for the laity of the church or anybody else who wanted to get into it. ShareCare is a one-day program. What we do is show all of the attendees the potential for healing that they have in their own hands, so they can help each other. We also give them an introduction to the imagery within their own body, so if they're starting to have a problem, they can talk to their organs. Very often the body will tell them what they need to do to correct the problem. That's what ShareCare is. It's a program of sharing care with each other.

When I got down to Florida, we gave ShareCare its name and expanded its application. For instance, often we'd get couples who had been married twenty, thirty years and didn't get along very well. We taught them how to treat each other, and that sort of re-cemented their marriage.

Anyway, I did the workshop at Unity and took in about $1,500.

At that time, I had four kids and my wife was in school, so I thought that was pretty good money. I came down three times after that first one, and on each occasion I was well received. Finally, Hal said, "Do you have a student you can send down here? The church is interested in starting a holistic-health clinic. Do you have a student that could do what you do and develop a clinic?" This request came at a time when I was looking to leave Michigan State. I said, "Why do you want a student when you can get the old man himself?" And that's how I came back down to Florida.

We set up the health clinic in West Palm Beach. I made one stipulation: I insisted that the Church agree that, as soon as we could afford it, we would create a free, store-front clinic to teach biofeedback in a black neighborhood. I remembered our free clinic over in Clearwater and St. Petersburg from years before, and I missed that kind of contact with the community.

Now, many black males tend to have high blood pressure—it's probably one of the biggest health problems they have. If they take blood pressure medicine, they're liable to become impotent. That's a big thing, so I thought we could get them to come to the clinic with the idea that they could lower their blood pressure with biofeedback without having to take medication that could mess up their sex life! I also thought that, at the same time we were doing the biofeedback, we could help to dissipate some of the anger they're carrying and perhaps we could calm things down in the neighborhood.

We were going to use a method that Patricia Norris developed at Leavenworth Prison that doesn't require expensive equipment. All you do is pick up a little outdoor weather thermometer at the hardware store, and you scotch-tape it onto the patient's finger. Then you have them imagine that they're very relaxed and lying on the beach and the sun is shining. What they need to do is notice how the temperature of their finger goes up as they imagine this. That lets them know that they are controlling their blood pressure because basically the temperature in the finger can't go up unless the blood supply increases. In other words, the arteries dilate. When the arteries dilate, the blood pressure goes down. The arteries dilate not only in your finger—that just happens to be where you are measuring it—but throughout your body. For people with a circulation problem due to high blood pressure, that's a very good idea. For normal people, it's also a very good idea—just to exercise the ability to do it.

It's the thought of the warmth that makes it work, not particularly the relaxation. If you had them imagine that they are ice skating and really enjoying it, or skiing, or any other activity where they get cool, the finger will cool down. The relaxation is important in order to get the concept going through their head. They've got to let go of their day-to-day thoughts to make it work.

That was my idea: to use this method as a lure to get black folks to come to the clinic. Hal agreed with it, and the Board of Directors of Unity *claimed* that they agreed with it, too. As things developed, it turned out that they had other things on their minds than helping black folks. For the moment, anyway, they agreed that we would go ahead with the free-clinic plan as soon as we made enough money in the regular clinic. The only problem was, we didn't put a figure on what "making enough money" would be. The first year I was in the clinic, we grossed roughly $125,000. The second year, I got up to $220,000–225,000. That still wasn't enough. The third year, I brought in about $325,000 for them and that still wasn't enough, so I told them to JAM IT WHERE THE SUN DON'T SHINE. We got into a row about it. Hal finally said, "John, the real reason we don't want to do it is because these people come to earth and they have a karmic debt to pay and that's why they're out there like that. You'd just be interfering with the payment of their karmic debt."

Another thing that happened that really irked me had to do with a girl who came to the clinic from Miami. She had been in a car wreck with an illegal alien so there was no insurance coverage. She had gone right through the windshield. Her arms and legs were completely nonfunctional. Her head had been crushed in. She had been a young ballet dancer, but now she could just barely move her eyelids or show a little bit of a smile. Her mom and dad brought her to see me because their insurance coverage had run out. The insurance company said, "You're plateaued now, so we don't pay for anything else." In other words, she'd reached her maximum recovery, and everything from then on had to be covered by mom and dad. Well, the fee at the church clinic there was a hundred dollars per visit with me. The visits with me were forty-five minutes to an hour long. The parents just felt like she was smiling more after the sessions and that I got rid of some of her pain. They said they'd like to come once a week but that they couldn't afford it. I asked the church if they'd let her come for nothing. *Pro bono.* They said *they* couldn't afford that. That seemed kind of strange because I thought that church people were supposed to *help* the needy. We discussed it for a while, and then I asked if I might put a front-page notice in the church bulletin. I said I'd give a before-and-after picture of her and say that we would accept donations to help with her treatments. They said that would be okay, so I did it. I wrote a nice article for them, and four thousand bulletins went out. We wound up collecting a grand total of eighty-five dollars. Eighty-five dollars! Can you imagine? That really bothered me.

I went back to the minister and asked him if he wouldn't please give the word in church and maybe this would help—perhaps we could start a fund to help poor people. Then he let the cat out of the bag, and I found out what all that "karma" crap was hiding. He said, "Well, John, every dollar that goes into a fund like that will be a dollar that the church doesn't receive. We can't have that." And this church catered to millionaires! But they have their charities on a schedule, and it has to be the right one and it has to be a high-prestige item. So I quit the clinic. Right then and there. That's when we started our own place. It was in the latter part of 1985.

Unfortunately, we still haven't been able create a free clinic. But we did set up our own foundation, and part of what we do is provide funding for people who can't afford to come to our Clinic.

Just around this time, when we were all struggling to start this new institute, a real tragedy hit my family. Mark was my third child and my second oldest boy, a real sweet guy.

I got a call on a Friday, about eleven at night, from my son Mike down in Key West, "Dad, Mark got hit by a car and it's pretty serious."

I said, "What happened?

Mike said, "He died."

Mark was about as loving a kid as you could find. He had been practicing at one time to be a rock star. He played lead guitar and he had promised, "If by age twenty five I haven't hit the big time, I'm going to stop doing it and find something else."

He was twenty-seven at this time, and he had been working for the Pinellas County Retarded Citizens Center, teaching woodworking and guitar to retarded citizens. Yes, a vehicle hit Mark, but it wasn't the fault of the lady driving it. She happened to be coming from the police station because she worked there as a switchboard person. Mike and Mark were riding bicycles, Mark in front and Mike behind him. Mark must have hit a stone or some loose gravel because he just veered out in front of her. Mike described how, as he went to hold him, Mark was bleeding and coughing a lot and kind of choking. Mike said, "Cough, and it will get the blood out of your windpipe." He coughed and then he was dead. He would have died anyway.

I was scheduled to teach a four-day class on SomatoEmotional release the following Thursday. Everybody around the Institute was saying, essentially, "Your son just got killed, so maybe you want to cancel the class."

I said, "No, what am I supposed to do, stay home and cry? I'm going to go teach." What I told the class was, "You all know about my son Mark getting killed, and I may choke up periodically. Just put up with it, and I'll give you the class. By the way, I'd like to take a moment and, whoever wants to, just send energy so that Mark can be on his way to do whatever he's supposed to do. Don't let his mother's negative energy hold him back." I don't know how many people did it. There were forty odd in the class, and I could feel their energy all around me. Then we went on with the lesson.

About two weeks later, at exactly 4:00 a.m. I sat bolt upright in bed. The clock says the hour, and here is Mark standing right in front of me with his leather jacket on and he's got his lip curled up. He looks like the guy who's trying to be the rock star again. He says, "Dad, I want to thank you for getting all those people to give energy to me so I could get away. You were right; mom was holding me back; she wasn't going to let me go onto what I need to do. And there's another thing I want to tell you: I came down here to teach you. That was my job. You aren't here to teach me. Now you've got it all, so it's all right for me to go. The one thing you're still a little bit stuck on is 'Forget the details—they don't matter. Go for the generalities, the concepts; don't worry about the data.'" Then he just disappeared.

About a week later, we were in a hotel, and my wife, Dianne, said there was a knock on the door. She opened it, and there stood Mark, just big as life. She saw him as clearly as I did. She said, "Mark?"

He said, "Yes. I just wanted to come and say goodbye."

He turned around and walked down the hall and got smaller, and smaller and just disappeared.

I totally believe this stuff. Sure, we both could have hallucinated it, but he was my son.

Even this tragedy didn't get in the way of us continuing the growth of the Institute that year. The Upledger Institute was founded primarily to teach CranioSacral Therapy and to see patients. Even during the early years at Michigan State, I wanted to teach the techniques to any professional person who wanted to use it. I considered CranioSacral Therapy to be an adjunctive therapy at that time. If it doesn't do anything else, it increases sensitivity. If you're a dentist and you practice it, you're going to have more awareness of what you're doing to your patient. Then, for instance, you might be able to help them through the *temporo-mandibular-joint* (TMJ) problems that often arise during dental treatment. There are so many ways you can use it. I thought it would be valuable to pediatricians, obstetricians, psychiatrists—in fact, anybody in healthcare practice. But as soon as I started making it generally available, I began to run into the resistance from the osteopathic medical profession that I've described previously.

While I was working for Unity Church, I had occasion to treat a certain woman for a serious scoliosis—a bad back. We'll call her "Mrs. Sandra Trumbull," and we'll call her husband, "Mark Trumbull." Mark had his own business-consulting firm. His father had been a vice-president for a Detroit automobile manufacturer. When his father died, he left Mark with a big trust fund.

Now, at the church, I was teaching four craniosacral classes per year, but Mark saw what I did for his wife Sandra's scoliosis and said, "You should get this out to the world."

I replied, "I'm doing it. I'm doing four classes a year with forty to fifty people in each one. That's one-hundred-and-fifty to two-hundred people a year."

Mark said, "Do you have any idea of how many therapists would be interested in it?"

"No. How many?"

"I'm not sure, but I am sure it's a lot more than two hundred. I would like to run a demographic study and see how many people potentially would like to learn it."

"Okay, do it."

He came back with a number something like 300,000. Well, who was I to challenge this guy? He had his own business-consulting firm! I really didn't care much about the actual numbers, but I was already becoming disheartened with the church, and now Mark Trumbull comes along and says that there are 300,000 people who potentially want to learn CranioSacral Therapy. The idea naturally suggested itself to him that we should start our own organization and get to work teaching them!

I told Mark I needed to think about it. This was around the time that I found out what was actually behind Unity's stalling about the free clinic. I came back to Mark and said, "Let's do it! How do we begin?"

He said, "If you can get me ten teachers by the end of this year, we'll have a going concern."

So I got him the ten teachers. We held a couple of tutorials. I invited people from the classes I had taught back at Michigan State as well as people from the church-sponsored classes. I selected the teachers from the tutorials, and The Upledger Institute was launched.

There were serious problems at the beginning, though they had nothing to do with CranioSacral Therapy or even with difficulties from the profession. It turned out that Mark, who was a "poor little rich kid" essentially, had no idea of how to run a business—he was used to having unlimited funds. He got us deeply in debt almost from the start, though I must say that he stood up for most of it. He made sure that he was co-signing the loans we took out, so when push came to shove, we were okay.

Mark caused more problems than the debt, however. He neglected to pay the payroll taxes for our first year! We had to get Bill Sable, who had done my accounting up in Michigan, to come down and rescue us from the tax people.

Apart from financial woes, the positive energy and creative excitement at the institute were infectious! Once Bill had bailed us out, he said, "I don't know why, but I want to stay here and work with you." And so he did.

My son, John Matthew, who was still a student up at Michigan State at the time, called one day and said, "Dad, I want to come and work for you."

I said, "You'll have to talk to Mark. He does the hiring."

"Okay, I'll come down."

It just so happened that during the two weeks that he was down here to arrange things with Mark, I was supposed to give a class in Palm Beach at the Brazilian Court Hotel. The class was set up for thirty people, but only twenty-two showed up, even though there had been thirty people on the waiting list. None of them had been notified! John Matthew immediately set to work figuring out what had happened. He discovered an error in our computer tactics. It became clear at once that he would be able to troubleshoot and manage this aspect of the business very nicely. Originally, he had been a math and physics student at Michigan State University, but he didn't like being in a lab all the time, so he wasn't really headed to becoming a scientist. He did have a good head for systems, however. Working for me allowed him to use his skills and abilities and at the same time be with people as much as he wanted. It was ideal for him.

After a little while, I decided to let Mark go. Actually, I didn't know if legally I could do that. We had started the business together. But he had been doing some stuff that was just unbelievable. At one point, he stopped paying the teachers. They were calling me and telling me that Mark had been lying about having checks in the mail and so forth. It got so that none of the teachers trusted him.

The last straw was what I call "The Paris Fiasco." Mark wanted to do a workshop in Paris like the one presently called "Beyond the Dura." I said, "Mark, our people don't have the money to go to Paris. You can't just assume the attendance will be high enough to cover our expenses. We're working with low-to-middle-class folks here. They're therapists. We can't do that."

Well, he didn't listen. He went ahead and put a $10,000 deposit on the hotel for the workshop. And, of course, the class didn't happen. Eight people registered. He cancelled the hotel booking, and I suddenly found out that we were out the $10,000 deposit. It was not refundable. So I fired him. I went in and said, "Mark, it doesn't look like you can do anything right, so pack up your stuff and get out of here." In fact, I was bluffing. I had no idea whether I could kick him out or not. But he was intimidated properly, and so he left. Then I said, "John Matthew, can you take this over?"

He said, "I don't know."

So I said, "We'll try it. I'm sure you can do better than the guy I just got rid of."

John Matthew worked out fantastically. Since he took over, for instance, we've founded numerous international branches of the Institute, something that could have happened earlier but was just stalled with Mark. It occurred pretty naturally, not because I had any particular ambition in this regard. We set up a Dutch branch because I was teaching in Hawaii, and five or six people from Holland were there. We got to talking and they said, "We'd like to have an institute in Europe." Mark was still with me then. Mark negotiated with these folks for a year and couldn't come to an agreement. When Mark left, John Mathew said, "One of the things I want to do is settle this thing in Europe. Can I go to Holland?"

I said, "Sure."

Two days later, I got a call from the Dutch guys. "Your son is great. We've got it all worked out."

That's how it started. From the Dutch, to the Germans, to the Italians. Then the Japanese came to us. John Matthew managed to negotiate successfully with all of the people.

As things progressed with the Institute, it became clear to me that all the therapists who were coming to us were not just looking for another battery of techniques. They were searching for the spiritual aspect of their own work. Given that CranioSacral Therapy does have a spiritual dimension, it was like a snowball that grew and is still growing quite on its own. It works like this. Somebody comes back to the hospital where they work after having had a CranioSacral Therapy class or two, and they start treating patients, and after a while their peers are saying, "WOW! You're so different. And your patients are doing so well. What did you do?" Then they want to do it, too. CranioSacral Therapy just kind of propagates itself simply because it's compassionate, it's essentially without risk, and it fosters a wonderful feeling of spirituality, the lack of which I think frustrates a great percentage of the human race at this point. I had some spiritual experiences to get me ready for it—Harriet Jerome came before Delbert, if you remember—but doing CST all these years, I have become deeply, deeply, deeply spiritual and very trusting of my own spiritual knowingness, if you will. I think the work has done that for me. But it isn't the work as a method or a technique; it's what the work gets you into doing. And that is trusting a sense that help comes from above, or however you want to put it personally. Help comes to you spiritually when you need to do healing work.

As I look back on my life, I can see that whenever I have needed that kind of help, it's been there. I am so in tune with it now that I have absolutely no concern about things going wrong. I know that if I put in the effort, my effort will be rewarded, provided it is in the right direction. The only concern I have is to be sure that the direction I'm heading in is in keeping with what is expected of me in terms of what is good for all of us. As long as I'm doing that, and as long as I'm not letting my ego or my selfishness interfere, then I know that things will work out, even when I am faced with what seems like failure. For instance, look at our project for Vietnam vets. I'll go into more detail about this later. In any case, I had wanted to do something with them as long ago as the early 1990s. Nothing happened when I first proposed it, except in little dribs and drabs. And I think that if we had been successful at first in getting support, we probably wouldn't have been able to do it right. We needed time for two reasons. First, we had to prove to the spiritual guides that we were sincere by just keeping on trying to make it happen. Second, because we didn't have the opportunity to do the program, we deepened our own knowledge and abilities, so that we were quite well-prepared to do it by the time it actually became possible.

I think the secret to it all is keeping one's ego out of the way.

Then being open just comes naturally. I don't remember a time where I really thought that I was good enough, smart enough, or strong enough to start telling people that I'm better than they are. I don't recall that ever. Setting my ego aside is not an effort that I make. Quite the opposite: I think it takes one hell of an effort for me to put my ego in the way. Jesus! I'm this little itty-bitty grain of sand on this whole big beach.

When people come to me with big egos, I just figure that they should go back out in the world and get their starch knocked out of them—then they can come back again. I don't particularly want to be the one who does that job for them because, in order to bang their egos around, I'd have to consider myself able to judge them. What I do is just disqualify myself. Sometimes, of course, I can tolerate them because I see something underneath their egos that might be worth working with.

Actually, now that I have said all this, I suddenly realize that I have had a couple of lessons in ego. Yes indeed—it just pops back into my mind. Way back when I started practicing in Clearwater, I worked for two years covering the hospital emergency room, twenty-four hours on, twenty-four hours off. It turned out that I was pretty good at saving lives under those conditions, and I started thinking, "Boy, I'm really a hotshot." Then one day I just happened to be around the hospital on a Saturday afternoon when a chiropractor called (you know, osteopaths weren't even supposed to talk to chiropractors in those days—and now I'm married to one!). He said, "I have a patient in serious trouble. I've been treating him daily for three weeks and he's getting worse. Is there somebody I can talk to? I need to send him to the emergency room."

I asked, "Well, what's going on?"

He said, "He's got foam coming out of his mouth."

I said, "Is it blood-tinged?"

"Yes. It's got blood in it."

I said, "You're in real trouble, buddy. You'd better send him over here right away and hope he lives till he gets here." The patient's name was Bill. He was in his mid-sixties. He was obviously in heart failure. I worked with him for about four hours in the emergency room and pulled him through. I had a nurse with me named Murphy who just thrived on this sort of thing. We were being so dramatic and heroic and all that kind of petty bullshit. And here is this guy—he makes it! But then I get called in the middle of the night. I had to come back and do a supra-pubic catheterization on him because he couldn't get rid of his urine. So I did that. Next day the chief of medicine says to me, "John, you did a bang-up job. This guy's alive because of your brilliant work."

And I believed him. But a week or so after I discharged him from the hospital, his wife brought him to see me in my office. He was doing okay from a physiological perspective—I mean his vital signs were okay—but his wife wanted to know when he was going to be able to play pinochle with her and their friends again.

I asked, "Well, can't he?"

"No, he can't remember the cards. He doesn't know anything." Apparently he had lost much of his brain function during his heart failure. And I'm thinking, "Jeez, he's not doing well," and it's beginning to dawn on me, "Who the hell was I to save this guy and make him be alive?" Because that's just what I had done: I had made him be alive. The family eventually ran out of money. I sent Bill down to the VA hospital in St. Petersburg. He died down there after a few months. His wife wound up a penniless widow. She kept coming to see me periodically, and I realized that I had done that to her. I made her life a misery. I prolonged his death by a year, or a year and a half. It wasn't right. For all my heroics, I had done the wrong thing. That really made me think a lot.

Another comeuppance that comes to mind had to do with a drunk—let's call him Jack. Jack had cirrhosis of the liver. I liked the guy. I really wanted to help him. At about 4:00 o'clock one morning, a nurse called me from the emergency room and said, "Jack's in here and he looks really bad. We think you'd better come in and see him." Usually, under circumstances like this, I would give orders over the phone and see the patient the next day, but if the nurse said she thought I should come in, it meant things were pretty serious indeed. I lay back down in bed and said to myself, "Oh Jesus, is saving his life worth me getting out of bed?" And I knew right then that I had to disqualify myself from emergency room work because I was making the kinds of decisions that belong to God. I think maybe my ego was starting to swell at that time. I had so many people praising me for the work I was doing in general medicine, emergency-room medicine. These two experiences really cut me off at the knees.

To finish the story: I did go in. And he made it okay. But what happened was I kept thinking, "How did I get the power to make this kind of decision?" Because if I had decided to stay home and sleep and get some rest—which I really felt I needed to do—he'd have died. And that's not something I think I ought to be in a position to decide.

The truth is, there are many circumstances where a physician can be tempted to play God. I told the story earlier about how Grandma fell down and broke her hip and the surgeon that attempted to repair it did a pretty awful job. Later, as chance would have it, when he showed up at the emergency room with a heart attack while I was the only doctor on duty, I had the chance to exact "divine" vengeance. I restrained myself, however, did my duty, and saved his life.

There was one more time that I really got nailed, egotistically speaking, for playing God in a slightly different sense. It happened not long after I started working at Michigan State. Again, I was getting a lot of accolades for what I was doing. A doctor named June McRae heard me talking about using carbon-dioxide inhalation for autistic kids to enhance their respiratory activity. An elevation of carbon dioxide in your respiratory centers causes you to breathe more deeply and strongly, which means that you will take in oxygen more efficiently. I had noticed that autistic kids generally are very shallow breathers. I thought that perhaps they suffered from an oxygen deficit and that this was part of their problem. I put them on CO_2 therapy: ten percent carbon dioxide with oxygen, three times a week for about ten minutes each time. It seemed to help.

I was talking about this at one of the CME programs at Michigan. Dr. McRae came up to me and said, "You should be trying 25 to 30 percent CO_2 and you'll see that they start getting rid of their neurotic behaviors." She introduced me to the work of a psychiatrist by the name of Meduna from the University of Illinois. He had developed carbon dioxide therapy initially to replace electroshock therapy. It's not nearly as traumatic. Then he found out he could cure stuttering this way. And he took it into the prisons to reduce anger, and he started getting doctors to use it as anesthesia for obstetrics. Well, anyway, she wanted to show me how to do it. She brought her tank of thirty percent CO_2 down—she lived about a hundred miles north of Lansing—and we started playing around with patients.

What I realized in watching the patients was that with CO_2 inhalation they were exhibiting a lot of the phenomena that we are getting in SomatoEmotional Release now. This piqued my curiosity. I decided to try it on myself. I did several rounds and I went through a lot of different things with it, but then one day, after I took maybe ten breaths, I said to her, "My back feels really stiff."

She said, "That usually means that you're taking on too much responsibility."

I said, "What do you mean too much? I've got four kids in school, my wife's in school, too, and I'm making a professor's salary, which isn't very much." I also mentioned all the other duties I had taken on as well as the project at the autistic center.

She said, "You're responsible for all that?"

"Yeah."

She said, "Gosh, I thought only God handled that much stuff."

WHOOSH! My ego was starting to build and that just took it away. Next she said, "Maybe you've got a God complex."

I think since then I haven't had any ego problem. Of course, there are circumstances when I certainly will push my own point of view. I'll fight, I'll argue, I'll stand up for what I think is right, but it isn't because my ego's calling. It's because it feels like it's the truth to me. I don't want to just stand by. It's got more to do with a sense of justice than with my ego.

I often think about why my work hasn't become as well known as the work of some of the other so-called New Age practitioners. It's because they go out and really hype what they do, and I don't do that. To me that's artificial. As far as I'm concerned, I'm doing what I'm driven to do, and I don't want to make my work a monument to John Upledger. This is work that will benefit the human race and also animals, and it should stand on its own merit.

Some people say, "John, you've had eighty thousand people go through your basic training seminars and it's the best kept secret in the world." But it's not a kept secret at all. It just isn't hyped. Because hyping is artificial. And the work isn't artificial. I don't want anything artificial attached to it. The best way to destroy it is to make promises that it might not be able to keep. But if it's good work, it will prove itself, it will grow at its own rate; it will have a solid foundation.

I refuse to hard-sell it, to compromise my practice in order to waste time on TV and radio and all that crap. When a healer becomes a public figure, their practice goes down the tubes. When's the last time your famous New Age physician saw a patient? When's the last time he or she did anything in terms of what they're preaching? They become a mouthpiece. And that's not what I want to do. I don't want to become a mouthpiece. I don't want mouthpieces representing CranioSacral Therapy. And if CranioSacral Therapy stops working, I want everybody to know that, too. If it can't have a life of its own, then I'm sure as hell not going to give it a false one. I don't want to commercialize it.

Sometimes we have a problem about this within the Institute. Just recently, we hired a new PR person who doesn't quite understand these things yet. The other day she asked me if we could bring in a crew to do a little filming while I was teaching a class. I hesitated a long time and finally said, "Okay. You can bring them in for half an hour." Well, when they got here, I didn't let them do this, and I didn't let them do that. They shot some footage, but I'm sure they're going to be disappointed with it. I wouldn't let it interfere with the class. These students paid their money to come to this class, and this class has to offer them stuff of a certain quality. I'm not going to compromise that quality just to get some choice footage.

The bottom line for me has always been that I must not let institutional responsibilities interfere with my hands-on practice. CranioSacral Therapy isn't just some "subject" that we teach and study. It's real and it's alive. It changes all the time. And I have to be there working with it to find out how and what it is at the present moment!

Ten-year-old Johnny Upledger proudly wears the uniform of the Roseville, Michigan, Chamber of Commerce marching band. By the fourth grade he was playing in a local high school band.

As a teenager (far left) hanging with pals on the streets of Detroit. John continued to nurture his love of music by playing in neighborhood jazz clubs.

Ever the classic himself, John rides away in his second car, a 1932 Ford.

Classmates Fete John Upledger

JOHN UPLEDGER

Prior to his departure to begin studies at Alma College, John Upledger, selected as the outstanding student in the June '49 South Lake graduating class, was given a farewell party by 35 of his fellow graduates.

John, who was graduated from South Lake with 19 credits, received honor awards for solid geometry, international relations, sociology, journalism, football and The Beacon.

In addition he was presented with a gold pin for journalism and was awarded the Danforth Foundation "I Dare You" honor certificate for being "the outstanding boy in his graduating class."

John is the son of the John Upledgers of 22020 Elizabeth. He attended South Lake from the third through the twelfth grade.

Deemed "Outstanding Student" of South Lake High School graduating class of 1949, John enjoyed accolades for honors in geometry, international relations, sociology, football, and a special tribute for his work in journalism.

An Alpha Sigma Phi fraternity formal at Wayne University in 1952. (Wayne University would be renamed Wayne State University in 1956.)

Graduating from Wayne University in 1953 with a B.S. degree in Psychology.

John calls U.S. Coast Guard Cutter *Cartigan* home for two years.

In 1954, John (second row, far right) graduates from the U.S. Coast Guard Hospital Corpsmen School in Groton, Connecticut.

Even in the Coast Guard in 1956, John rarely let an opportunity to play the piano pass him by.

The family man graduates from the Kirksville College of Osteopathy and Surgery in 1963. With wife Beverly, daughter Leslie, and sons John Matthew (upper right) and Mark. Michael would make his appearance just a few short months later.

John Matthew, Mark, Michael, and Leslie Upledger.

Osteopath by day (far left), Dixie Doc by night.

At the speakers' table of a 1979 American Osteopathic Association meeting in Dallas, John (third from left) lets his unconventional side slip out.

Dr. John Upledger (far left) heads a multidisciplinary research team from Michigan State University to study craniosacral system issues in children at the Center for Autism in Flint, Michigan. That initial research ultimately led to his testifying at a Government Reform Committee meeting of the U.S. House of Representatives on the potential benefits of CranioSacral Therapy for autistic children.

This gathering of professional colleagues represented what would become The Upledger Institute's first satellite office established in Europe in 1990.

In the 1980s, Dr. John began educating CranioSacral Therapy practitioners through-out the world. His methods are now practiced by more than 80,000 healthcare practi-tioners in over 56 different countries.

Reflections caught in the baby grand.

Jamming with his son Mike.

Spending a moment with wife Lisa, Mardi Gras-style, at Beyond the Dura, a biennial international research conference hosted by The Upledger Foundation.

Kicking it up at a Mardi Gras-style dinner dance with
Claire Sylvia, author of *A Change of Heart*.

Tapping into the healing benefits of sea, sand, and sun.

This is what it's all about—the joy of treating children.

Congratulating Dee Ahern, auction winner of his Michigan State University lab coat. Proceeds benefited the nonprofit Upledger Foundation.

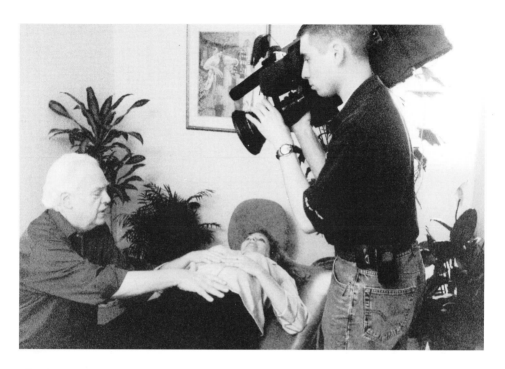

Working with the media to spread the word about the benefits of CranioSacral Therapy and SomatoEmotional Release.

Dolphins continue to influence Dr. John's research, work, and play.

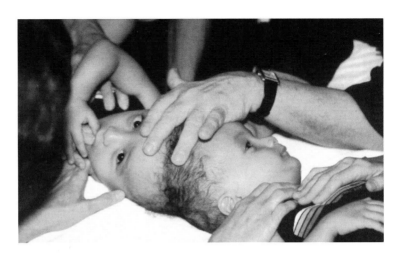

Treating conjoined Egyptian twins Ahmed and Mohamed Ibrahim to CranioSacral Therapy.

All in a day's work.

With wife Lisa at his seventieth birthday tribute in 2002.
Friends and colleagues gathered from around the world to
honor Dr. John's life and the remarkable role he has played
in healthcare.

Father and son, John Matthew, at Dr. John's birthday tribute in 2002.

INNOvators
TIME 100: THE NEXT WAVE

[Alternative Medicine]

>>> Natural forces are the healers of disease. <<< HIPPOCRATES

[CRANIOSACRAL THERAPY]

A New Kind of Pulse

JOHN UPLEDGER HAS NEVER SHIED FROM risk taking. As a Coast Guard medic in the 1950s, he once performed an appendectomy in the eye of a hurricane with the help of an onshore surgeon who guided him by radio. "To the best of my knowledge," he says, "no one's done that before or since." Today Upledger, 69, keeps on setting precedents. An osteopath by training, he is the founder of a form of nontraditional medicine called craniosacral therapy that is rapidly gaining adherents.

While assisting in a spinal operation in the 1970s, Upledger was startled to notice a strong pulse in the membranes that surrounded the patient's spinal cord. He determined that the pulse—which did not appear in the medical books—was coming from the cerebrospinal fluid that bathes the brain and spinal cord. He came to believe that anything that blocked the flow of this fluid could cause physical and mental distress. "All these membranes affect brain function," he says, "and when they're not moving properly, there can be harm."

To free up the restrictions, Upledger applies light resistance to parts of the body that seem to be stuck. These frequently include the bones of the skull, which Upledger says remain mobile

◀ JOHN UPLEDGER
His treatment addresses an astonishing range of ailments by using gentle manipulation to restore normal circulation in the cerebrospinal fluid that bathes and nourishes the brain and spinal cord

throughout life—a point many medical doctors dispute. During a craniosacral session, the therapist may gently lift a person's head to allow a skull bone to shift and the normal flow of fluid to resume.

How well does it work? Upledger says the treatments have relieved conditions ranging from headaches and chronic back pain to autism and learning disabilities in children—and there is no shortage of testimonials. He is currently working with Vietnam veterans suffering from post-traumatic stress disorder at his clinic in Palm Beach Gardens, Fla., a facility that has trained some 60,000 craniosacral practitioners. And while many M.D.s remain skeptical of the therapy, others have followed the lead of pain-control centers and physical-rehabilitation units in sending Upledger their patients.

"What we do is take away obstacles," says Upledger, "like removing stones from the road." And that, he might add, has proved far easier than cutting out an appendix in the center of a storm.
—By John Greenwald

TIME To meet more Innovators and nominate your own candidates, join us at time.com/innovators

Time magazine applauded Dr. John E. Upledger as one of America's "next wave of innovators."

Current Projects

The Upledger Institute has been in existence for twenty-one years, and I am now seventy-four years old, but it seems that I keep opening new projects and new areas of interest all the time. I think we should end this book with a look at some of our more recent adventures. Let's begin with the dolphins.

***

Dolphin Research

I started paying attention to dolphins way back when I was in the Coast Guard. It happened soon after I had my first assignment as a hospital corpsman on a ship in the Gulf of Mexico that I wrote about before—the *Cartigan.* Now, you have to understand that, being from Detroit, I was used to swimming in Lake St. Clair and the Detroit River. I'd never heard of sharks or dolphins. I didn't know what they were. Well, I guess I knew what sharks were! Anyway, we were out in what seemed like the middle of the Gulf on one of those rare occasions when the water was calm. There were fins just above the surface of the water, following the boat everywhere we went. At a certain point, the skipper got on the bullhorn and announced, "Okay, swim call."

I'm thinking, "But the water's full of sharks! He must be crazy!"

Then Buzz, the gunner's mate, went up on a twenty millimeter. I said, "Whatcha doin' up there, Buzz?"

He said, "If a shark comes, I'll shoot it."

"We're really going to be swimming out there?"

"Oh yeah," he says. "No problem."

About ten sailors jump over the side and I'm thinking, "If they can do it, I can do it." So I jump in. Nobody's got any clothes or bathing suits on. I'm swimming around but I'm really scared. All of a sudden a big, big fish comes up next to me—a big gray fish with a fin on top. "Oh, shit! A shark." Well, the fish came up and just kind of nuzzled up against me and, as soon as it did that, I wasn't afraid any more.

That was my first dolphin experience. After that, every time we'd get swim call, the dolphins would be with our boat. Every time! It didn't matter where we were, they were with us. We used to scratch their backs and play with them. And that's how I got tight with dolphins!

After I finished osteopathic medical school, I began my practice on Clearwater Beach down here in Florida, as I've told you. I had a little, eleven-foot sailfish (a sailboat without a cockpit), and the dolphins used to follow me whenever I went out on my sailfish. I began to understand the idea of communicating with them by telepathic means. They could send me a concept and I'd just have it. I spent a lot of time doing that kind of thing with them. I'd be sailing along on my little boat. I'd be out there, and there'd be a dolphin here and a dolphin there, and suddenly I'd understand that they were trying to tell me something. I remember so clearly—there were little, local things they were trying to tell me—like don't sail in a certain direction, there's a storm that way. What I got very clear about from them was that the human race will ultimately evolve into a situation where we won't need words anymore. We will just send concepts back and forth to each other.

I was out with the dolphins almost every day for a period of about a year and a half or two years. After hospital rounds in the morning, I would be in the office from about 10:00 a.m. to 12:00 noon and from 2:00 p.m. until whenever I finished in the evening. I would always have two hours at lunch time. We lived right on the water, so I'd just go home, eat a sandwich, jump on the boat and be gone for an hour.

How did I learn that they could be helpful with healing? They themselves taught me. In fact, they taught me that they could do many things and that they were wiser than humans. It became clear that they possessed some kind of spiritual knowledge.

Around the time that I was sailing out with the dolphins, I met a fellow named Timothy Wiley, who had written a book called *Dolphins, Extraterrestrials, and Angels.* Timothy was living in Sarasota at the time. One evening, I was having dinner with Timothy, and conversation got around to dolphins. He told me the following story.

"I always thought that if you needed help while swimming out in the ocean, the dolphins would help you if they could. I used to go swimming every night around 5:00 o'clock." He had a little cottage on the beach. "I decided I would swim out and pretend I was drowning and see if they would help me. I floundered around but they didn't pay any attention. So I swam back to shore and thought about it."

By the next afternoon, Timothy realized that they knew he had been faking, so this time he swam out until he was really floundering! He swam so long and so far that he could hardly move his arms. Two dolphins came up, one on each side, and offered him their dorsal fins, and then another dolphin came up from underneath and pushed him up a little bit, supporting him till he got a hold of the dorsal fin. They took him into about three feet of water and dropped him off.

Those were the seeds. The idea was planted in my mind that, at some point in time, I would explore the possibility that dolphins might be able to help sick people get better. I put it to myself exactly that way: I didn't think that dolphins were intentionally healers, but I said to myself that they probably could help you get better.

The opportunity to test the idea didn't present itself for a long time—not until I got back to Florida after my years at Michigan State. We had just stabilized our Institute when a woman named Laura, who had taken several of my classes, got hold of me. She had heard me talk about interacting with dolphins and becoming buddies with them and letting them touch me and so on. She said, "I grew up in Virginia Beach and we had a lot of dolphins there. I swam with dolphins as a little kid, and I've just taken a job at the Dolphin Research Center as research director. I think you and I could probably do some good work together." The Dolphin Research Center is in the Florida Keys on Grassy Key. It was quite convenient for us.

That's how we started at the Dolphin Research Center. The idea was just to explore and find out what we could, because, by then, I had heard a lot of stories and myths about how dolphins can fix this, that, or the other thing.

The Dolphin Research Center is a place where you can go and swim with dolphins. The general public can come in and pay so many dollars and get a swim with them. They had several ponds with probably eighteen or twenty. They let us bring patients in and work with the dolphins in a pond that was, I'd say, half the size of a football field. Maybe a little smaller than that. When we were there seeing patients in the water, the trainers from the Center would let three or four dolphins come into that pond, and the dolphins would decide what they wanted to do. Maybe they'd decide just to come in, look around, and leave, but sometimes they'd come and stay and begin working with us. The trainers tried to maintain control of the dolphins coming into the pond, but soon the dolphins began exercising a degree of free will. We might be in there working with a patient and a certain group of dolphins that the trainers had let in, but outside of the gate, there might be another dolphin that wanted to come to participate! When the trainer wasn't looking, he might sneak through the gate, and there he'd be, putting his nose on the patient to the trainers' chagrin. But it was as if the dolphin had been "called" to help this patient as he/she would disobey the trainer.

The dolphins are pretty shifty when they want to be. The top of the fence is at water level, and I did see them jump over it a number of times. The trainers claimed that dolphins *never* do that, but they did—I saw it! It was as though the dolphin intuitively understood that a particular patient had a problem it knew how to work with. If the trainers wouldn't let that particular dolphin in at that particular time, the dolphin would take it upon itself to get in there, by hook or by crook.

That's how we learned pretty quickly who was in charge of the dolphin therapy. Usually, when there's a CST session conducted by multiple therapists, one therapist assumes the responsibility as the lead. It gives direction and coherence to the therapy. But when we're working with dolphins, the dolphins are the lead; they know what needs to be done to help the patient the most. The dolphins have different ways of sensing this and communicating with the patient's body. So the human therapists are there as tools, to help the dolphins do what they need to do, to turn the patient to give a dolphin easier physical access, to stabilize the patient in the water, and so on.

The dolphins are really benevolent animals. They're determined to heal our patients and, because of their physical makeup, they have more profound tools than human hands. Dolphins emit an ultrasonic frequency four times higher than that which is used by hospitals to shatter kidney stones, and that sound is delivered through water, a more efficient medium for transmission than air. This is a method we understand—ultrasound—and dolphins are naturally able to harness that to alter human tissue.

Through their ultrasonic abilities, it is very clear that dolphins can make very deep and subtle physical changes on our patients. But there's also a really strong energy component. There's an emotional lifting of the patient, a lightening of the emotional attitude, a gentle relaxation which makes healing more possible.

Another aspect of the dolphin therapy is that dolphins are good at sensing imbalances in our energy fields, and they can help us balance them out. When the dolphins look at you, they see your field in terms of the color spectrum. If you have a void in it somewhere, that means you're not healthy. They repair that for you, but it's still your job to get yourself healed. They don't do everything for you, but they are intelligent enough to know that they can help, and kind enough to want to.

We brought a wide variety of patients. We had automobile-accident victims with residual paralysis; we had a couple from Europe with a child who had a genetic bone defect—*osteitis deformans*—that made him abnormally susceptible to broken bones. This child was, I believe, twelve years old, and had suffered something like fourteen major fractures thus far in his life. The dolphins came up and worked on him, and I asked his parents to keep me informed when they went back to Europe about how he was doing—whether he continued to break his bones. About six months later—no more fractures. They promised to let us know if the susceptibility returned, but I haven't hear from them since and it's been several years.

There was one incident where the dolphin, in effect, criticized the work of one of our therapists! The therapist was holding both feet of a little boy, and I was working on his head. Another therapist was holding his pelvis. There had to be three of us to support the child in the water while treatment was happening. Now, a dolphin usually will come up on the free side of a patient and stick its nose wherever it wants to. But this time, the dolphin came up and pushed the therapist off the little boy's left foot and put his own nose on it, and almost immediately the child's whole body just seemed to buzz. The dolphin stayed there less than a minute. The therapist tried to put his hand back on, but the dolphin, after circling a few times, came back and pushed him off again. That happened three times. After that episode the boy was fine.

We had another case where a girl had lost the use of her right arm in a car accident. We worked with her in the water, and I was astonished because, when the dolphin finished—we were all working together, the dolphins sending energy either by touch or through the water—she climbed out of the pond using her right arm to help herself up the ladder.

Another case involved a woman who also had been in a bad automobile accident. Her pelvis was pushed up on one side about three or four inches and, as a result, her leg was extremely short and she couldn't use it. Her pelvis hurt all the time. A dolphin glided up and put its nose on that side of her pelvis, and I could feel her body change. You could see her leg lengthen. When she came out, her legs were nearly equal length and she was able to use both of them.

Yet another case with the dolphins, one that we've gotten some publicity from, is that of Graham, a little boy with cerebral palsy. He started the dolphin therapy along with normal cranial work at age four. At first, he was really afraid of the dolphins; they were so much bigger than him. The dolphins sensed this, and they were really smart about it—they came up and nuzzled the therapist's hand where she was holding Graham. At that gesture, she thought that the dolphin wanted access to the boy's lower back, so she moved her hand, and the dolphin followed her placement. It knew that it would be less frightening for the boy to begin the therapy through the medium of the therapist's hand, and the ultrasonic waves would still work fine.

By the end of one intensive session, his mom, Barb, told us that she was already seeing improvements in Graham; he was standing up straight for long periods of time, when before he was hunched over. He was laughing at appropriate times in adult conversation. Before the therapy, he couldn't laugh at all without having acid reflux and vomiting, but now he was laughing and having a good time for as much as twenty minutes at a time with no problem.

Barb had the right attitude about the therapy, she told us, "I've tried lots of different things, but the one that seems to make the most difference in him being at peace in his body is CranioSacral therapy. We're not looking for any miracles; we're just looking for him to be happy in his body. The dolphins make Graham happy, they give him a little bit of joy where before he had only known the suffering of disease. And for me, that's enough to make it worthwhile. "

But there are other methods to figure out what the dolphins are doing. We brought a psychic out there who talks to Orca whales, and she spent a lot of time talking with the dolphins. She said that it's their natural thing to send in regular universal energy that will heal anything. They don't need to know what's wrong. They conduct a vast cosmic vibration or prana or orgone or elixir or whatever damn thing you want to call it, and that helps the body heal, whatever happens to be the problem.

All of this came about because that student of mine happened to be connected to the Research Center. In fact, many important things in my life have happened just because I didn't interfere when some seemingly chance event got them started. Somewhere along the line, I got it through my thick skull that if I went with the flow, good things would happen; so, if something lays itself out in front of me, I'll do it rather than say to myself, "I don't know about this" and let it go.

I've spoken in this book extensively about "guides." A couple of years ago, I would have said positively that the guides are behind all of it, and I still think that's true. But Valerie Hunt got me to understand that one shouldn't depend too much on one's guides. God is really guiding you, and they're just God's spokespersons. Don't worship your guides too much. You got the "Big Guy" up there that you really need to be beholden to. Valerie said that the spirit guides are just there to help you do what you're supposed to be doing. That bothered me a lot for a while, because I was rather attached to my guides. She wasn't telling me I had to let go of them, but she was moving them down to another, somewhat lower level. I finally accepted that after a few months of mulling it over.

Perhaps what Valerie said about the guides is true about the dolphins too—that we shouldn't make too much of them, get caught up in myths or wishful stories, or do the New Age thing; but let me tell you this: I have no idea regarding the true limits of what dolphins can do. For instance, after working for a while at the Dolphin

Research Center, I made friends with a particular dolphin named AJ. AJ would come up and lie down right next to me on top of the water. The trainer said that this was really strange. One time, I put my hand out, and AJ put his back up so that his blow hole was right under my hand. (Dolphins are actually of the same family as whales—they can stay under water for long periods of time and, when they surface, they expel air and water through a hole on their backs that we call their "blow hole.")

The trainer had already warned me in no uncertain terms that the dolphin would probably kill me if I put my hand on his blow hole. But I hadn't put my hand anywhere: AJ had put his blow hole under my hand, so I told the trainer to back off, that if I died, it would be my own responsibility.

Well, I didn't die. What did happen was that AJ established quite an amazing rapport with me, so that I could call upon his energy if I needed it, even if I was far away from the Dolphin Research Center. If I was back at my Palm Beach Gardens office, for instance, and I ran into a case that was particularly difficult, I could just ask for "dolphin energy" to come and help me, and I would feel it coming through me, and the patient would often make a great improvement at that particular time. It's like a lightness that comes in, with a little bit to it. The most important thing is: you immediately feel the result in the patient.

During the winter, immediately following the time when we stopped treatments at the Dolphin Research Center and when we were no longer working with dolphins at all, I went over to Edinburgh, Scotland, to do a symposium. There were about a hundred therapists from the UK in attendance. If they had difficult patients, they would bring them in, and I would work on the patient up on a little stage. I would think out loud while I was working, so they knew exactly what was going on.

The third patient I worked on was a little boy with cerebral palsy, and I ran into a real steel wall inside his head. I just couldn't get through it. So I said out loud, "Okay, I need a little dolphin energy here," and the structure quickly loosened up. During that day, I called for dolphin energy perhaps three or four times, and each time, whatever difficulty I was having cleared up right away.

At the end of the day, the technician who was making a sound recording of the seminar called me over and said, "Listen to this." Every time I said I needed a little dolphin energy, there was a big blast of static on the recording! And the static remained until I heard myself say, "Okay, that's better," or whatever else I said to indicate that the dolphins had succeeded in doing their job. That happened each time I had called on the dolphin energy. The next day, the same thing happened.

Well, after that second day, a woman came up to me and said that she was a professor at Edinburgh University in the department of physical therapy. She proclaimed that she didn't believe in any of the dolphin nonsense; however, every time I asked for dolphin assistance, her hearing aid, which she'd been wearing for twenty-five years, started buzzing! She wanted to know if I knew why that was happening? I said I didn't know and thought to let it go at that; but I was now aware, at any rate, that dolphins can send their energy across the Atlantic if I asked for it, and that it was energy indeed if it could cause interference with a tape recorder and a hearing aid.

About four weeks after the seminar, after I'd returned to Florida, I received a package from Scotland from this professor. She had sent me her hearing aid! Enclosed was a note saying that about three or four days after the seminar, she realized she didn't need it any more. She said she could hear a clock tick now with what had been her deaf ear. She was sending me the hearing aid so I could analyze it and find out if the dolphins had changed it. I would have liked to, but I didn't know how to do it.

The Vietnam Program

How did I get started with Vietnam veterans with Post-Traumatic Stress Disorder (PTSD)? As usual, it seemed to be programmed by the guides. I was conducting a symposium in October, 1992, in Hartford, Connecticut. One of the attendees brought in a robust-looking man, somewhere in his fifties. His name was Jim. I asked him to lie down on his back on the treatment table with his shoes and belt off and his pockets reasonably empty. The table was up on a riser so everyone could see. An audience of about two hundred CranioSacral therapists, with a wide variety of professional training, surrounded the riser.

I told Jim that I wanted to evaluate him with my hands before he said anything about his problem. He nodded his assent. I touched the bottoms of his feet with my fingertips. As soon as I made contact with him in this way, I was drawn easily to his heart. I was sitting on a roller stool on his left side, so I was easily able to move closer to his heart and comfortably place one hand under his left chest and my other hand on top of it. I literally held his heart between my hands. I directed energy into his heart. He immediately went into another time and another place. I began dialoguing with no difficulty.

Jim flashed back to a time in Vietnam when he and some six other soldiers had been trapped for about two days by the Vietcong. Jim described the situation as though he were there. For part of the time, he spoke as if situated in his body there in Vietnam, and for part of the time he spoke as if he were a spirit looking on from above. He only occasionally talked from what we usually call memory! I shall integrate all of these sources as I describe our treatment session.

A U.S. helicopter came on the scene to rescue Jim and his buddies. Jim insisted that men who were still alive should board the helicopter before he did. There were several dead-buddy bodies lying on the ground. After the other troops were boarded, Jim himself started up the rope ladder. As the helicopter tried to climb, it couldn't ascend. The load was too heavy. Jim immediately dropped from the ladder, and the helicopter rose and departed.

At this point, Jim recalled a great adrenaline rush. He did the impossible. He went on a killing rampage and wiped out all the surrounding North Vietnamese soldiers. His recollection was that there were about ten of them. He relived the looks on their faces as he surprised and shot them, one at a time. Now there was no more enemy. Jim felt wonderful. At this point, his consciousness came back to the symposium for a minute or two. He told us (me) that he wasn't really a hero. He just jumped off the helicopter ladder so that he could go on killing. He was addicted to killing and he felt invincible.

Now, away again from the symposium and back in Vietnam, Jim saw himself from above, walking down a path after his killing spree. He saw a North Vietnamese officer lying on the side of the path. This officer was wounded and apparently helpless. In his own body, he drew his knife and cut the North Vietnamese officer's heart out of his chest and continued his walk along the path, carrying the heart in his hand. Soon he came to a footbridge over a stream. He threw the heart into the water and continued walking—right back into the Hartford, Connecticut symposium!

Next Jim had a vision of the heart-less soldier floating down from the ceiling and coming towards him (towards Jim), pleading for the return of his heart so that he could continue his journey to the next phase of his life. As the officer approached, initially Jim felt hatred, but then he became curious. He wondered why he, Jim, and the heartless officer were so bent on killing each other. They had no reason to hate each other. They had just been told by their governments that they were enemies and that therefore they should kill one another.

Jim began to weep in front of the whole class. This was all wrong. He felt so guilty. I asked him how he could help the officer. Jim said he would give the officer his own heart. With that, I felt a large absence and vacancy quickly form in Jim's chest. He began to weep again. I asked the audience to send healing energy to Jim so that he could develop a new heart. Within minutes his chest vacancy filled with warm, pleasant energy. He smiled and thanked me and the others very profusely.

I heard from Jim in about a week. He said he felt great. It seems that before the symposium, he had experienced frequent episodes of what he called "escaping from reality"—flashbacks of Vietnam like the ones he experienced on the treatment table, but they happened uncontrollably and sometimes resulted in seemingly inexplicable situations. He told me that just before the symposium, he found himself in a trench that he had dug around his house but had no recollection of digging.

When Jim communicated with me after the seminar, he asked if we would treat some of his buddies who were as bad as he had been. He and I then worked out a first program for Vietnam vets with Post-Traumatic Stress Disorder, and it was a huge success. Jim has since gotten a master's degree as a rehabilitation therapist and works in a New England rehab center.

So in the 1990s, we started giving week-long intensive programs for veterans. Those sessions went well, and then after the second Gulf War, we saw a place where our services could do some good. We started a much larger, formalized treatment center for soldiers and veterans at a Naval Hospital in California. We really scaled up the operation in 2005, when a new unit opened.

One thing I know for certain is that once I decide to go ahead and investigate something, I do it without misgivings or fear. That's my way. But if you want to talk about fear for real, you need to think about the experience of people who have to deal with it at its most intense level. Nobody experiences fear more vividly than some of the soldiers in combat, and often that fear does not go away when their time at the front is over. It stays in the body.

That's why we've had so much success using CST to treat Post Traumatic Stress Disorder. War wounds have both physical and emotional components, and most therapies treat only one or the other. When a body is injured, it's not just physical trauma that gets trapped in the tissues. Intense emotions accompany the injury—shock, fear, and even guilt—and these also get lodged in the body. When you remove the vector of the physical impact, you can release its emotional components as well.

To treat PTSD, you have to recognize its symptoms and address each one accordingly. There are seven common aspects of PTSD, and we've adapted our CST therapy, respectively, to each of them. Through these you can see how CST works on both the physical body and the conscious body.

Insomnia can result when the joints of the head and neck become jammed due to extreme physical stress. CST is used to release these pressures and improve the efficiency of fluid outflow at the occipital-cranial base—the base of the skull. When this is successfully applied, our subjects sleep much better.

Hypervigilance is a hallmark of PTSD; it is a state of heightened awareness in which any surprise or unexpected noise causes an excessive response that the subject cannot control. It comes from being on high alert too much, the fight-or-flight response. We use CST and its offshoot, SomatoEmotional Release, to locate and release energy cysts throughout the body. We concentrate particularly on the reticular activating system of the brain and spinal cord, which are responsible for the secretion of adrenalin and other stress hormones and biochemicals. When we can reduce the system's level of ready alertness, both hypervigilance and hyper-responsiveness are alleviated. In a moment, I'll tell you about Ed, who really needed this treatment.

Intrusive thoughts continually interrupt a PTSD victim's ability to concentrate and may even prove intellectually disabling. CST is used to balance fluids and release restrictions on the right and left sides of the cranium, thus enhancing the circulation of both blood and cerebrospinal fluid. As a result, nutritional supplies to brain cells are improved and toxic waste products are removed. The cortical areas that help control conscious thoughts are also revitalized and become more effective.

Flashbacks involve the mental re-experiencing of the horrific events that caused PTSD initially. Each time they occur, they are just as terrifying as the original experience. Unlike normal memories, these do not mellow with each recall, nor can the person experiencing them describe them in words. While this kind of fear response can be considered appropriate at the time of the original traumatic event, it is certainly not appropriate ten years later in a safe setting. Studies have shown that, in PTSD, the left hemisphere of the brain is less functional than the right, and the hippocampus—thought to be a important factor in memory control—had gotten smaller on the left side than the right. Cranio-

Sacral therapists work to equalize the mobility and fluid flows of both sides of the brain. They also pass energy from right to left, focusing on the left-side speech area. After using cranial techniques, we have seen clients become able for the first time to describe the flashback event and, as this ability improves, the flashback comes under control and the experience can be recalled voluntarily. Eventually, the power of the event fades and the flashbacks discontinue.

Panic attacks also mark PTSD, and they usually fade as we treat the hypervigilance and the flashbacks.

Long-term fear results in a PTSD patient exposed to a short but scary episode. By way of comparison, the non-PTSD person might well react with momentary fear to the same episode. This long-term fear becomes chronic anxiety.

Understandably, depression and suicidal thoughts are common in PTSD-afflicted individuals. CST focuses specifically on releasing abnormal compression at three junctions: where the sphenoid bone and the base of the occipital bone meet, forming the floor of the cranial vault, the joints where the first cervical vertebra and occipital bone unite at the base of the skull, and where the lumbar and sacrum come together in the lower back by the tailbone. Once pressure in these areas is alleviated, depression lifts and suicidal thoughts stop.

A good example of our work with a Post Traumatic Stress Disorder case is Ed.

Fear sometimes has to do with immediate physical danger, but very often it is just the result of the way we are conditioned. My mother likely conditioned me not to feel fear, something that stuck no matter what, but Ed didn't have that and his experience in Vietnam made him feel fear all the time.

Ed had gone through just about the worst kinds of combat

experiences that anyone can undergo without actually being killed or physically impaired. He had killed many Vietnamese and spent subsequent years in a state of constant alarm—at any moment in Vietnam, and then at home in the USA, he felt that he might be under attack and have to fight for his life. As a result, he was having a great deal of trouble bringing his alarm system—his *reticular activating system*—under control.

The reticular activating system is the part of your nervous system that sets you on edge, ready for "fight or flight" at any time. His was tuned way up because he had been in so much combat. It kept him in a constant state of being ready to kill or be killed. When it's like that, there's a lot of adrenaline in the blood and a lot of stress going on all the time throughout your body. Ed's reticular alarm system was wound so high that you could walk behind him, snap your fingers, and he'd turn around and be at your throat in an instant! We were trying to get into this mechanism, get it to go down to a normal, noncombat level.

I started dialoguing with him and letting him know that Vietnam was *then* and this was *now*, and that all those horrible dangers were no longer present. I also was trying to get him to understand that when one's alarm system runs on high alert all the time, it causes premature aging: the body is unable to produce enough energy to replace what it's spending to maintain such a level of alertness.

I was using this argument in dialogue with Ed's alarm system. I was talking directly to it. It had its own personality. It was saying, "Why should I reduce my vigilance? Being alert is keeping me alive!" I had to convince Ed's system that A) we were out of Vietnam and that he was no longer in this kind of danger; B) if something critical *did* come up, the system could bounce back up again and stimulate the whole body to go back into that "fight or flight" mode; and C) if he didn't reduce his level of constant alertness, he'd age and probably die prematurely from an aged liver, a worn out pancreas, an overworked heart, or the overuse of some other organ.

I had Ed visualize a dial, going from zero to one hundred, with one hundred representing maximum alert, and zero, the totally relaxed state. My idea was that I should be able to feel his bodily tissues relax under my hands as the alarm dropped to about twenty-five or thirty. As far as I'm concerned, that's a good place for the reticular activating system to operate; but every time I got Ed's down below fifty, he would get tremendous chest pains, and then the dial would bounce back up again because his chest hurt like hell. We went through a cycle like this a couple of times, and I realized there was something important going on here. Then he started dialoguing with me on a deeper level. I was speaking with his *voice of fear*. He said he was afraid to let it go lower because he'd get killed. I tried to get him to release the fear, because it was hanging onto him like an octopus inside his chest. Suddenly, I just gave him a big, hard whack on the chest with the palm of my hand, and the fear just sort of shattered and came out of his body and, after that, the alarm system stayed down and he was okay. I felt it come out like wind. A few people saw some black stuff. He just changed remarkably within seconds, for the better.

The Vietnam program, in general, is set up for us to work on six guys at a time: six vets on six tables in a rather large, rectangular room. I have three therapists for each veteran. Two therapists are assigned to each for a whole day, and the other therapists float; that is, they just go around and see where their services are needed.

In the four programs that we conducted at first, the veterans were booked into a motel over on the beach—it was a mom-and-pop place, no glitz or special rules. We paid for their lodging. We sent a van over there to pick them up in the morning and brought them to the room that we had prepared for them. They were introduced to their two therapists for the day, and we sat around a while and did some "talk therapy." Actually, most of these vets had been in talk therapy before. They preferred to chat about their current situations. They'd been through all that other stuff with psychiatrists too many times, so we all sat around and yakked, really just to get comfortable with each other. That would start around 9:00 and, depending on the group mood, continue until 10:00 o'clock each morning. Then we'd break and go to the tables for hands-on work. A buffet lunch was brought in so the guys could eat when they wanted to. We'd work to at least 5:00 o'clock. Then the van would take them back to the motel. We did that for a first five-day week, took the weekend off, and a second five-day week similarly.

Since those sessions took place in the nineties, we've had immense success running intensive programs at the Naval Hospital in California. These programs were started by a retired Navy pilot and a local therapist, and they're for veterans of our most recent wars, the ones in Iraq mostly. Now we're treating not just Vietnam vets, but also Iraq vets.

This one captain, John, was an F-18 pilot who bombed Baghdad on the first pass. He confided to me that he felt really bad because he dropped all these bombs and killed all these people when he didn't even know who they were or what they were doing. That caused him to resign the military after twenty-seven years of service. I don't know how he found our work but, once he did, he tried it and loved it; became a certified practitioner. In October of 2005, I went out to the California Naval Hospital and ran a symposium, wherein I treated probably ten patients in front of the whole medical staff of the hospital.

This one guy Richard I worked on at that symposium really

made an impression on me. His job was to sit in the back of a truck with a fifty-caliber gun and, if he saw anything suspicious, to fire—kill it. Well, as they were rolling along, he was shooting a whole lot of people, but then he saw this guy up on top of a roof who didn't look like a soldier, so he didn't take him out. He simply couldn't bring himself to shoot him. A couple minutes later, a bullet comes from there and goes through his buddy's leg.

Richard had this on his conscience. Plus, he had been in situations where he had taken on unbelievable amounts of toxic stuff. As a consequence, he was suffering from depression, loss of memory, disorientation, rooms spinning. We started getting the toxins out—we were pumping the hell out of his CranioSacral system. By Friday morning, he had a whole basket full of sausages, eggs, and stuff. In fact, he was in the kitchen cooking breakfast for everybody, happy as a lark. He went straight to the admiral and told him what a change he'd had not only in his health but his personality and belief system—everything.

Finally, this government bigwig was sent from Washington to this California Naval Hospital to observe our "nonstandard" treatment. He was the second-in-command to the officer who was in charge of all the military health care. When he came in the beginning, he thought I was full of bullshit. We'd have eye contact, and then he'd just look away. But by the third day he was talking to me. He had observed the improvement in these guys and listened to them when they talked, and in the end he sent a positive report in to Washington. In fact he wanted to know if he could take one of our introductory courses himself. I sent him a free ticket to a CST1 class.

He's coming back out there—he's supposed to do psych evaluations on our patients—the day before the therapy and the day after, so they can measure how this works.

We're lucky that our program has such enthusiastic support at this Naval Hospital. The Commanding Officer there, Captain Sandra DeGroot, declared one day, "This is the hope of the future." She's really supporting the program, and it's making a huge difference in the lives of veterans.

The other therapists participating in the program were all trained in Advanced CST and its offshoots, including the release of energy cysts, SomatoEmotional Release, and Therapeutic Imagery and Dialogue. In relation to these techniques, when it seemed appropriate for the patient, we'd get into imaging and dialoguing, because if you can image what you are releasing from your body at the same time that it's happening, it can be much more effective.

Often, you don't have to give any instruction about imaging to get it going. If two or three therapists are working on a person, and if they get the position exactly right, the patient will flip right back into the related scene. We'd have Vietnam guys screaming all over the place without having said a word about imaging; but they would start imaging, and, as they did, we would offer the opportunity to dialogue. If they took us up on it, fine; if they didn't, we kept on going, using our hands on their body to perpetuate the image until they reached a point where we could help them release it. Our success rate was extremely high. To this day we are in touch with several of our veterans. Most are doing very well. All have improved significantly.

Organ Transplants

Another recent adventure of mine has been with organ transplant patients. I'll be damned if I know how this really began. I think it probably came along because I objected violently when they put a baboon heart into a little girl. By that time, I was convinced that tissues have their own consciousness. Taking a baboon consciousness and putting it in a six-year-old girl just seemed monstrous. What if she lived? What are we going to have? That bothered me a lot.

The whole thing, it seemed to me, came down to this: Let's say that you receive a heart from somebody else. You're not just getting a pump. A heart is not just a piece of machinery. You're receiving the personality of that person's heart, and it now becomes a part of you. The question is not only will your organism accept the alien physical organ, but is your being willing to accept this new personality? And it turns out that the answer is sometimes yes, and sometimes no. It depends on the individual. The same thing is true of a kidney, a liver, and so on. The cells of the transplanted organ have profound memories of things foreign to the recipient.

I'd been working with a patient we'll call Richard Jones for various problems, and it finally reached the point where he needed a heart transplant. Now, Richard was a very successful business man—a realist and a tough-minded kind of guy. He just couldn't believe me when I told him that his new heart was going to be something more than an organic gadget to pump blood.

His operation was performed by some of the best medical people available, but after his transplant, he started having all sorts of problems, and his high-class cardiologists and neurologists couldn't fix him. Primarily, he was having trouble with his legs. Finally, and reluctantly, since he already knew what I thought about heart transplants, he came to see me about what was happening. And since I already knew what *he* thought about heart transplants, I said, "Richard, if you want me to help you, you're going to have to give me a real shot at it." I wanted him to participate in a full two-week program.

He said, "I will give you whatever you need," but in the end, he was only willing to stay for a week—he'd only go that far. Okay.

Richard's new heart, it turned out, had belonged to the body of a thirty-eight-year-old housewife. When I began working on him, I could feel what I perceived to be an energy of rejection encasing the left side of his chest where the heart was. It had been clear to his regular physicians that his body was rejecting his heart physically, and they had prescribed medication to handle that immune-system aspect of it. But I could still feel the negative energy in the field between what I would consider the heart's energy field and the rest of his body. Our team in the program worked on him silently, and we were, in fact, able to get rid of that rejection energy. As soon as we did that, his legs got better. We performed various "peace-making" activities to harmonize his relation to the new being that was now in his body—all silently. But the beauty of the whole thing came after his week with us when I got a call from somebody at his home who wanted to know "what we had done to him"!

I said, "What do you mean?"

"Well, he's running around here picking up linen and washing dishes and doing all kinds of things he never would think of doing before." Apparently, he was behaving just like an ordinary housewife! Since he had returned from the program, he had become, in general, a softer kind of guy. Richard, to this day, can't accept the idea that his new heart is anything more than a pump, but, to put the whole thing in a nutshell, we got him to make peace with his housewife's heart without his knowing we were doing it, and it worked anyway.

Here's another story. One morning I got a call from a woman in the Southwest, let's call her Marge. She said that another woman— Ella—had come to visit her because she had received her (Marge's) deceased son's heart. Marge had heard somehow about my work with transplant patients, and the two of them wanted to come and visit me. I said I would be happy to see them. I invited them to come and be prepared to stay for a week. I didn't charge them anything because this was very much exploratory territory for me.

This is what they told me when they arrived. Marge had an eighteen-year-old son who, before his death, had been a heroin addict and a repeat sex-offender. Marge and the boy's father had broken up; the boy was living with his father and going downhill fast. One night, Marge determined to "rescue" her son by bringing him to live with her. When she came to pick him up, he packed a knapsack and apparently came along willingly. They hopped into her car. After a few miles, she stopped for a red light, and the boy suddenly opened the door, jumped out of the car, pulled a gun out of his knapsack, and shot himself in the mouth. The bullet went right through the back of his head. She got on her cell phone and immediately called 911. An ambulance arrived very quickly. He wasn't dead, but it was clear when they got him to the hospital that he wouldn't last long. Marge had the presence of mind to decide to donate his organs; she signed the proper papers as the boy passed on.

About a year later, Marge got a phone call from Ella, who was a farmer's wife in Iowa. Ella said, "I received a heart transplant some time ago, and I have been tracking and tracking and tracking to find out who it belonged to. I think I have your son's heart." It turned out that they were able to confirm that this was the case. I don't know how the heck they figured it out—it's supposed to be a secret thing—but Ella said, "Since I've had my heart transplant, I have been thinking about suicide. I've been mean and nasty and depressed and all kinds of things that I never was before." Marge told Ella the story of her son's unhappy life and suicide.

As soon as Marge heard Ella's story, she immediately felt love for the woman because she had her son's heart. She invited her to come and live with her to try to work out what was going on because she thought that Ella was experiencing her son's state of mind. Ella left her farm and came to spend a few months with Marge. Eventually, they decided to consult with me.

I set out working with them concurrently on two adjacent tables. I had a few other therapists working with me, so we could all be in physical contact with both women at the same time as we began dialoguing with them. It wasn't difficult to get Ella's heart—the son's heart—to talk, and not only *talk!* The heart was raising holy hell because it wanted to die along with the rest of its body. It didn't want to go on living but found itself inside this farmer woman, and, as the heart put it, "she's a damn Christian fundamentalist, and I can't have any fun any more!" Well, we finally convinced "Heart" to put up with his circumstance, and we got Ella, who was indeed a fundamentalist, to start dialoguing with Heart, but it took quite a bit of negotiating. A big problem, besides the boy's own resistance, was that we had to make peace with Mom. We began to blend the bodies of the two women together, and this worked very nicely because in some sense they were sympatico. But there was a big difficulty with their attitudes, because Ella was dead set on converting Marge, not only her son, to her fundamentalist views. Marge soon resented Ella's intimacy with her son's heart, and she particularly resented her efforts to convert him! So they had it out, and we had to work pretty hard to help them go completely through it. We simply told them, initially, "You're destroying each other. You have to stop this. Ella, you have to stop trying to convert Marge to your way of thinking. Just let her be her own person. Ella, you'll have to get used to having the heart of a person who isn't a Christian fundamentalist."

The problem was complicated by the fact that Marge remained spiritually connected to her son's heart, so what was happening to Heart was, in effect, happening to Marge. And here was Ella trying to convert both of them, and Heart was almost exhausted from all this bombardment.

The reconciliation occurred through just plain old talking. I said, "Here you are. Heart, you and Ella are going to keep on living together. Please, there's no need to fight about it. You can all accept each other; you can all live peaceably side by side." I just kept responding to all of their objections and trying to make peace for them. After a while, through sheer persistence, it worked.

There's one more piece to this story that's really interesting. We worked on (what I have to insist was) the three of them for two or three hours a day for five days. On the last day, or the second to the last day, David, one of the therapists, had his hand under the sacrum of each woman. Marge's sacrum was hurting her a lot. As we were continuing our task of bringing peace among Marge, Ella, and Heart, all of a sudden, David's eyes started to pop out of his head. He called out, "Ella's sacrum is starting to buzz. It feels like it's got a nest of bees in it." And Marge was smiling, saying that *her* sacrum felt all better. But more than that, Ella's ferocious need to convert both Marge and Heart had just melted away and all was forgiven. With Ella's missionary efforts abandoned, both Marge and Heart could relax.

When I'm meant to learn by the guides, I find that they send me patients with the particular problem they want me to understand. After my understanding is complete, I won't see many of those kinds of patients any more. The guides are taking me along step by step. At a certain point, the transplant patients just stopped appearing. We had about ten altogether, and then it just dropped off.

It was as though all this were happening as a lesson for me and, when I learned it, no more transplant patients were needed. There is, however, one key transplant story I want to tell—that of Claire Sylvia, who, in fact, had introduced me to the issue of transplants in her book, *A Change of Heart.* I eventually met her, and she has become a patient and a good friend.

Claire had been a dancer in New York City. She began suffering from pulmonary hypertension. She reached a point where she could hardly walk up a flight of stairs and was put on a list to get a heart-lung transplant. (Usually, when you receive a lung transplant, you receive a heart at the same time, because to introduce new lungs to a strange heart makes the whole procedure more difficult.) Eventually, she got her new heart and lungs.

As was usual practice, the hospital did not inform her as to the identity of the donor, but several circumstances made her extremely curious about who was now inhabiting her upper torso. First, when she was convalescing in the hospital, she found herself looking at several plump, little dark-haired nurses and getting a bit sexually aroused, even though she had never been a lesbian! Second, as soon as she got out of the hospital, she began to have urges to consume meals of fried chicken and beer, though, as a professional dancer, those items were not exactly staples in her diet! But she indulged the impulses. And then, third, one day she paid a guy to give her a ride on a motorcycle—again, something she had no interest in before. What was all this about?

Well, over the next few months, she experienced several dreams that seemed to be providing information about the donor, and she consulted a psychic who made some helpful suggestions. On the basis of these indications, she took a trip to Connecticut to do actual research. The psychic told her to look in the library for a local news-paper of a certain date, and there, sure enough, was the story of a boy, eighteen years old, who had been killed in a motor-cycle accident. There was enough information in the article for her to locate the boy's family. She learned that they had, indeed, arranged for his heart and lungs to be donated, so it was very possible that she had received her transplants from him. The family showed Claire a pic-ture of the dead boy standing with his girlfriend, and she was exactly the physical type that had been turning her on. The boy was, nat-urally enough, a motorcycle enthusiast. And here's the clincher: his favorite foods were fried chicken and beer.

Now, Claire did very well with learning all this. She worked with a psychologist for quite a long time, and she came to see me just because she wanted to check her body out. I went over her and couldn't say that there was anything outstanding at that particular time because she had managed to go through the whole thing pretty well in therapy and had accepted what had happened. Sadly, after a little while, she required a kidney transplant because all the drugs she had taken for her heart transplant had wiped her kid-neys out. But that came later and is part of the story I will get to.

At the time I saw her, Claire had recently broken up with the man who lived with her. Among the circumstances of their break-up was the fact that she felt she no longer loved him and that many ordinary things he did had begun to annoy her. They really did care for each other, however, and were still on good terms. When he learned that she needed a kidney, he volunteered. His kidney matched her needs. She accepted his offer and received the trans-plant.

Well, as soon as she woke up from the operation, she felt not only grateful to him, but her love for him was reawakened. Part of him was now literally inside her. They started living together again, but now *she* started performing precisely the tasks that he used to do around the kitchen that irritated her! She lived with him for a couple of years, and then they finally separated.

I'll give one last transplant case because I think it reveals another angle on all of this. I was teaching a class in New York during the period when transplant patients were coming to me regularly, so I told the class that, if anybody had a transplant patient, I'd love to examine them. One woman said she knew a man who had just received a kidney. He'd been out of the hospital about a week, and she was sure he'd be happy to have me examine him.

The patient was a theater director in New York. I went over to his home and examined him from head to toe, and I couldn't find any sign of rejection energy or anything like that. Everything seemed to be peaceful and happy with his body and mind. Finally, I said to him, "I find nothing here to tell me you are having any kind of problem with this kidney."

He kind of laughed and said, "I know."

I said, "How do you know?"

He said, "It's my brother's kidney. We've always been very, very tight." It was almost like getting a clone of his own kidney.

One piece of advice I would like to give regarding transplants is for patients and their physicians to start working with the transplant issue as soon as they get out from under the anesthetic. I think they should just start talking to the new organ, saying something like: "Kidney (if it's a kidney), you're in a whole new environment now; you've been transplanted into another person's body, but you can adapt and be accepted." Then the physician should talk to the host's body and try to get it to accept its visitor. Transplantation is a little like immigration: it's like someone moving from Okinawa to Italy. You can't expect that he or she will get along right away.

Recently, I have had another idea about transplants: the possibility of "pre-emptive" dialoguing! Let's say a person is in a medical situation in which the treatment is going to put them at risk in some way, or put some organ at risk, or that you are on some medication that, over time, is going to damage your kidney or liver. Right at the beginning, a therapist could start dialoguing with the organ in question and explain that a problem may arise. It should be explained that the treatment is to save the whole body and, though it may impair a specific organ's function, you are requesting the whole not to rebel, should an organ replacement be required. I've also thought of starting with a person who's waiting for a transplant and trying to get that body to accept the concept of a foreign tissue. You can't very well talk to the organs of someone who's just been in a car crash, but a medical patient could be pre-conditioned. People who sign papers allowing their organs to be donated could, at that time, tell their organs what is happening and instruct them that if there ever should be an accident and they find that they are suddenly located in a foreign body, to accept their knew role!

I know very well what kind of a job it would be to get this idea accepted as part of the organ-donor program! I have no illusions about that. But I just thought it would be a good idea to put it out there. Anyone who signs an organ donor agreement could be given instructions to consider saying, "Hello kidney, hello liver, hello heart, I have signed this paper—if I'm killed, you should know what's going to happen. You could find yourselves in another body!" I know the prevailing attitudes, though, and I'm sure I'd be laughed out of any professional discussion of this.

You'd be amazed at how many doctors, even transplant surgeons, will tell the patient authoritatively that the heart is only a pump, it doesn't do anything else, there's nothing else involved. In a way, that's considered their wisdom, protecting the patients from their own fantasies. We live in an age that is so afraid of its own ghosts it can't even entertain, let alone admit, that spirit and energy exist and that information travels outside recognized and sanctioned channels. In a way the supposedly enlightened modern time is really a kind of superstitious dark age.

Cell Talk

Kayla

I've been talking to patients' original organs for a long time, and eventually it became time for the next phase, Cell Talk. A good way to broach this subject is to tell the story of Kayla.

Kayla is eighteen years old at the time of this writing. She's extremely bright and talented. I first met her while she was inside her mother's womb. I started treating her mother for injuries suffered in an automobile accident that happened while she was pregnant with Kayla. After she was born, I saw Kayla periodically for one thing or another, but mostly I treated her mother, and Kayla would sit in the room. Well, one Sunday morning, I got a call from Kayla's mother. She said, "John, can you help me?"

"What's the matter?"

Kayla had taken sick two months earlier. She ached all over and had very little energy. She was spending most of her time in bed and was missing a lot of school. Kayla had gone, first, to her primary care physician, and, from there, to an infectious-disease specialist. He had put her on about eight different courses of anti-biotics, one after the other—none of them worked. He sent her to a rheumatologist, who thought she had some sort of autoimmune disease, but he wasn't sure. They made an appointment for her to go up to the Mayo Clinic. The visit was scheduled for a few days after Mom called me. I said, "Okay. Bring her over. I'll see what I can find."

Well, Kayla came over. Kayla was thirteen or fourteen at the time. Kayla is—well, I would like to have her for my own daughter. She's that kind of person. She lay down on the table out there in my little study, and I put my hands on her feet. She was obviously in a lot of pain. What I got was an immediate sense that there was a virus in there somewhere. That just came into my head. To explore this intuition I used a technique called *arcing*—a light-touch used to perceive subtle energy abnormality in the patient's body by scanning fully with receptive hands. As I traced all the way from her feet, I picked up chaotic energy or entropy in both knees, the left pelvis, the left bronchus (just off the side of the sternum), and the posterior aspect of her head—inside of her cranium. All of those places seemed to me to have a very disorganized energy. I would define that energy as an inflammatory process. I said, "I think you have a virus."

So I worked hard to clear those stuck places, one by one. And I'm calling them "stuck places" because, for me, Kayla's normal energy couldn't get through them. They were inflamed, they were swollen, there was a certain amount of "fluidic stasis," if you will. Well, I opened up all of those places. It took me an hour and a half. As I worked, she started feeling pretty good. Then I gave her a regular spinal manipulation to loosen the structures and tissues that had been caught up by all of the discomfort she was having. Mom called the next morning and said that she was "great."

The following Wednesday, she went to Mayo. They did some blood tests and Mom called me on Friday. She said, "You were right. She has a cytomegalovirus."

I asked, "What did Mayo tell you to do?"

Mom said, "She has to go to bed and rest until the virus burns itself out."

I said, "How is she doing?"

Mom said, "She did really well until Thursday, but then it started coming back. It's not as bad as it was."

I said, "Bring her over."

I treated her on the weekend a couple of times because I was fully booked at the office. I worked through the blocks again. Then I began to get the idea that viruses create stasis so that the immune cells can't get in to get rid of them. They also hide inside of normal cells and they're hard to pick out. A virus in a normal cell will put out ten or twelve abnormal protein markers on the cell surface. A normal cell has about ten thousand protein markers on its surface, so you've got to be pretty alert if you're an immune cell to pick ten abnormal markers out of 10,000! Well, I broke down all those blocked areas again. I don't remember if it was the second or third time I saw her, but it struck me that if I could talk to organs, why couldn't I dialogue with immune cells? I put my hand on her thymus [a gland in the upper chest and lower throat that is largely responsible for directing and producing immune cells] and I said, "Thymus, will you talk with me?"

I explained to Kayla, "Just let the voice of Thymus come through. Don't censor it or change it or feel obligated to answer. Just whatever comes. Immediately, "Yes" came through from the thymus.

I said, "Thymus, I think that there are viruses hidden around in this body that are so clever that you might need my help to find

them. Would you be willing to dispatch a whole bunch of monocytes and macrophages [these are types of immune cells] to places
where I put my hand?"

"Yes."

It seemed best to send a unique signature energy that is just
mine, so I said, "Can you tell that this is just my energy?"

"Yes."

"Okay. I'm going to move my hand down to Kayla's knee. I
want you to send a bunch of these immune cells. Just tell them
where to go. Clone them! Make millions of them to come down
here."(I did suggest macrophages and monocytes because I thought
they would be the most effective. Monocytes can become
macrophages and they can move much faster than macrophages.)

Within one minute, I could feel a buzzing under my hand on
her knee.

"Now clear out anything that even looks like it could possibly
be diseased or 'not-self.' Please, please, please take care of it."

And I could feel it happening.

"Now can I move to the next place? You can leave the
macrophages here to finish up and send me a whole new batch for
the next one."

I went very quickly, but with real intensity, from place to place.
And finally, I ended up on the back of Kayla's head and she said,
"Oh, my God! I feel better!"

I said, "Kayla, you heard what I did. Right?"

"Yes."

"What I want you to do is look through your body every morning and see if you can locate places that might be virus pockets.
Then I want you to politely ask Thymus to send the macrophages
and monocytes wherever you find those pockets."

She practiced this self-treatment at least twice a week for

several months, and she's doing very, very well. She showed a friend how to do it whose mother had CMV (cytomegalovirus). The mother came and took our two-week intensive treatment program and we taught her how to cell-talk. And she's running around doing fine. So that's what got me started on what I now call "Cell Talk."

We'd been doing organ talk, and brain talk, and pain talk, and now even talk to the glands that produce cells, so why not talk to a single cell?

Since then, we have had great success with virus infections and other problems in which dialogue with body parts and cells is a possible way to go. A skeptical patient always has more difficulty than an accepting one in achieving success. Give that whatever interpretation you want.

Further Cell Talk: Ethel

The next experience with talking to cells involved Ethel, the mother of Rebecca, one of our therapists at the Institute. Rebecca told me that her mother had gone for a physical because she was tired all the time. They found that her liver enzymes were all screwed up, so they sent her to the Mayo Clinic where they did a biopsy. The biopsy gave her a diagnosis of autoimmune disease of the liver, which means that her own immune cells were attacking and killing her liver cells. Rebecca said, "If she came down here from Indiana, would you take a look at her?"

I said, "Sure." So she made a special trip. I had only one appointment with her. Now Ethel is seventy-two years old and a very nice lady. I had her lie down on a table, I put my hands under her head, and I said, "Just relax." Her eyes started to show REM (rapid eye movements) right away and her eyelashes started to flutter. I said,

"May I talk to your thymus gland?"

"Yes."

And I went through the ritual of "Don't censor your thoughts, etc., etc., I want to hear from the gland, not from you." I do whatever I can to get the person out of the way and the organ speaking. I've been known to say some pretty far-out things and to use strong language when necessary. The ego is a pretty stubborn character. A skeptical person might say, "How can my liver speak?" I might answer, "Hey, buddy, move out of the way and give the poor organ a chance. You've been hogging the stage for forty years. How could anyone else speak?" I might say, "If I sang a sweet song, would the pancreas like to make its pleasure known? Is it shy?" Whatever it takes ... I let inspiration guide me.

On this occasion it didn't take much. I said, "Thymus, did you know that at the Mayo Clinic they did a biopsy of Ethel's liver and it said that immune cells are destroying the liver cells? Did you know that? My understanding is that you're in charge of such things."

"Yes, we know. They're doing it at my suggestion."

I said, "Are you trying to destroy her liver?"

"No! We're just trying to destroy the cancer cells that are forming there."

"Oh. She's starting to get cancer of the liver?

"Yes. We're killing the suspicious cells so she doesn't get that."

I said, "How did the cancer start?"

"About four years ago, she had a lot of radiation exposure."

I found out that, four years before, she had had colon cancer and had been treated with radiation.

I said, "Good. You keep on destroying those cancer cells. But there are so many of them that her liver function is starting to deteriorate. Did you know that?"

"No. We weren't aware of that. We were just focusing on the cancer cells."

"Would you mind if I talked to the stem cells?"

"No, go ahead."

"Would you mind if the stem cells went down there and made normal liver cells? You wouldn't destroy those, would you?

"No, no, no, no, no."

"Be sure that you instruct your macrophages and your natural killer cells and your lymphocytes not to mess around with new, good, normal liver cells."

"It's a deal."

I put my hand over her sternum and said, "Okay, Bone Marrow, you got stem cells in there?"

"Oh yeah!"

"Can you make me a whole bunch of them? I probably need a couple of billion of them."

"Sure."

"We have a problem with her liver."

I explained the problem with the liver and the cancer that was destroying it, as well as the fact that we needed more liver cells.

"Stem cells, can you accommodate Ethel's need for healthy liver cells?"

"Sure, sure. We didn't know that was going on."

So I said, "Okay. Send a bunch of stem cells right now down to the liver."

My hand was right over the liver and within a minute I felt BZZZZZZZZZZ.

Before two weeks had gone by, I got a call from Rebecca. She had received a letter from her mother saying that she had a retest on the liver profile (blood test). The results were almost normal and she feels much better. About a month after that, I received a set of Ethel's liver function test results and they were totally normal. The dialoguing with "hands on" was all we did. Nothing else. No other therapeutic modalities were used. If you don't like "cell talk" as an explanation, you tell me what's going on. I'll settle for results.

I started a class, which we call "Craniosacral Therapy and the Immune Response." I figured that the folks in the class ought to know most of the immune cells and what their characteristics are, so that's what we're teaching in that class, and then we have them treating each other. We are shrinking tumors, taking care of fibroids, getting thyroid glands that are swollen to go down, and, really, it's almost shockingly easy. All you've got to do is talk to them. Most of the time, the cells are focusing on what they're doing—like treating the cancer. That's necessary, but they don't realize the ripple effect. You have to alert the rest of the body to the ripple effect. In order to do that, you've got to know whom to alert. That's what the class is about.

Stem-Cell Talking with George

I am presently working on a case that involves talking to stem cells in a rather extreme way. Recently one of our therapists saw a six-year-old boy named George who had had half of his brain surgically removed. She performed routine CST adjustments, and then she wondered whether there was any more that could be done. She asked me if I would look at him.

George had been subject to uncontrollable seizures since he was an infant, so, when he was about three years old, the surgeons at Johns Hopkins removed the entire left hemisphere of his brain. Incidentally, it only reduced the number of seizures, it didn't stop them. I'm not sure how his parents heard about our work and got the idea that we could be of some help, but suddenly here I am, and here they are at our Institute. I walk into the treatment room and there's this little six-year-old lying on the table. He can't talk and he can hardly move his body. Mom and Dad are standing nearby. Mom says he never laughs or cries. He's pretty much (to use the common unkind expression) a "vegetable." Before the removal of the left side of his brain, he had begun to speak and had normal motor control of his body between his seizures.

Put yourself in my place. I've got a mom and dad staring at me and a child here on the table with half a brain and I'm wondering what I can do for him. The thought came to my mind, maybe I can dialogue with his stem cells. Stem cells are quite plentiful inside brain tissue. When I put my hands on his head, I could feel that the left side of his skull was sort of "sloshy" with what was probably cerebrospinal fluid. There was a big vacant space and the fluid was accumulated there.

I started to dialogue. I said, "Stem cells in the right brain, will you talk to me?"

Now, of course, the boy couldn't talk, so the stem cells couldn't answer through his voice, so I had to get a sense of their response just through feeling his head. I did get an encouraging response—a kind of buzzing activity, but on the *right* side, not the left. That made sense because if the stem cells were going to go to work, it would have to be from the part of the brain that still existed!

I asked the cells if they understood that the left side of the brain had been removed surgically and, if they did understand that, would it be reasonable for them to try to create a mirror-image hemisphere on the left side? I, of course again, couldn't get an answer in words, but I could feel energy on the right side. But then I also started to feel a little buzzing on the left side. Apparently, they started to go to work immediately!

Next, I said to the stem cells (I was speaking out loud so Mom and Dad could hear what was going on), "You understand that the right and the left sides of the brain have different functions, so please try to create a left side of the brain that does the things that left hemispheres normally do."

Every once in a while, I'd glance over at Mom and Dad to see if they thought I was crazy, but they seemed pretty taken with what I was doing. I could feel the changes happening inside the little boy's head, so I addressed Mom and Dad, "I don't know what else I can tell you, but maybe he can recreate the left side of his brain. I would like you to do what I'm doing, speak to the stem cells on a daily basis. Just put your hands on George's head like this and tell them you'd like to have this left side of the brain created, okay?"

They were all for it and, after they took George home, they reported they did what I asked.

About two months later, I got a call from Mom and she said George was starting to talk and cry and laugh and even beginning to move around. Now, in spite of his condition, George was going to a school for handicapped children. They have teachers who specialize in finding ways of kids communicating by having them squeeze their hands—that kind of thing. George's teachers were amazed at how well he was progressing with his "school work." Obviously, he couldn't do ordinary school work, but they had been going through the motions and, while before he wasn't responding, now he was.

He's also improved a great deal from the neurological perspective. The question becomes, is he actually growing a left side of his brain, or is he perhaps learning how to do these things with the right hemisphere? I don't know the answer to that yet. I'm not ready to order tests that would tell us for sure. I don't want a CT scan or an MRI because both are invasive and dangerous to cells that are just starting to grow. Eventually, I will have an electro-encephalogram performed, because that's totally passive. Whether he's growing a new half of a brain or not, I certainly don't want to put it into an abnormal magnetic field, and I don't want to radiate him either, because both of those things can kills cells and alter DNA. The EEG just receives the electrical activity—but there's no rush. If the kid's doing fine, why get in the way or introduce the possibility of doubt or failure? The equipment might not operate on the same level as our work. Function is also independent of orthodox medical causality. I mean the kid is playing ball!

George and his folks were down here fairly recently and, when I put my hands on his head, I could sense something like a cauli-flower-shaped growth beginning to come into that left side where the fluid has been. Maybe I'm crazy, but what I could visualize was something small, maybe the size of half an orange, but with bumps on it, just like you'd see on the top of the cortex, and just starting to invade the left side vacancy. I could "see," on the left side of the *corpus collosum*—the connection between the right and left halves—something sort of flowering into that cauliflower-like shape.

That's what I can tell you at this point. It's just wild. If it really is so that he is growing a new half a brain, think about the impli-cations for people who've had brain injuries, or had part of their brains removed because of tumors. And all it requires is commu-nication—dialoguing with the stem cells. I think that stem cells are very happy to help. All you have to do is ask!

Remember Li'l Abner with the "Shmoos"? They were magical beings that would become anything you wanted them to become—but you did have to ask! I think stem cells are kind of that way. They don't always know what's necessary or what's going on. As soon as you point something out to them, it seems like they take action. If that's the case, then what we're looking at is a healing system that just needs a little request and perhaps some guidance; then it's willing to do things that we thought impossible. I won't begin to suggest what this says about our human situation and what's been missed by science.

Preliminary Cell Talk: Andy

Here's another story—it's about a little boy who was introduced to me by Pat Norris, Elmer Green's daughter. We'll call him Andy. Pat said that Andy had just cured his inoperable brain cancer! This happened years ago when I was doing some work at Menninger, but it is part of the background of the Cell Talk enterprise. Andy was about eleven or twelve years old. Pat wanted my opinion and asked me to see him. I could feel a lot of energetic confusion in his head, but I got that straightened out pretty easily. Then she gave me his history. He had been referred to her by the hospital to teach him how to die—to ease his death process—because the tumor was absolutely uncontainable. He had been operated on before. This was a reoccurrence and there was nothing more that could be done. He was going to die and she was being asked to help him do it with less pain psychologically. Well, she said, about the third time he came to see her, she was letting him know that everybody dies and that kind of thing, and he said, "But I don't want to die."

She asked him, "What could you do so you won't die?"

He said, "I'll come at the tumor with rocket ships and laser guns, and I'll kill that tumor."

Pat said, "Well, why don't you go ahead and do it?"
And he did, and the next time he came in, he said the only thing he needed to do was to have "Pac Men" come in and clean up the dirt.

At the next session, he said, "It's all gone. I need to get some more x-rays so we can make sure."

Pat called the hospital, but they refused to take the x-rays. They said it was ridiculous, there was no need to do any more testing on him, that she should just let it go.

Well, he went home that afternoon and threw himself down the stairs, pretending to trip, and landed on his head! His mom was at the top of the stairs and he screamed out to his mom, "Mom, Mom—I think I've broke my head!"

She took him to the emergency room and they x-rayed him for skull damage, and they couldn't find the tumor.

When I examined him, all I could sense was some kind of chaotic energy in his head. Actually, I probably was dealing with his fall and not with the tumor at all. When I was done, his mother asked him, "How did it feel when Dr. John was treating you?"

He said, "It was like a Vulcan Mind-Meld!"

Frankly, I think that anybody who does health care should know about this. I also think that moms ought to learn it because you can teach your kids to get well by their own efforts. When this gets out on the market, the drug companies are probably going to try to assassinate me.

———

Compassionate Touch

Our Compassionate Touch Program actually got started in Washington, D.C., in the early 1990s. Jim Gordon, who is a psychiatrist on the faculty of Georgetown Medical School, had a group of young teenagers that he sort of "big brothered." They were all black high-school kids and each one had witnessed a murder firsthand. Most of them were male. Lisa (my present wife) and I happened to be in Washington, I think for something having to do with the NIH, and Jim asked us if we would spend an evening with his kids.

Well, I didn't know what to do with them. I thought I would simulate a ShareCare session. (ShareCare, as I mentioned earlier, is our official name for the mini-seminars that teach basic Cranio-Sacral techniques to parents and other lay people.) We had about three hours to fill. I wound up just following my intuition. We were in a gymnasium with a stage at one end. Once I was on stage, I found myself explaining a little bit about what healing energy could be and could do. I thought I would give them an example, so I asked for someone to come up out of the group. Nobody wanted to do it. Eventually, one guy volunteered after a lot of cajoling. He had a sore shoulder, so I just brought him up there, sat him on a massage table, and put some energy into it. He felt better right away and was quite astonished. He was about to get off the stage, but I said, "No, no! You sit right here on the massage table." I said, "Okay, who's got a sore something else?" Things had gotten started now, so it didn't take as much cajoling. Soon, another guy found the courage to come up. He had a sore knee.

Most of these kids had really negative vibes. You could feel their anger five feet away. The room was loaded with negative energy; nevertheless, these two fellows were up on stage now, and I said to the first one, "You put your hands on his knee—one on each side—and you just send healing energy through. Just have the intention to send whatever kind of energy he needs to heal." It took maybe five or ten minutes, and the second kid said, "My knee feels better."

We did that three or four times, with the person who had just been healed healing someone else's problem, and pretty soon I had each kid in the room treating his neighbor. You could just feel the anger in the room dissipate. I must say, I was astonished. I thought, "Gosh, if it can work with these guys, it can work with anybody."

When I got back to Florida, I continued to think about what happened. I wanted to do more work like this, but I realized that rather than work with teenagers, who were already pretty resistant and angry, I should teach kids before they think it's not possible, and that meant enlisting pre-school children. I reasoned, if we do this with little kids, and they learn a valid technique from the time they were, say, four or five years old, nobody could ever brainwash them out of it. After they'd experienced it a few times, it would be part of them. So my goal, then, was to teach young children that they could help heal each other. I thought that it might counter the more conventional stages of frustration and violence. Kids who learn to heal will always have that magic, as an alternative not only to bullying, hazing, and vandalism, but to cynicism and alienation as well.

At that particular time, I was becoming better acquainted with Frederick Holtzberg, one of the executives in Aveda, the cosmetic company. Frederick had a large distribution center in Cincinnati, Ohio, and, when he heard about my experiences with the teenagers in Washington, he said, "Why don't you try out your ideas at the day school I run for my employees' children?" So we tried it there, and the word from the teachers was that the children really loved it.

At that time, we also had a CranioSacral Therapy student whose mother owned a nursery school in Buffalo, New York. The nursery was for poor children. Frederick's school, by contrast, was mostly middle-class. But it worked just as well for the poor children in Buffalo. So then—being as impulsive as I am—I decided that we would start talking this up in the CranioSacral Therapy classes and find out if there was a way to have the public schools let us in to try it on their kids. We had a few takers, but there was a big hang-up, and it was no surprise: people on the far-right and so-called social conservatives were particularly opposed to compassionate or any other kind of touch. They just didn't want us to teach children to touch each other. They thought that might create "sexual perversion." I, on the other hand, was of the opinion that sexual perversion comes when you're *not allowed to touch anybody* until you've got testosterone coursing through your veins. If you haven't touched anyone until after puberty, you've got a good chance of becoming a rapist. I tried to sell it that way. But the real selling point, as far as I'm concerned, was compassion. If your acts of compassion expand, your acts of violence are reduced. I came to believe that compassion and violence are inversely related. Unfortunately, there are persons in this society who are pretty wacky on these issues, so much so that real old-fashioned hands-on caring is neglected because touch for them has become associated with sexual perversion. Exactly those qualities of love and compassion that religious people should want to cultivate are blackballed and discouraged.

I've had many lessons about compassion over the course of my life. The first was when I shot that little bird and my father made me pick it up and look at it. Another was when I was hanging out with street gangs in Detroit. There was a guy who showed up at one of our parties who didn't really belong there. (Of course, my gang-buddies didn't know I was a member of three different gangs at the same time and didn't really belong there either!) This fellow was the Grosse Point-type—he was of the elite. Grosse Point is where the Henry Fords live. He didn't look like us, he didn't talk like us, and he didn't act like us. Three or four of the gang members took him outside and started to beat him up. I was with them, though I didn't participate. I just watched. Pretty soon, he was down on the ground and one of my best friends was kicking him in the ribs. I told him to stop. He kicked him again. I grabbed my friend, turned him around, and hit him in the mouth, and I knew in that moment that I didn't ever want to be a part of anything like that again. I didn't want to be somebody who would beat people up and make them hurt and maybe kill or maim them. I didn't want any part of that. I really felt sorry for this guy. I managed to make sure that we got an ambulance to come and pick him up and take him to the hospital.

That was a major jump in compassion for me. I found out that when I felt what that guy was feeling on the ground, I couldn't be violent.

Well, I took my ideas about teaching kids to help each other and my ideas about compassion and I developed a nice presentation and began giving it to all of the students in our CranioSacral Therapy classes. Some of the students were physical therapists in the public school systems. Laura Quast, for instance, worked in New Glarus, Wisconsin and brought our ideas before the Superintendent of Schools there. He liked the approach, and we were able to bring Compassionate Touch to the New Glarus school system. Even with his approval, Laura had to do some fancy footwork to make it happen. She went to the school board first and they were very cold, so she went to the schoolteachers themselves, explaining the whole thing, and got them on her side. Then she went back to the school board with four grade-school teachers, and the board finally approved it. From my own experience back at Michigan State, I can tell you that if you've got one school-board member saying "No," then others may shift and agree with him. Most public officials don't want to take a risk. What Laura did was make them see that this was going to be something that would reduce violence in the schools. She put it to them this way: "You can be one of the first schools in the country to participate in this program and show that it works."

At the present time, Madison, Wisconsin (about fifty miles away from New Glarus) is making inquiries about the program for their schools. My feeling is that eventually interest in Compassionate Touch will reach "critical mass"—then all of a sudden, "BOOM!"—it will show up everywhere. I really have a strong feeling in my bones and in my intuitive sense that this will will happen in the next couple of years. It's going to be all over the place.

As of October, 2003, we have "before" and "after" data on almost 1000 public school children. The most dramatic changes that we have seen in the children have been wonderful improvements in social behavior after just four days of the program. There have even been some efforts to measure the changes scientifically. We had psychologists devise evaluation forms for us to use. The teachers evaluate the children before and after the program, and then a year later.

I can't tell you just what the tests are, but the psychologists have modified standard tests that evaluate inter-social activities, social behaviors, helpfulness, temper-loss—that kind of thing. The results that we have seen show that after being initiated into the program, children are much more caring about each other and much more helpful when something like an accident happens.

The statistics strongly support the efficacy of the program. There is measurably less violence perpetrated in later childhood years by "Compassionate Touch" graduates.

I think that compassion is *communicable*. Everybody is born with a level of it that's part of our genetic make-up. It's even telepathic. Psychologists have observed that newborns and infants who are quiet and peaceful start to cry when somebody who is suffering or in pain walks into the room. It's as though they sense the pain in the other person and feel empathy for them. We are born with a "compassion instinct."

Well, if that's the case, then our teachings that kids in school must not touch each other go against our genetic makeup, and it's only natural that we become frustrated because we are not being allowed to exercise our basic impulses. That frustration builds up and develops into anger, and anger ultimately displays itself in some sort or other of violent behavior. There seems to be an inverse relationship between compassion and violence, as I noted before. The more violence there is, the less compassion, and the more compassion, the less violence. At a certain level, the suppression of tenderness is so aggravating to the system that it propagates violence.

The mother of a little girl who had experienced one of our classes wrote a letter telling how her child came home from kindergarten one day when she (the mother) was in bed with a migraine, and the girl asked, "Mommy, do you have a headache?"

"Yes."

"Can I put my hands on your head?"

"Sure."

In about five minutes, her headache was gone, and the child felt wonderful. I suggest that this ability to help is permanently etched in the little girl's brain and thus is communicable. She helped her mother's headache, and she can do it again and again and again. . . .

A boy told us about how his dog got hit by a car and was lying in the street. He went and put his hands on the head and the rear end of the dog and thought his happy thoughts—that's what we teach them to do: "Think happy thoughts"—and, after a few minutes, the dog stopped yelping and started licking one of his hands and got up and walked away.

Another boy told us about helping his big brother, who had fallen down and skinned his knee. He just went up and asked if he could help, and his brother accepted the offer and mumbled, "Okay." The knee got better right away. The boy was so proud because, he said, it isn't very often that you get a chance to help your big brother.

To prepare our therapists to teach Compassionate Touch in the schools, we give them a little basic training, approve them, and then send them out to train teachers and children. What I really want to happen is that the school teachers learn Compassionate Touch themselves so that *they* can teach the children as part of the school's regular curriculum. Then it'll go on throughout the year.

It has worked. Some of the teachers in New Glarus are willing to travel all over the country and testify about the benefits of the program. And the teachers themselves are experiencing the benefit. One of them said recently, "I've been using this technique on the kids when they get hurt, and I not only help them feel empowered. I feel better about myself."

One evening, I went with Laura Quast to work with the teachers in New Glarus before they engaged with the children. We began with a two-hour question-and-answer session with parents and teachers—sort of like a PTA meeting. The next morning, I held an "in-service" day for kindergarten, first-, and second-grade teachers, and any others that wanted to come. I explained Cranio-Sacral Therapy, energy, the physics behind the work, and I talked a bit about my own experiences. Then I did the same thing that I did with the black kids in Washington. I had a teacher come up who had pain. I took care of the pain. Then I had her sit there and work on another teacher. I had each teacher treat another after being treated. There were eight teachers, and they all got better. One of them was suffering from spondylitis—an inflammation of the whole spine. I had everybody make a chain. We put collective energy through her, and she got up off the table pain-free.

We spent the next day with the children—thirty to forty-five minutes in each classroom—that's all. Let's call it an hour, tops! The teachers knew what we were going to do, so they helped us out. We went into each classroom, and we told the kids that they had the ability to help somebody with a "boo-boo." Jimmy Green, one of our instructors who came along with me, did a great job. He got up in front of the children and asked, "How many of you have been to Disney World?"

Hands went up all over the room!

"Oh, so you know Mickey Mouse. Well, I was at Mickey Mouses's house, and . . . what do we have here in Wisconsin that's so good to eat?"

A chorus of kids answered: "Cheese!"

"Cheese! Well, Mickey spilled some cheese on the floor, and I was walking across the floor and—WHOOPS!—I slipped and fell on the cheese. I hurt my knee. Oh, my poor knee."

By now he had the children's full attention. Then he said, "Who would like to come up and fix my knee?" One little girl came up. And that's how it started. He had them treating each other and the teacher treating them. Within an hour, they all were hooked!

We tell them that they can help anyone who is hurting. We make sure that they know that they have to ask, "Are you hurt? Would you like me to help you? Is it okay if I touch you?"

We also do a little follow-up. We've developed a song for them to sing about "helping hands." We ask the teachers to reinforce the process by having them start each day in the classroom by singing it and, if a child has something good that happened with their "helping hands," to tell about it. Then she has them draw a picture about it, and they put it up on the bulletin board. It takes three or four minutes every morning. And for the benefit derived from it, that little bit of time is very, very tiny.

Here's the song. I played the piano for it. It goes to the tune of "O Where, O Where Has My Little Dog Gone?"

> *O where, O where are my helping hands?*
> *O where, O where can they be?*
> *With a rainbow going from one to the other,*
> *O where, O where can they be?*

(Spoken) Here they are! (all show their hands)

Then, to the tune of "Twinkle, Twinkle Little Star":

> *When you have a hurt somewhere,*
> *I will show you that I care.*
> *If you like my helping hands,*
> *You can tell me "Yes, I can,"*
> *And I'll send a rainbow through*
> *With my hands from me to you.*

And that's how Compassionate Touch got started. It's a way to help dispel a lot of the frustration and anger that's going on in the schools, and there aren't a lot of them. Of course, the approach has to be modified as you move from one grade to the next. You can't teach sixth graders to sing the "helping hands" songs. I'm sure that we can come up with something appropriate for them. And we will do that. We could even have compassionate rap. It's all energy anyway. We look at the kids, we throw out a little bit, we see how they respond, and then we change it. You adapt to whatever is coming back to you. We'll start teaching this very soon.

We'll have a couple of workshops for our CranioSacral therapists so that they can go to the schools and try to get a program started. I have no illusion that our Institute can cover all of this by itself. We can get it started and we can do the training program. Anybody that's been through our CranioSacral Therapy Two seminar can learn what it takes to teach the children. The question becomes, do these potential trainers have personalities that can get along with the children and the teachers, and are they able to convince the school board? We're picking carefully, but most people can easily learn the mechanics. I really look for this program to make a change over a period of time. I think the children that learn it now won't be as mean or as angry as they grow up.

I find it extremely interesting that these improved attitudes expand spontaneously. We taught the children to help each other when someone is in pain, but the teachers have commented that in the classroom, if somebody is having trouble reading, for instance, another child will come over and help. They never did that before. There seems to be something inherent in the process that generalizes helpfulness and compassion by itself.

Incidentally, we have seven public schools in the program at the present time. That's quite a feat because there's usually one member of the school board that says we shouldn't be teaching these little kids to touch each other, it will cause sexual perversion, etc. Another problem is also giving us trouble now: teachers are overworked and don't want to do the evaluations. To accommodate them, if the standard forms are too irksome, we now allow the teacher simply to write us a statement at the end of the year. We have the data on about five-hundred children as of October, 2005. That should still be a statistically significant sample. We have also had about a thousand children go through the program into 2006.

I think, as I keep saying, that everyone is born with an innate ability to help their fellow human beings and friendly animals. Society teaches that we can't do it and that to think we can is silly. But that's just plain wrong. Healing is something that you simply have to do, no questions asked.

Exciting
New Cases

The following are four very exciting cases that seem to be disclosing new areas of healing for me. The cases are all open—I have no idea how they'll turn out, but each is quite extraordinary in its own way.

Chester

Chester is a sixty-four-year-old fellow who has been on kidney dialysis three times a week, for about five years. I got to know Chester because he's the yard man at our home. During a routine blood test five years ago, he showed elevated levels of two substances that are used to evaluate kidney function. The substances are *creatinine* and *urea nitrogen.* If these levels are high, it's supposed to mean there's something seriously wrong with the kidneys. Now, I've read all of his medical records and I can't find a diagnosis for his kidney problem apart from these tests anywhere. His physicians apparently just felt that these measures were so high that they needed to put him on dialysis right away. He was drinking alcohol a lot at the time, so it was hard to tell whether he was really asymptomatic. He was working—he wasn't disabled—but he says that he was drinking about a quart of hard liquor, especially vodka, everyday. Sometimes that will mask symptoms. Anyway, he went to the doctor, for some reason, and they found these elevated levels.

Dialysis was performed three times a week at a clinic set up especially for the treatment of kidneys. His blood was drained, purified, and put back in him each time over a period of about three to four hours.

Within a couple of weeks after they started the dialysis, he quit urinating. This is to be expected because the dialysis strains wastes and toxins from the blood and the kidneys don't have to work.

During all the five years that he was on dialysis, he was on a list to receive a kidney transplant, but now he was sixty-four years old, and the limit for getting a transplant is sixty-five. Meanwhile, his heart was slowly weakening—heart and kidney function are closely related. When the kidneys aren't putting out the fluid, then the fluid accumulates and the heart has to pump against that back pressure. Dialysis doesn't help that situation, so it's expected that you can't live forever on dialysis. He was informed that he needed a heart transplant before he could get a new kidney. The doctor felt that, without a new heart, he would not survive the kidney transplant surgery. So basically Chester had a death sentence hanging over him if they didn't find him a heart and a kidney by his sixty-fifth birthday. Chester told all this to my wife while he was working in the yard, so I had him come in.

Well, it took us about an hour to get rid of his heart problem. All we had to do was pump the fluid and give him an energy massage. When he went to the dialysis center for his next treatment, they couldn't figure out what had happened. They wanted to know why he looked so much better now? I then did some acupuncture on him and, of course, our CranioSacral work. My wife, Lisa, and I started seeing him twice a week. His kidneys continued to improve energetically. Now he's urinating again—ten to fifteen ounces a day—but he's still taking dialysis. He's showing some improvement on his blood tests. In every way it's obvious he's improving instead of deteriorating, and the doctors at the center want to know why! Conventional medical wisdom says kidneys don't improve. Once they begin to go bad, they can only deteriorate further. But my feeling is that, at some point not too far in the future, we'll have his kidneys working satisfactorily. The problem is that it's impossible for them to work full blast right now because the dialysis takes out a lot of what would be urine. The ten to fifteen ounces of fluid that's left over, however, tells me that his kidneys are, in fact, performing.

We actually don't know what his kidneys are doing. If we quit dialysis outright, would they kick in completely? Don't know. The problem is that it's impossible to experiment to find out. I would love to get his dialysis down to twice a week to see how he does, but the dialysis clinic won't stand for that. Why? Because they say if he gives up one of his "slots," they'd have to give it to somebody else and, once that happened, it might be a year or two to get a slot back again if he needed it. So we've got to be pretty damn sure that things are working perfectly before we totally stop his dialysis. I would like to reduce his dialysis and see if his kidneys would accept the challenge by increasing urine output. And yet it is obvious that improvement is going on. Even though conventional medicine says that those kidneys are irreparable, I'm saying that they aren't.

Well, we relieved the back pressure on the heart. As a matter of fact, they sent him down to Miami Heart Center for an evaluation and they couldn't find much wrong with his heart at all, even though he's sixty-four years old and has gone through all of this stuff. My question is, will his kidneys be able to handle the whole job? How will I find that out? I really don't know. This is completely uncharted water.

The crux of the issue isn't medical, it's financial. At the Kidney Center, they charge him $1,600 a week. And the doctor gets $350 a month on top of that, and the blood tests are on top of that. Between his insurance and himself, they're raking in almost $2,000 a week on this guy, so they don't want to let go of him. I've concluded that the threat (if he cuts down dialysis to twice a week he won't be able to get the third slot back if he needs it) is a tactic to prevent him from getting away from them. And I think, honestly, the real reason they haven't found a kidney for him is that he's about to reach the cut-off age for a transplant and he'll be on dialysis for the rest of his life. I must say that, in my opinion, that's at least a part of what's underneath it all. But we keep looking for a way to reduce Chester's dialysis and see what his kidneys may then be able to do.

Conjoined Twins from Egypt

Probably the most remarkable case that has ever come my way involves a pair of Egyptian conjoined twins! They're connected at the head. There's some shared brain tissue, as well as some shared blood vessels that service the brains. Their eyes, when looking straight ahead, are at about a 60 degree angle to each other, so that when one of them's lying flat, the other one is off at an angle; they can't see each other; if one moves fast he can give the other a whiplash!

We heard about the twins from a Dr. Kenneth Salyer, who runs the World CranioFacial Foundation. Ken Salyer is a bone-remodeling plastic surgeon. He heard about the Egyptian twins and sent a team from his foundation to Egypt to look at them. They brought them to Dallas, Texas, where Ken's offices are. Ken wants to perform surgery to separate the twins, but it will have to involve a neurosurgical team to help with the brain and vascular separations.

Dr. Salyer's wife happens to have taken three of our Cranio-Sacral Therapy courses so, when the twins arrived in the U.S., she convinced him that it would be a good idea to try to do Cranio-Sacral work on them. Dr. Salyer invited me to Dallas in the beginning of October, 2002. I went there and spent three days with the twins.

What I found immediately was that it was as if the two skulls had sutures between them. I theorized that I could mobilize those sutures, just the way one mobilizes the sutures between the plates in a single skull. Mobilizing the sutures between the two skulls of the twins meant that I could, in a sense, if only very slightly, begin to separate the two skulls.

My feeling was that it was during the gestational period in the uterus something like the following might have happened to what should have been normal identical twins. With identical twins, at a very early stage, there is a "sticky" protein called *connexin*. At the proper moment, this protein receives a message and loses its stickiness so the two fetuses can separate. I think something must have happened so that the stickiness was not removed and the twins continued to grow while they were still joined. The skulls probably accommodated the juncture; the blood vessels were doing what they normally do, because they usually develop in response to the demand that's placed on them locally.

We all have two *jugular draining systems*—two jugular veins, one on each side of the normal neck—draining from our brain, but each of these little guys had only one. It was on the left side of each twin, so the vascular systems of the two were not independently formed. Also, their metabolisms weren't functioning separately. One kid was eating and pooping normally and the other was not doing much eating or having much bowel movement. Both twins were living off the nutrition that only one of them was taking in, and that was passing through the common vascular system. The twin who wasn't eating was considerably smaller than his brother. We also found out that the heart of the one who wasn't eating wasn't working effectively: it was beating at about 180 to 200 beats per minute. That is too fast to allow for filling between contractions, thus the heart becomes less effective. The heart in the stronger twin was pumping more slowly and thus furnishing blood for both of them. Because of the way one twin seemed to be dependent on the other, the surgeons were really concerned about the possibility of separating them.

I learned all this when I got there but, with a little work releasing the vagus nerve, I was able to get the smaller twin eating and pooping. This nerve was compressed close to where the two skulls were joined; to be precise, on the flat side where one of them was always lying. Within three or four days after I got that to open up, the dependent twin was eating more and passing bowel movements. I also was able to get both hearts pumping effectively rather than just one.

Andrew Fryer (a pediatric cardiologist who is a CranioSacral Therapy student of ours) together with his wife, Sally (a physical therapist in one of our advanced programs) took an interest in the twins. They live in Dallas. After I left, Sally decided to keep working with them. I showed her what I thought she should be doing. She saw them three times a week for more than a month until she and the twins came here to Florida to be part of our intensive program.

When they got here, we put them in front of a mirror where they could see each other. What was weird about that was they had a psychologist in Dallas who said, "Don't ever let them see each other because if one dies, that will put the other one in mourning."

My response was: "The hell with that." We have a big floor mirror in the intensive room, so we sat them down in front of that mirror and let them play. They looked at each other and started touching each other and doing things—becoming fully aware of each other's existence and relationship to themselves.

When they went back to Dallas, I got a call from Sally, our therapist who was working with them there. She said, "One of these twins is now talking Egyptian and the other one is talking English. Neither one of them is doing both!"

I exclaimed, "God, how did that happen?"

"They had the two Egyptian nurses here and the Egyptian pediatrician came with them. They were always talking Egyptian and of course, we were always talking English. You'd think they'd learn both, but each one was different. That lasted for about three weeks and then they started overlapping."

During that program, my goal was to separate their heads as much as possible, but also to get all of their physiological systems working independently. Many of their systems other than the ones I have already mentioned were still at least partially linked in function. We went through their bodies and, one by one, separated the functions of their digestive systems, livers, spleens, hearts, lungs. We were able to create enough physical separation between the skulls so that you could get a finger in the "dent" that appeared where the two come together. The two skulls were put together like a suture, and by manipulating them, I got them to sort of spread out. As we did that they both began to act differently, more autonomously.

The whole thing was quite successful. The smaller twin began growing more rapidly. After we relieved some compression from the tops of their brains, they both started using their motor systems and began to crawl; one had to crawl forwards while the other was going backwards, and then *vice versa*, but they seemed to have figured out how to do it just fine!

After they left the intensive program, I got a call from Sally. She said that about two days after they got back to Texas, she was able to put them onto one of those "physio-balls" that you inflate like a big beach ball to do exercises on. Their heads connected over the top of it; they rolled the ball with their hands, and they have learned to walk that way.

The idea about creating the separation between the two skulls was related to my notion of the "sticky protein." I talked it over a good deal with Ken Salyer. I said that if I was right, then perhaps there would be a genetic structure that would kick in once the actual physical connection was broken, and whatever systems remained linked might begin to separate by genetic means. Ken thought that was a pretty good idea. He agreed with me on the possibility, so a bit after the intensive program, Lisa and I went back to Dallas.

We had three therapists working on each body while I worked at the joined skulls. I used tractions and a lot of energy and deployed my hand almost as a laser to separate the two. My feeling is that it's kind of like toffee—if you keep pulling it and pulling it, what will happen is that the connections in the brain and the connections in the blood vessels will get narrower and narrower. The greater the separation we can get that way, the easier the surgical job will be.

Before we started with them, the surgeons were probably not going to operate, because they thought it would kill both of them;

but once we had worked on them, they began to think there was a good possibility that the two kids would be okay.

I mentioned before how the kids only had two jugular veins between them. Well, we began dialoguing with them to get them to grow another jugular vein each. The CT scan that was done before I started with the twins showed thin venous structures running down where the missing big veins ought to be. Let's say they are about a sixteenth of the size they ought to be. I thought that we could get them to expand: they had the path there, so we just had to develop it into a highway! And, indeed, there was a slight enlargement.

At that point, the operation was going to be scheduled for the late spring or summer of 2003. What they were planning to do—and I was afraid that this might be a setback for them—was to put them in the hospital for about six weeks. Ken Salyer wanted to put a balloon under the skin where the two heads join and stretch that skin so that he could use it to flap over the surgical sites after the surgery was completed. After that looked like it was okay—when that skin developed and separated—then they'd be ready to operate. My plan was to go back to Dallas again because I didn't think the airplane ride would be good for them.

The idea was that they would stay in Dallas for one year post-op, and then go back to Egypt. This was all being financed by the World Cranial Facial Foundation. No fees were involved at all. We donated our time, too, and we raised some money to bring them from Dallas to Florida and back again. We also got the hotel to donate the rooms and so on. During the week that they were in Florida, we had fifteen interviews with reporters and TV stuff. We were on Fox news. There was a pretty good shot of me talking for about three or four minutes while they were focusing on the twins.

The news media really seems to be interested in things like this.

In of June, 2003, the twins were hospitalized for the preliminary surgery. Sally Fryer visited them there and treated them three times a week. Before they entered, they were in tremendous shape but, when Ken Salyer put the "balloon" under their skin, he did so with too much pressure, and the skins started to "dehisce." (When the skin disconnects from what's underneath it, it may turn black and die.) They were trying to get more skin and instead they lost some. After that first surgery, the twins slept for three days.

Eventually, late in the summer of 2003, Dr. Salyer achieved the desired stretching of the scalp skin, and the neurosurgeons were able to plan their separation surgery. This would involve separating brains and blood vessels, as well as dealing likewise with meningeal tissues and so on. Dr. Salyer's work took about three months. When it was finished, the twins were removed from Dr. Salyer's hospital to the hospital where the neurosurgeons were to operate. During the whole stay in the hospital where Dr. Salyer worked, CranioSacral Therapy was administered three times a week by Sally Fryer and her crew.

The neurosurgery was successfully carried out in October, 2003. It went better than the surgeons had anticipated. I do believe that CranioSacral Therapy deserves some of the credit for the ease with which the surgery was accomplished and for the fact that there have been very few post-op problems. When the neurosurgery group deems it safe, the twins will be moved to Dr. Salyer's hospital where his constructive surgery can be done. I am writing this in late October, 2003. After Dr. Salyer is finished, I hope that we can get the twins back to the Upledger Institute in Florida, where I am confident that our intensive work will counter post-operative complications and possible long-term disabilities.

One last update: In early November, 2003, both twins were

doing very well and were transferred back to Dr. Salyer's hospital and care. As of the time of the writing of this book, the twins were happy and living individual lives. Mohamed and Ahmed Ibrahim returned home to Egypt in November 2005. As of January 2006, the boys were receiving daily physical therapy and were expected to begin English school. The family is thrilled to report that the boys are happy, active, and making great developmental strides.

Matthew

Matthew is an eleven-year-old boy whose parents brought him to us in December, 2002. He has been totally dependent on a ventilation machine since birth. When Matthew was born, they couldn't get him to start breathing, so they put him on a ventilator immediately. They did a tracheostomy to make an incision for the ventilator to go in and informed his parents that he would never be able to live without the machine. The diagnosis was "congenital central hypoventilation syndrome," which is just medicalese for the fact that he couldn't breathe.

Matthew's mother is a physical therapist, and she wrote me to ask if I thought there was anything I could do for him. I said I didn't know but I was willing to try. She brought him down, and I just tuned into his rhythm a little bit and asked his craniosacral rhythm if it would reply to yes/no questions. I requested that if the answer were "yes," it should stop abruptly, and if the answer were "no," it would just keep on going. Well, it stopped abruptly, so I took that for a "yes" and assumed we were on the same page.

I asked, first of all, whether all the parts necessary for a functioning breathing system were present and available in Matthew. It said, "Yes." Then I asked, since all of the parts were present, was it just that they'd never started? Again the answer was, "Yes."

Now I asked if something had happened in his mother's uterus that prevented him from learning how to start breathing. Affirmative. I said, "Well, if I can help get you started breathing, would you be willing for me to do it?"

"Yes."

I asked, "Would you love it if you could breathe on your own?"

"Yes."

I started putting energy through the respiratory centers in the brainstem, and then I ran down the vagus nerves because they influence the bronchi and their dilation and constriction. I also started working with the rib cage and all the nerves that come out of the spinal column that control the rib cage muscles, and I worked with the *phrenic nerve* that goes down to the diaphragm. In short, I passed energy through all the things that have to do with breathing and, when I was done, I said, "Okay, let's take the ventilator off." We did and, as I gave verbal instructions about moving his diaphragm and rib cage, Matthew started breathing. He had never done this before.

Mom almost passed out right on the spot. She was really afraid, because everybody was telling her that he would die if he went off the ventilator, but here he was breathing on his own. I was telling him to push his belly in and out, helping him breathe consciously, and he was doing it! But was he getting the oxygen he needed? We checked his oxygen/carbon dioxide ratio—it was excellent.

When Mom got hold of herself, realizing that he was actually breathing, she asked, "Well what should I do?"

I said, "Take him off the ventilator for about an hour, maybe four times a day for a couple of weeks, and call me and let me know how he's doing."

She followed that plan, and Matthew did just fine. They came back to see me in about three months. By that time, he was able to stay off the device for four hours at a time without any difficulties, all the while breathing consciously. The next step was to see if he could breathe spontaneously without having to work at it.

They visited me again, and I had him breathe consciously for me on the table, and then I started to train him to breathe "nonconsciously" by distracting him. He learned very well, and by the end of the session he was breathing quite normally. I had him appear at our "Beyond the Dura Conference," at the beginning of June, 2003. At the conference, we have a "patient panel" where patients get to demonstrate their condition. Matthew walked on stage with no ventilator and talked to everybody. Matthew's mom wrote me a note a few weeks later. She said that, for the first time in his life, she let him out of her sight without the ventilator. She said they went to the mall, and he went wandering off, and she was scared to death but she decided not to interfere, and he was just fine.

I was concerned at first that he might have trouble sustaining spontaneous breathing while asleep, but it appears not to be a problem.

When he was down here for the conference, he confided in me that he knows that he's going to be okay, so he wants to be a football coach.

Before he went on stage, his mom gave his history so, when he walked up and started to speak, everybody was very moved and many almost cried. Matthew still had the surgical aperture in his throat from the tracheostomy, and he has to put his finger over the hole to talk. The thing I have to do next is convince a surgeon that he won't die if we close up the hole. It would be nice if we can get him past having to do that finger thing when he talks.

I think what we'll do is put some material over the hole and keep it covered for a while and, once he's had his hole covered for two or three weeks, his mom can go ahead and find a surgeon willing to close it permanently. As of the writing of this book, that has happened.

———

The Olympic Diver

The next one is Mary Ellen Clark, an Olympic diver. Mary Ellen came in September '96 with a bronze medal from previous Olympics for the high dive. This time she had to break training from some time in July, as I recall. She was three months without training, and the reason the coach wouldn't let her train was because, after diving in, she was so dizzy that she swam to the bottom of the pool. She could drown if she was that disoriented.

She went everywhere. She'd been to twenty places in the U.S. to try to get rid of this. She underwent everything there was. What I did was evaluate her body and found out that there was a lot of tension coming up her neck; the dural tube was tight but the tightness wasn't coming from there. Everybody was focusing on her head and her ears. I wound up on her left knee. She had an old injury that went up into her pelvis, and she was so strong that her pelvis worked even with the bad leg. Her leg worked too. But it threw her out of kilter so that the muscles coming up the right side of her paravertebral area, the area next door to the spine, were tight and they were pulling her skull back so that, when she moved a certain way, it interfered with the blood flow to the brain.

The other piece was that the sacrum was stuck, and that was tugging down on the dural tube—the tube of membrane that comes down through your spinal canal from your head. As that was pulled, it was pulling the temporal bones backwards and causing her to be dizzy. So there were two factors: her temporal bones were out of line (and that will always give you vertigo); and she was getting fuzzy-headed because the blood supply to the right side of the brain was being impaired. It all came from this left knee injury she got when she was practicing on a trampoline.

One footnote: when I started letting her train her lower body, I said, "What are you going to do?"

She said, "I'm going to do a lot of leg pushes."

I said, "How much do you train with?"

She said "Oh, 625 pounds."

Oh my god, here's this 5-foot 3-inch little girl!

<hr/>

Fritz

This next story has a very bizarre "psychic" twist to it. It is quite fantastic and also terrifying, really.

A gentleman from Zurich, Switzerland, came to see me a few years ago because he had had a bad neck accident. We were able to take care of that without any complications. He'd been all over Europe trying to get his neck fixed and finally heard about me. Now he comes by about once a year, and we've become pretty good friends. Fritz is about my age, 71, or 72. He used to be a big-time executive with an international company, and he traveled all over the world managing regional offices, so he's been to a lot of places.

In the summer of 2002, I received a letter from Fritz saying he'd had surgery for a ruptured aneurysm in an artery in the forehead. He had recovered from that surgery extremely well, and he thanked me for my craniosacral work with him, to which he attributed the ease of his recovery. (By the way, from Swiss neurosurgeons I have ample confirmation of the fact that a healthy craniosacral system is a real plus in preparation for surgery. Fritz had given a copy of *The Inner Physician and You* to his neurosurgeon, a Professor Prost. Prost wrote me a letter to the effect that he had performed over 20,000 surgeries and recognized exactly the "fluid wave" we talk about, and he doesn't understand why anybody has trouble believing in it.)

While they were operating on Fritz for the aneurysm in his forehead, they found another aneurysm in another artery. After he had healed from his first surgery, they wanted to go in to repair this second aneurysm, which they did. But after the second surgery Fritz wrote me to say he wasn't recovering very well. It had been six weeks and he was still having major problems.

Now here's the really weird part. Fritz had seen a psychic some years before, and the psychic said that whatever happened to him, he should never let the medical people do an MRI on him. No reason given. Just: NO MRI! No matter what! I suppose the psychic had been correct on some other matter, because Fritz obeyed, and he refused to let them do an MRI to find out why he wasn't healing properly. They operated again without an MRI, and what they found out was that *they had left a needle inside him!* Also the clamp on the aneurysm had slipped. So they did the repair. But can you imagine what would have happened if they had turned on a magnetic resonance imaging machine with a steel needle still inside his head!?

Fritz came to visit very recently and stayed for two weeks. We got a rid of a lot of the traces of old things—skiing injuries and so on. But the fact that Fritz had three surgeries in a period of ten weeks is pretty remarkable for a man of his age. He's not incapacitated in the least. He is bright as a whip. I worked on his head and released the strictures that had formed post-surgically to make sure his brain had enough room. He was able to feel it as I was doing it. The truth is that this is a wonderful thing to do—to release strictures in the membrane surrounding the brain after surgery. It takes me back to the days when I used to "scrub" with Dr. Tyler on brain-surgery cases and then make sure, the next day, that the membranes hadn't contracted. Well, Fritz's membranes had contracted a bit, but I was able to stretch them out again and his brain is functioning just beautifully.

Jazz and
What It Means to Me

Before I sign off with this memoir, my wife, Lisa, says I have to say a bit more about what jazz has meant to me and how it has really been an integral part, not only of my life, but of my work. And I think that's true. (Lisa herself plays the drums a bit.) Things have happened in the course of my life and my work that are pretty much the way they happen in a really good jazz jam session!

I started playing jazz when I was really very little. I owe it to my dad, who opened me up and gave me the freedom to improvise. By the time I was a young teenager, I had many opportunities to hear other guys improvise and to play music just the way they wanted to. When you are improvising with other musicians, it's just as if you are reading each other's minds while you are playing. Often I'd walk out on the bandstand, being hired for a gig at a wedding or perhaps a stage show or at a jazz club, and it would be the first time I'd met some of the players, and by the time the first number was over, we'd be looking right into each other's heads. And we'd be playing beautifully and it would sound like we'd been playing together for years.

Jazz helped me feel free about being creative, and not only about music—but in my profession as a doctor. I do the same thing when

I'm treating a patient as when I'm playing music. Jazz has helped me to *read* people. Just as I learned how to read jazz musicians, I learned how to read people by feeling them out, so to speak, not so much by listening to them but by *touching* them. And I think that touch has a lot to do playing jazz. As a pianist I'm always using my hands.

Jazz also has given me a tremendous release.

Some time, not too long ago, I had a trio—piano, drums, and bass—and we played one night a week at a local place called the "City Club." The gig lasted for about six months. After it was over, I wanted to keep the trio going but I wasn't real happy with the bass man. What happened was this. I was about to leave town— I'm not sure where I was going, probably to California. The limo driver taking me to the airport was a very nice black guy, El Green. As I listened to him talk, I got a hunch that he was a musician, so I asked him. He said, "Oh yeah, man." We got to be friends. Pretty soon I found out that he had a contract to do ten one-hour TV shows for the local channel, and he said he wanted to do one with me on classical jazz. By this time, I'd played the piano for him and he'd heard me play Duke Ellington, and so forth. Lisa and I started practicing for the date and he began coming to hear us—but we still didn't have a bass player.

Now here's where it gets really wild. Our air-conditioning contract, it turns out, required that there be a routine periodical inspection; and the inspector (who was really just a kid) appeared one day while I was working in my home office. Lisa showed him around and he noticed our piano and drums and said, "You got music in this house!"

Well, he did his inspection, but meanwhile I had four therapists in my home office with me on Chester, and he (the inspector) came into the room with some paper he needed me to sign.

I said, "Just a minute, I'll be right with you," but he says, "No hurry. Can I just stand here and watch?"

After a couple of minutes, I saw that he was watching really intently, so I said, "How would you like to just grab his feet?"

So the guy brought a chair over, sat down, and started holding Chester's feet as I instructed him to, and I asked him to push energy up into Chester's body. He did, and I could feel it way up into his head, and I thought this guy's got talent!

Now it so happens that I often have a cellist in the room, because sometimes you can stimulate kidney activity by playing it. The cellist was there. After a little while the inspector kid caught sight of the cello and said, "You know I'm a musician."

I said, "Yeah?"

He said, "I play bass, so could I try playing your cello?"

He took the cello, played it like a standup bass, and he was really good—so he's now our replacement bass man!

They're opening a new Ritz Carlton Club about two miles from us, and we've already played there one night a week for three months.

Philosophies, Stories, and Lessons

CranioSacral therapy has been my life's work, and I've come to realize that it arises from openness. The whole thing in a nutshell, doing this work, is you put your hands on and you blend. You be one with the person you're working on. The intelligence of that person starts coming through into you and it comes into your consciousness. Then if you're smart enough not to follow your rationality, you just do it.

I don't have preconceived notions. When a person lies on the table, I don't want to know what's the matter. I want to evaluate him or her first and then we go from there. I'm just doing what I'm told. The patient's body is where the information comes from.

The refusal to admit, let alone explore, this is just about the biggest problem I have with conventional medicine. Arrogance has to be totally dismissed. You have to let go of your ego completely and you have to be like a blank check that can be used in a lot of ways. It's acceptable here, here, here—but it's always blank. She's going to put the writing on it. That's how it works.

I'll give for an example of a brand new patient I've had. The diagnosis she brought with her is pseudotumor of the spinal cord. Pseudo is fake; what it means is that there's fluid involved in a cystic apparatus, but there's no cell or tissue in there to make it a tumor. It's just fluid. They call it a pseudotumor. Back when I was working at Sun Coast Hospital in Clearwater, Florida, I used to operate with the neurosurgeon, and we did some pseudotumors. In those days, you used x-ray because that's the only thing you had. The pseudotumor looked like a tumor because the dye that you used in the x-ray went around it. The assumption was that it was a tumor, but invariably it was a cyst. They called it a pseudotumor because it's, in a way, an imitation of tumor. I've seen enough of them that when I hear a diagnosis of pseudotumor, what that means to me is that they don't know what it is, but it looks like it's got fluid in it.

With this woman, it was pretty easy. She had tremendous pain from this place, coming around from the front of her chest, and it was about the level of sixth to the eleventh thoracic. It was on the righthand side and it was about an inch wide. I picked this up from my own feelings about what I was contacting. As I got the fluid out of there. she began feeling better immediately. I've worked on her three or four times now. We just treated it like a cystic tumor that's full of cerebrospinal fluid rather than tissue. We get that to move out and stay out. The whole point is, if I can flatten it and then hold it flattened for a while, it will begin to glue itself together and not be pushed apart by the fluid pressure.

When I treat her, I put a hand in the back and a hand in the front and I imagine energy going through there that will move the fluid. This is what I'm talking about when I describe passing energy in CST. Let me explain it in another way. I've been reading about quantum physics, and I'm a big fan of Erwin Schrödinger. In the early 1900s he wrote the first formula to be accepted in quantum physics. He got a Nobel Laureate for it. What I'm coming up with very much resembles his model of waves, particles, and uncertainty theory; that is, if I want something to disappear, I put enough energy through it, and what happens is, astonishingly, it disappears. That how strong intention is—it works on a quantum level.

Anything that is clogging a system—even fluid—is of course made up of atoms. Every electron in an atom has a specific electrical charge, and it's always negative. The neutron and the proton in the nucleus of the atom are made up of quarks; each quark has exactly the same positive charge as the electron has a negative one. What happens when I put a lot of energy through living matter in the form of intention is that the energy increases the activity of the atoms and of the quantum quarks. When an electron and a quark collide they lose their mass and turn into energy. Now what I'm doing is sending quanta of subtle heat energy that increase the amount of this activity. That means there are more collisions between positive and negative particles and anti-particles and, when they collide, they turn into energy and lose their mass. The energy comes out as heat. When you're doing this and you're feeling the heat coming out, you're engaged in a quantum process.

Entropy is the negative energy that causes things to age, to ultimately die or fall apart. It's countered by what Schrödinger called information, aka syntropy, which is the part that keeps you alive. The balance between entropy and syntropy is going to dictate whether you're going to be degrading or revitalizing. Schrödinger also said that when you feel the heat come out, it's bringing entropy with it and therefore you're revitalizing wherever it came from.

Between those two concepts—the heat coming out and the quarks and electrons turning into energy and then removing entropy—probably there is some unknown connection. The entropy and the quark electron activity are related. I'm willing to guess that they are probably different ways of looking at the same central phenomenon but coming in from two divergent directions.

Anyway that's what I'm doing with this patient. I'm dissolving the fluid in her pseudotumor and, at the same time, I'm trying to get rid of the entropy that prevents the tissue from healing back together again.

It's all my intention. That's it. That's as far as I can go—and I really don't give a damn whether the quantum stuff or any other story about why something happens is true or not. If I intend it and it works, I don't need to know more than that. If I am blessed and I wake up one morning after a dream about something and understand how to do it, that's wonderful. We are not automatons; we are mysterious beings with many dimensions. I don't need a statistical survey or lab test to tell me what I know or what I don't know or what I supposedly can't know. Dreams, intuitions, and listening are the way I get most of my information. Sometimes I just awake in the morning with it. You put your intention where you want it.

Does that ever piss scientists off! They're still trying to do a double-blind study, double-blind on the universe—but it's impossible. They find out that one guy feels palpation and the other guy feels something else, so it must be nothing.

My point is, I'm using my intuition to get into the fluid and to dissolve it and get it to turn into energy, using the principles that I just gave you. Physicists don't get challenged on hypotheses like relativity or quantum theory or uncertainty principle, but if you put something like that out in medicine, they'll crucify you. Whether these things are true or not, they heal people. That's what counts for me. I don't need to be able to go all the way with it. There are too many sick people needing our help to waste time with academic experiments. We're doctors, not accountants.

A lot of my ideas go all the way back to Dr. Howell at Kirksville. He taught me about scale; everything recapitulates itself at different intervals of scale. The atom has a nucleus. If you look at it in a bigger arena, the nucleus is the sun and the electrons are the planets. If you want to understand life, Dr. Howell taught me, you have to understand size and domain.

Usually my general methods tend not to make scientists happy, but then again, more and more as the years go by, that's improved, and the world has begun to change. We've had a few neurosurgeons taking our curriculum. We get more cooperation from them than some specialists; generally, neurosurgeons don't feel as though we're getting on their turf. A neurosurgeon will do surgery and then sometimes send his patient down here for CranioSacral work because that will help the surgery, and it makes him look good too. But, at the same time, he doesn't want to know what we're really doing.

I shouldn't generalize. We've had just three neurosurgeons who have taken our classes and they're fine with this stuff. The neurologists are the ones who really hate me. They hoard their incurable diseases. They'll tell you this is terminal, this is irreversible, and then their patients come down here in panic and we reverse the damned things. Boy, that really honks them off. I've had neurologists call me and put me through quizzes about, do you know where this nerve goes, do you know what that nerve does, do you know where the nerve centers are, etc.? I'll say, "Is this a State board to renew my license or something?" I get smart with them. I haven't met a conventional physician yet who scared me.

One More Story

Well, that's as far as I have gotten in my life and in my work. All of our programs at the Institute continue to develop and, since I am still working with patients on a daily basis, I continue to explore, and my own story continues to move onward.

Previously I have mentioned that Dianne (my second wife) and I were not getting along. My rather radical medical inquiries became increasingly incompatible with Dianne's belief systems, and this divergence took on real momentum around 1990. As her education progressed along more classical academic lines, I investigated creative and alternative healing methods. Beliefs that come from the heart speak to the heart and determine emotional life. Ultimately we ended our marriage.

I met my present wife Lisa during a CranioSacral Therapy I class, though at the time I didn't see what was coming. Lisa is a Florida-licensed chiropractor with a great affinity for our work. I met her the second time literally on the table, as she was a demonstration patient in CranioSacral Therapy II when I was presenting palate and tooth issues. I suppose you could read symbolism into this, but I wouldn't. Or put it this way: Working together we initiated a healing process, and at the end of the demonstration she said, "So what do we do now?" She meant, of course: "What's the next step in my treatment?" But she told me later it had a second meaning that she wasn't consciously aware of at the time: "Where do we two go from here?"

Soon our paths converged again. She joined our staff in 1991 when we had an opening for a therapist. She ended up sharing an office with me, but that was mostly done to demonstrate that I am not biased. They are. I told them they're biased. Because she was a chiropractor and a woman. Yeah, chiropractors and osteopaths despise each other; they developed together, but they split after the Palmer, the guy who invented chiropractic therapy, accused the osteopaths of not being pure. So now I hire a chiropractor, and a woman, and we don't have an extra office to put her in, except one way down, which would isolate her, or to put her in my office.

And then one day, we were standing there and all of a sudden we were in an embrace. Kissing. That felt good. It was very straightforward. It took two days for us to become romantically involved. We were married on October 5, 1996. Short and sweet.

Lisa and I share treating patients and practicing CranioSacral work, evolving together in work and life.

There's one more little anecdote I'd like to share before I close.

I remember one time very early in my practice I was flying out of Florida on Delta Airlines. All the passengers were on board, the door was shut, and we were just sitting there waiting for takeoff. But after about ten minutes a stewardess came through and asked, "Is there a doctor aboard?"

Usually I don't volunteer for such things, but this time I said, "I'm a doctor. What do you want?"

She said. "There's a man having a heart attack out on the jetway."

She opened the door and I went out there. He was lying on

the jetway floor about half-way to the terminal entrance. There was a nurse taking his pulse. I looked at him and just followed my intuition. I put one hand under his heart and one hand on top, and I just thought, "UHHHH, GET BETTER!" Within seconds the cyanosis (the blueness) began to pass from his lips; soon his pulse got regular, and he sat up. It took maybe ten minutes. By the time the paramedics got there with their ambulance, he was able to walk over and just get on the cart. They insisted on taking him to the hospital, but I don't think he wanted to go. The nurse said to me, "What kind of doctor are you, anyway?"

I just looked at her and said, "A good one!"

Contact Information

For information on healthcare continuing education workshops for professionals and educational materials (modalities include CranioSacral Therapy, SomatoEmotional Release®, Mechanical Link, Visceral Manipulation, Lymph Drainage Therapy^{SM}, Therapeutic Imagery and Dialogue, and related techniques):

The Upledger Institute, Inc.®
11211 Prosperity Farms Road D-325
Palm Beach Gardens, Florida 33410-3487

Phone: 1-800-233-5880 or 561-622-4334
Fax: 561-622-4771

Website: www.upledger.com
E-mail: upledger@upledger.com

Dr. John E. Upledger is founder and medical director of The Upledger Institute, Inc., based in Palm Beach Gardens, Florida. Dedicated to the natural enhancement of health, the Institute is recognized worldwide for its groundbreaking continuing-education programs, clinical research, and therapeutic services.

Throughout his career as an osteopathic physician and surgeon, Dr. Upledger has been recognized as an innovator and leading proponent in the investigation of new therapies. His development of CranioSacral Therapy in particular earned him an international reputation. In 2001 he was featured on CNN and in *Time* magazine as one of America's next wave of innovators.

Dr. Upledger is a Certified Specialist of Osteopathic Manipulative Medicine, an Academic Fellow of the British Society of Osteopathy, and a Doctor of Science in alternative medicine. He has also served on the Alternative Medicine Program Advisory Council for the Office of Alternative Medicine at the National Institutes of Health in Washington, D.C.

Barry S. Kaplan, M.D., is a classically trained psychiatrist and a Life Fellow of the American Psychiatric Association who practiced for many years before widening his horizons to include the phenomena of mind/body connections and their influence on human health and behavior. When his wife had a stroke at a relatively young age, the couple sought help from John Upledger after finding that the traditional medical community had nothing more to offer. That meeting led to Dr. Kaplan's eventually heading up the Upledger Institute's "Intensive program" and to his feeling that John Upledger's story needed to be told to the world.

Poet and independent scholar Charles Stein is the author of *Persephone Unveiled: Seeing the Goddess, Freeing the Soul* (North Atlantic Books, 2006) and eleven books of poetry including *The Hat Rack Tree* (Station

Hill Press) and the forthcoming *From Mimir's Head.* His examination of the poet Charles Olson's use of C. G. Jung, *The Secret of the Black Chrysanthemum* (Station Hill Press), is a classic study of that poet's work. Stein edited *Being = Space x Action: Searches for Freedom of Mind in Art and Mathematics and Mysticism* for North Atlantic Books. He holds a Ph.D. in literature from the University of Connecticut and a B.A. in ancient Greek from Columbia University. He lives in Barrytown, New York, with classical guitarist Megan Hastie.

Greenwood landscape 2017
@Yahoo.com